EMMA WILLARD
DAUGHTER OF DEMOCRACY

Emma Willard

EMMA WILLARD
DAUGHTER OF DEMOCRACY

By
ALMA LUTZ

With Illustrations

PUBLISHING CO. INC.

BOX 9883 • WASHINGTON DC 20015

Published by arrangement with
The Emma Willard School

Library of Congress Cataloging in Publication Data

Lutz, Alma.
    Emma Willard : daughter of democracy.

    Reprint of the ed. published by Houghton Mifflin,
Boston.
    Bibliography: p.
    Includes index.
    1. Willard, Emma (Hart) 1787-1870. 2. Emma Willard
School, Troy, N. Y.
LA2317.W5L82 1975   370'.92'4 [B]   75-37635
ISBN 0-89201-018-5

TO THE MEMORY OF
MY MOTHER AND MY FATHER
BOTH FIRM BELIEVERS
IN THE HIGHER EDUCATION OF WOMEN

PREFACE

A LITTLE over a hundred years ago, Emma Willard, then a young schoolmistress in Middlebury, Vermont, realized the injustice and short-sightedness of the unequal educational opportunities offered girls and boys. It became her life purpose to free women from the ignorance to which they had been bound by custom and narrow scriptural interpretation.

When she presented her 'Plan for Improving Female Education' to the New York Legislature and to the public in 1819, she became a national figure, and her experiment, the Troy Female Seminary, founded in 1821, exerted an ever-widening influence on the development of our country. Because of the change wrought in public opinion by her daring and persistent stand for the higher education of women, seminaries and high schools for girls, and, later, women's colleges and coeducational universities, became a permanent part of our national life.

The work which she started so courageously in 1814 and continued so steadfastly throughout her life unfolded beyond her fondest hopes and is still being carried forward to-day. Not only women, but men and the whole Nation have reaped the benefits of the intelligent useful womanhood developed under her plan of education.

Although, during her lifetime, Emma Willard was unable to devise any means by which her Troy Female Seminary might endure as a permanent institution, it has continued down to the present day and is now known as the Emma Willard School, in Troy, New

York. It was there that I as a student first became interested in Emma Willard.

It has been my object in writing the life-story of Emma Willard to give her the important place she deserves in her country's history and in the movements for the higher education and advancement of women, and, at the same time, to revive the charm of her dynamic personality.

All those to whom I have turned in my search for material have been most helpful and I wish to express my appreciation of their interest and coöperation.

I am especially indebted to Miss Eliza Kellas, Principal of the Emma Willard School, in Troy, New York, for access to all material at the school; to Miss Helen Hart and Mr. William C. Hart, of Williamstown, Massachusetts, and to Mrs. Emma Hart Dickinson Chambers, of West Hartford, Connecticut, for their recollections of their great-aunt; to Mr. Hewlett Scudder, of Schenectady, New York, and Mr. John Phelps, of Baltimore, Maryland, for permission to quote from letters; and to Mrs. Alice Upson Cowles, of Kensington, Connecticut, for her help in looking up family records.

John Lord's 'Life of Emma Willard,' published by D. Appleton & Co. in 1873, has been invaluable in its preservation of many important letters. For permission to quote from these letters, I am indebted to D. Appleton & Co. For the use of Emma Willard's letters to Mrs. Sigourney, I am under obligation to the Hoadley Collection of the Connecticut Historical Society. For the use of other original letters, I am indebted to the Emma Willard School, the Dreer and Gratz Collections of the Historical Society of Pennsylvania, the Congressional Library, and the New York Historical Society.

ALMA LUTZ

CONTENTS

ILLUSTRATIONS

This book is bound in the style of EMMA
WILLARD'S *Journals and Letters from
France and Great Britain* (Troy, 1833).

CHRONOLOGY

1787. February 23, Emma Willard born in Berlin, Connecticut.

1802. Attended Berlin Academy under Thomas Miner.

1804. Taught children's school in Berlin.

1805. Winter, attended the Misses Patten's school in Hartford, Connecticut. Summer, taught older boys and girls in upper room in her father's house.

1806. Winter, took charge of Berlin Academy. Spring and autumn, attended Mrs. Royse's school in Hartford.

1807. Spring, Assistant at academy in Westfield, Massachusetts. Summer, Preceptress of academy in Middlebury, Vermont.

1809. August 10, married Dr. John Willard.

1810. September 28, birth of her son, John H. Willard.

1812. Financial reverses.

1813. August, death of her father, Samuel Hart.

1814. Spring, opened Middlebury Female Seminary in her own home.

1818. February 5, sent her 'Plan for Improving Female Education' to Governor De Witt Clinton, of New York. December 31, received encouraging reply from him.

1819. 'Plan for Improving Female Education' presented to New York Legislature by friends and published. Waterford Academy for Young Ladies granted a charter by the New York Legislature. Spring, moved to Waterford, New York, and opened academy.

1820. First public oral geometry examination for women conducted at Waterford Academy. Governor Clinton again asked Legislature for financial aid for Waterford Academy, and was refused. Published 'Universal Peace to be Introduced by a Confederacy of Nations Meeting in Jerusalem.'

1821. Received offers of financial aid from Troy, New York. March 26, Common Council of Troy raised $4000 by special tax for purchase of building for female seminary. Spring, Troy Female Seminary opened in temporary quarters. September, Troy Female Seminary established in permanent quarters. Published 'Will Scientific Education Make Woman Lose Her Dependence on Man?'

1822. Studied science with Professor Amos Eaton, who subsequently took charge of science department at the Troy Female Seminary. Published 'Ancient Geography.'

1824. Sister, Almira Hart Lincoln, began teaching at the Seminary. September 18, Lafayette's visit.

1825. Opening of Rensselaer School. May 29, death of Dr. Willard. July 1, Lafayette's second visit. October, opening of the Erie Canal.

1826. Son John entered West Point.

1828. Published 'Republic of America.'

1830. October 1, sailed for Europe on the Charlemagne. October 24, landed at Havre. November 2, reached Paris. November 7, received call from Lafayette. November 9, met Mrs. Opie and Mr. and Mrs. James Fenimore Cooper at Lafayette's soirée. December 5, attended Opera with Lafayette.

1831. January 18, death of her mother, Lydia Hinsdale Hart. Published collection of poems, 'The Fulfilment of a Promise.' February, presented at French Court. March, met Madame Belloc. April, arrived in London. May, met Maria Edgeworth, Robert Owen, Samuel Coleridge, Washington Irving; visited Scotland. June, sailed for America; wrote 'Ocean Hymn.' August, returned to the Troy Female Seminary. Almira Hart Lincoln married Judge Phelps.

1832. Worked for the establishment of a female seminary in Greece.

1833. Published a series of addresses, 'Advancement of Female Education,' and 'Journal and Letters from France and Great Britain.' Opening of Oberlin Collegiate Institute, which admitted women.

1835. Publication of Mrs. Willard's and Mrs. Phelps's translation of 'Progressive Education' by Madame Necker de Saussure. Opening of Wheaton Seminary.

1837. Organized Willard Association for the Mutual Improvement of Teachers. Published 'A System of Universal History in Perspective.' Opening of Mary Lyon's Mount Holyoke Female Seminary.

1838. Turned management of Troy Female Seminary over to her son John and his wife Sarah, who acted as Principal. September, married Dr. Christopher C. Yates.

1839. June, left Dr. Yates and went to live with her sister Mary in Berlin, Connecticut. Opening of first State Normal School in Lexington, Massachusetts.

1840. Worked with Henry Barnard to improve common schools of Connecticut. Elected Superintendent of common schools of Kensington, Connecticut. Wrote two poems, 'Our Fathers' and 'Bride Stealing,' for bicentennial celebration at Farmington, Connecticut.

1843. Granted divorce from Dr. Yates by Connecticut General Assembly.

1844. Spent some time in Philadelphia. Summer, returned to Troy Female Seminary. Published 'Temple of Time' and 'Address to Pupils of Washington Seminary.'

1845. Attended convention of County Superintendents at Syracuse, New York. Taught a series of Teachers' Institutes in southern New York. Published 'Chronographer of English History.'

1846. Traveled through Southern and Western States. Published 'A Treatise on the Motive Powers which Produce the Circulation of the Blood.'

1847. Published 'Chronographer of Ancient History' and 'Historic Guide to the Temple of Time.'

1848. Published 'A Letter to Dupont de l'Eure on the Political Position of Women.'

1849. Published 'Respiration and its Effects, Particularly as respects Asiatic Cholera' and 'Last Leaves of American History.'

1850. Address for Columbian Association of Teachers, delivered at Smithsonian Institution.

1853. Published 'Astronography.'

1856. Published 'Late American History.'

1857. Published 'Morals for the Young.'

1860. Published 'Appeal to South Carolina,' in *New York Express*.

1861. Memorial from American Women presented to Congress, through her efforts.

1862. Published 'Via Media.'

1864. Published 'God Save America' and 'Universal Peace.' July, captured by Confederate soldiers while on railroad journey.

1865. Opening of Vassar Female College at Poughkeepsie, New York.

1870. April 15, died at Troy, New York.

EMMA WILLARD
DAUGHTER OF DEMOCRACY

• •

CHAPTER I

THE HERITAGE OF CONNECTICUT

ON the floor in front of the wide fireplace in the Hart farmhouse sat a girl of twelve, drawing geometrical figures with charcoal on the white Connecticut-marble hearth. Deep in thought, she marked off another triangle, then paused to work out the proof of the theorem. Emma Hart had made up her mind to study geometry, and she was teaching herself.

For a girl to study geometry in 1800 was presumptuous. Such an indiscretion incurred the frown of society, and was considered not only unladylike, but actually menacing to the welfare of the race. Public opinion held the female mind utterly incapable of comprehending mathematics. Self-constituted interpreters of God's will proclaimed woman's study of mathematics contrary to nature and divine decrees. Others sadly shook their heads, prophesying dire calamities ahead, when women, engrossed in solving mathematical problems, would neglect their husbands and families.

The little girl, pondering over her theorems by the fireside, was destined through her ever-growing zeal for knowledge to break down to a large extent the prejudices and preconceived ideas of the world in regard to the intellectual ability of women.

Emma Hart came of a race of pioneers and courageous

thinkers. Her ancestor, Thomas Hooker, a minister of
the Church of England who had been silenced for non-
conformity, followed members of his congregation to
America and settled with them at Newe Towne (Cambridge), Massachusetts. Soon, rumors of the fertile
meadows of the Connecticut Valley reached Massachusetts Colony, and Thomas Hooker became an ardent
advocate of migration to this new country, which offered better farming land and relief from the crowding
around the Massachusetts coast towns. There was much
opposition to the proposed migration, John Cotton eloquently arguing against settlers leaving Massachusetts
after taking an oath to defend it, and picturing the suffering and hardships which would attend the opening of
the wilderness. For a time, the General Court forbade
the migration, but eventually consented, and in 1636,
Thomas Hooker led one hundred members of his church
through the wilderness into Connecticut, where they
founded the town of Hartford. The journey from Newe
Towne to Connecticut was made in June, when the
weather was warm and sunny. Over an Indian trail to
the west, through deep forests and tangled underbrush,
over swamps and streams, past Indian villages, the band
of pioneers traveled slowly, with wagons and tents,
driving a herd of cattle with them. Sturdy men, courageous women unused to wilderness hardships, children,
aged grandfathers and grandmothers were in the party.
It was a peaceful, cheerful migration. Toward evening
they camped in the forest, built fires, foraged for game,
milked their cows, braved the blackness of the night
and the howling of wolves until at the end of two weeks
they reached the banks of the Connecticut River. Here
they found the fertile meadows with clear-cut jagged
hills in the distance. They found maize, beans, and

squash planted by Indians in clearings and saw Indians dragging nets of yellow salmon from the river. It was a promising wilderness in which they settled.

In the colony was another ancestor, Stephen Hart, a deacon in Thomas Hooker's church. Tradition says that Hartford derived its name from a ford in the Connecticut River discovered by him and named Hart's Ford. Hart's Ford may be found on old maps. A few years later Stephen Hart was one of a party that discovered the fertile Tunxis Valley and settled there, founding the town of Farmington.

Still another ancestor, John Hart, the grandson of Stephen and Emma's great-grandfather, faced that tragic pioneer experience, an Indian massacre. Sent away from home on an errand when a boy of eleven, he returned to find his home a smouldering mass of ruins and his whole family killed by the Indians. Later his son, Samuel, migrated from Farmington to Christian Lane, the Great Swamp settlement. Sunday after Sunday, he and his fellow settlers and their families traveled fifteen miles on foot and on horseback over Indian trails to church in Farmington. There was danger from Indians and wild animals, and the men went armed.

The Hart family was an important one in the development of Connecticut. This colony, isolated from English control and important colonial centers, such as Boston and New York because of difficult, slow transportation, built up an independent government, adopting very few of the institutions of the Old World. The result was that in 1662 it was granted the most liberal charter of any colony, a charter giving the people power to elect their own governor and make their own laws. Through successive generations the Harts were representatives in the General Assembly and active in town meetings. With the heritage of Connecticut behind her, little wonder that Emma Hart early became an eager student of her country's history and an ardent defender of its liberal principles.

Captain Samuel Hart, Emma's father, was an outstanding figure in Berlin, Connecticut, because of his ability and courageous, independent opinions. When a boy, he prepared for college, but the death of his father left him at the age of thirteen with the care of his mother and sisters, and he was obliged to give up his plans. Always a student, he continued his education by reading with keen enjoyment the English classics, history, philosophy, and works on religion. He followed the common occupation of that period, farming. At nineteen he married Rebecca Norton.

Not many years later, the first signs of serious trouble between the British Government and the Colonies were discussed in Berlin. Feeling was strong against the coercive measures of Parliament. The Quartering Act and the Stamp Act aroused the indignation of the whole neighborhood. Young men organized 'Sons of Liberty' societies with the motto, 'Liberty, Prosperity, and No Stamps.' Then came news of the Boston Massacre; three years later the Boston Tea Party fanned their fighting spirit; and then, closely following, came word of the Boston Port Bill which closed the port of Boston to shipping and moved the Massachusetts seat of government to Salem. Now it was time for Connecticut to act. At an enthusiastic meeting in Farmington, June 15, 1774, attended by people from Berlin and New Britain, it was voted:

That the act of Parliament for blocking up the port of Boston is an invasion of the Rights and Privileges of every American, and as such, we are Determined to oppose the same, with all other arbitrary and tyrannical acts in every Way and Manner, that may be adopted in General Congress: to the Intent we may be instrumental in Securing and Transmitting our Rights and Privileges Inviolate, to the Latest Posterity.

That the fate of American freedom Greatly Depends upon the Conduct of the Inhabitants of the Town of Boston in the Present Alarming Crisis of Public affairs: We therefore entreat them by everything that is Dear and Sacred, to Persevere with unremitted Vigilence and Resolution till their labor shall be crowned with the desired success.

This was not all. A committee of thirty-four prominent men in the various parishes was appointed

To take in subscriptions of wheat, Rye, Indian corn and other provisions of the Inhabitants, and to collect and transport the same to the Town of Boston, there to be delivered to the Select Men of the Town of Boston, to be by them Distributed at their Discretion to those who are incapacitated to procure a necessary subsistence in consequence of the late oppressive Measures of Administration.

Work went on as usual on the Hart farm, but through it all ran an undercurrent of excitement. The battle of Lexington and Concord, Bunker Hill, the Declaration of Independence stood out above the routine work in the fields. Connecticut was furnishing Washington with supplies collected in Farmington. Contributions for the army were often received after the Sunday service, and the people gave whatever they could spare — sometimes money, sometimes Indian corn, flax, wood, shoes, or stockings. Governor Trumbull was the man of the hour. Colonel Selah Hart, at the order of the General Court, provided stores of lead for the Colony from the mine of Matthew Hart. Near by in Hartford, English soldiers were held as prisoners. Then Connecticut was threatened. The burning of Danbury, the British fleet menacing the coast towns, Burgoyne in the west — all this brought warfare near.

Meanwhile Samuel Hart's wife had died and he had married Lydia Hinsdale. There were now ten children in the family. His oldest son, Samuel, ran away to join the army as a fifer, and he, as captain of the company formed in Berlin, was sent to defend the coast towns. Often afterward he told the story of how he barely escaped death when, with a group of soldiers, he was observing the enemy through a telescope near New Haven. 'We had better leave this place. We may be exposed to their guns,' he had just remarked, when his comrade was shot down.

There was another story he loved to tell of the messenger galloping into camp, waving a white flag, and shouting, 'Burgoyne and all his men are ours!'

The Revolution over, Captain Samuel Hart settled down again on his farm in Berlin, watching always with interest the deliberations of the leaders of the new nation. He represented his town in the General Assembly and held other civil offices. When the Congregational Church was organized in the parish of Worthington in 1772, he was made its first clerk and treasurer in spite of the fact that he was known to hold liberal religious views, especially in regard to the final salvation of mankind. Salvation for the few elect, eternal damnation for the many, was the popular doctrine.

Eventually, his liberal views brought him into conflict with the disciplinary methods of the church. It was the custom for every man to be assessed for the support of the minister, just as he was assessed for the support of civil officers. Refusal to pay this tax meant imprisonment. While Samuel Hart was treasurer of the church, two of his neighbors became Separatists and refused to pay the tax. As treasurer, he was obliged to issue warrants for their arrest. The severity and injustice of this measure troubled him. At a meeting of the church, he pleaded for tolerance, but his suggestions were voted down. Thereupon he himself paid the taxes and charges against his two neighbors, released them from prison, resigned his office, and later withdrew from the church. Appeals and even threats to keep him in the church were unavailing. 'You must not leave us,' pleaded a prominent church member. 'We cannot spare you. Without your abilities to direct us, what can we do?'

'There are two things in religion which I despise,' answered Samuel Hart, 'the one is force, and the other flattery.' He was firm in his decision to withdraw, and then that persecution began which has always been the penalty for divergence from orthodoxy.

It was not until 1807 that formal announcement of his withdrawal was written on the records of the Ecclesiastical Society of Worthington:

Captain Samuel Hart, watch withdrawn. He and several others attended another church.
Dec. 11, 1807.

The church referred to was the Universalist Church, which appealed to him because of its belief in universal salvation and the eternal progress of all souls.

Such a decision as was made by Samuel Hart, in opposition to church authority and with the penalty of popular disapproval, took courage. It meant sacrificing for his convictions his social standing and his prospects of advancement in the community. Many regarded him as a heretic and shunned him. He was barred from holding public office. Yet there were some who recognized his sterling qualities and privately sought his advice in personal matters. It is not surprising that, less than

fifty years later, we find his daughter Emma courageously taking her stand in the face of ridicule and
bitter criticism for her ideal — the higher education
of women.

Emma's mother, too, had a share in moulding the
character of her daughter. Lydia Hinsdale traced her
ancestry to Robert Hinsdale, who settled in Dedham,
Massachusetts, in 1637, and was one of the men who
petitioned for and supported the first free school in the
country. There, and later in Medford, where he was one
of the first settlers, he held many public offices. Moving
farther west, he became one of the original proprietors
of Deerfield. Her father, Captain John Hinsdale, was
a soldier of ability and was spoken of as 'literary.'

Lydia Hinsdale married Samuel Hart when he was a
widower with seven children. Although only twenty-
three, ten years younger than her husband, she took
charge of the household with the efficiency and executive
ability of the typical New England housewife. She was
well educated for the times and skilled in needlework.
Quiet and gentle, yet firm, practical, thrifty, and extremely industrious, she supplemented the idealistic,
scholarly qualities of her husband. With seven stepchildren and a growing family of her own to bring up,
with her husband's mother and her own parents to care
for, with all the household duties — cooking, baking,
milking, making butter, carding wool, spinning, weaving, and so on — demanding her attention, she was able
to manage her household comfortably and harmoniously. Each child did his share of the work, and com-
radeship and good-fellowship dominated the family life.
As one of the daughters wrote in later years, 'No dissension or domestic jar was ever witnessed between the
parents.'

Emma, who was born on the twenty-third of February, 1787, was next to the youngest, the sixteenth in this large family. 'If baby had been a boy, we would rather have named him for General Washington,' her father is said to have remarked to the Reverend Benoni Upson, his friend and the pastor of the Kensington church, 'But under the circumstances, she will be baptized as Emma.' Whereto the minister replied, 'Feminine form of Emmanuel, which signifies "God with us."'

CHAPTER II

LOWER LANE

THE simple farmhouse where Emma Hart was born in Lower Lane, Berlin, looked out over meadows to the clear-cut, rugged Connecticut hills. It was a square house, three stories high, red brown — the color of unpainted, well-weathered wood. A large center chimney warmed the rooms on cold winter days. The kitchen with its wide fireplace, shining pewter, and long pine table was the most used room in the house. Up the spiral stairway, on the second floor, was the large loom room, always a busy place, for there were many children to clothe and the girls did their share of the carding, spinning, and weaving. After the men had done the shearing, the women sorted the wool, setting aside the best for the father's clothes, the next best for the other men in the family, the third part for themselves. The rest was made into flannel and blankets, while the remnants were used for mops. In many families the scraps and burred clippings were burned, but it was Mrs. Hart's custom to have Emma and her sister Nancy gather them up in baskets and then scatter them about on the bushes in the pasture so that the birds might find them and use them for their nests.

Flax was another product of the farm. It was broken and dressed by the men and then spun and woven into linen by the women. The days were always busy. Besides the regular household tasks for the girls and farm work for the boys, autumn brought quantities of apples and pumpkins to be pared, strung, and dried. In the spring, the kettle of maple syrup hung over the fire, boiling for sugar. The wild berries ripened and were gathered and preserved. Now and then the large iron kettle filled with soap grease was set over a fire built in the yard, and the girls watched it boil till the soap 'came' and 'spun aprons' from the stick their mother lifted from the kettle. On hot summer days, they sat in the cool of the house, braiding white straw into hats, while they discussed the fashions, or the bright tin dishes made at Edward Pattison's shop down the Lane, or perhaps Mrs. Lucy Brandegee's silkworms, how she fed them on leaves from her mulberry grove, how she spun, dyed, and wove a red silk gown to give to Martha Washington.

There were corn huskings and quilting bees. Often the men of the community helped a neighbor build a house or a barn, while the women not to be outdone served them bounteous meals, making a holiday of the occasion. There were large family gatherings at Thanksgiving when children and grandchildren returned to the Hart home. The older children were married now and had their own homes near by. Asahel, Jesse, and Charlotte lived in Berlin. Asahel was a tailor, Jesse a cabinetmaker and later the owner of a tavern. Charlotte had married Orrin Lee, the blacksmith, who like all blacksmiths in those days made everything in iron and steel that was used — nails, hinges, latches, shovels, hoes, scythes, plows. Sometimes Rebecca, who had married William Cook, made the journey from Danbury by stage. Samuel and Mary, now Mrs. John Lee, lived in Blue Hills, Kensington. Samuel was already prominent in public affairs and in the Democratic Party.

These family gatherings stood out as red-letter days for the children, Nancy and Emma. The rows of pumpkin pies, the puddings, the doughnuts, the turkeys roast-

ing on the spit, the cracking of butternuts by the fireside
were holiday memories.

There were days when Nancy and Emma and their
little sister Almira played in the meadow among the big
patches of bluets and under the blossoming apple trees.
Often they gathered wild strawberries in little baskets
that they had made of oak leaves pinned together with
thorns. Sometimes, looking across the valley at the clear
outline of Mount Lamentation, they would tell each
other the story of Mr. Chester lost for days, long ago, in
the dense forest on the mountain. They would watch
the peddlers go by, their horses loaded down with big
baskets of shining tinware which came from Edward
Pattison's shop down the Lane. They wondered about
the peddlers and where they went. They had heard it
said that the peddlers traveled far west and south and
even took wagonloads of tinware to Canada, bringing
back furs which were made into muffs at Edward Pattison's shop. Everybody wanted the bright new tinware.

Uncle Elijah Hinsdale had a mulberry orchard and
raised silkworms. How exciting it was to go with him
into the silk house, to see the worms feed on mulberry
leaves, and watch the silk being reeled! Think of wearing dresses made out of cocoons!

Sometimes at Brother Asahel's on Worthington
Street they saw the big yellow stagecoach drawn by four
horses dash past. The blowing of the bugle, the snap
of the driver's whip, the fleeting glimpses of passengers
as the coach rumbled on were reminders of a world
beyond Lower Lane.

Night after night during the long cold winter months,
the Hart family gathered in front of the blazing logs in
the big kitchen fireplace. There were games for the
younger children and stories — stories of Stephen Hart

and Thomas Hooker, of their journey through the wilderness to Connecticut, of the Charter Oak, of the wedding of Isaac Lee and Tabitha, the daughter of the rich Isaac Norton who was the grandfather of Captain Hart's first wife. Isaac Lee was the hero of the neighborhood. There were stories of his Herculean strength, how he tossed barrels of cider into his cart as other men tossed pumpkins, how he threw the big bull, and excelled in all athletic sports, particularly wrestling. Now he was Colonel Isaac Lee, the friend of the leading patriots. He had been a delegate from Berlin to Hartford in 1788 to ratify the Constitution of the new Republic. Courtly and dignified, with his cocked hat, white wig, blue coat with shining buttons, black velvet breeches with knee buckles of silver, white silk stockings and silver-buckled shoes, he was an imposing figure, treated with reverence everywhere. Children bowed and curtsied as he passed them on the street, and were eager for stories of their hero.

Most popular of all were the stories of the struggles and hardships of the Revolution told by Captain Hart, while Emma sat on his knee wide-eyed, eager, and absorbed, fired with an intense patriotism which she carried with her all through her life. He told of the British burning New London, of his part in defending the coast towns, of Uncle Orrin Lee as drummer boy, of Uncle Samuel Lee who nearly starved in a prison ship, of spies, of Washington, of the daring, impulsive young Lafayette, of Paul Jones and the Bon Homme Richard.

Then there was reading. Sometimes Mrs. Hart read aloud from Chaucer, Milton, or Shakespeare, or Captain Hart read while she busied herself with her knitting. Often one of the children read to the family from a geography or biography, stopping in difficult parts to

ask questions. Perhaps Captain Hart had borrowed a
book from a friend, or brought Rollin's 'Ancient History' home from the Worthington Library. Books were
rare in those days, expensive and hard to get, and the
Harts treasured every one that came into their home.
All of the library's books were read at their fireside —
Plutarch's 'Lives,' books of travel, the works of Addi-
son, Steele, Pope, Thomson, Watts, Gibbon and other
historians. Emma attributed her love of books to this
library and remarked in later years, 'Luckily this old
library possessed few novels, and I had read its books
before my rage for fiction began.'

All these books brought new ideas into the Hart home.
Questions arose about religious and moral principles,
and these were talked over. Politics and current events
were always considered. There was talk about the new
President, John Adams, about Hamilton, about the
views of that popular Democrat, Thomas Jefferson,
about the French Revolution and Napoleon. A woman
in England, Mary Wollstonecraft, had written a book,
'The Vindication of the Rights of Women.' It said new
things about women and women's education. They
rang true; but the world was not ready for them, and
her tragic, impulsive career brought discredit upon her
theories. Thomas Paine had published a book, the 'Age
of Reason.' It stirred up the minds of men and made
them wonder about the things they had always believed. Captain Hart was a thinker; he was liberal; he
liked to thrash out new ideas.

And so, glimpses of the wide world came to the little
girl Emma, as she sat by the fireside, winter evenings,
and developed in her a passionate love of reading, an
ability to think for herself, and an unquenchable desire
for knowledge.

CHAPTER III

SCHOOL DAYS

ALTHOUGH fireside education was such an important factor in Emma Hart's life, she was not limited to that, but early attended the district school. Connecticut was one of the first of the Colonies to provide public schools for primary education. The Reverend Thomas Hooker, Emma's ancestor, had advocated the education of children that they might learn to read the Scriptures. The early school laws, however, specified that instruction was to be for male children only. All that was considered necessary for girls was a slight knowledge of reading, which would enable them to become familiar with the Bible and the Catechism. They learned to read at home or in dame schools conducted by elderly women in their kitchens for a few pennies a week. Emma's father, who always maintained that the State should educate its children, was sent to the Legislature as a special delegate to ask for educational measures.

During the Revolution, interest in education waned, but with the formation of the Republic, the need of more general education was felt, since the success of the government depended upon the intelligence of the voter. Although there was still opposition to the spending of public money on 'schools for shes,' district schools began to be opened to girls for a few months in the summer when the boys were busy on the farms. Gradually, girls were allowed to stay on through the winter months.

It was one of these district schools that Emma Hart attended at Worthington Center. The school building was small, dilapidated, and weather-beaten; the schoolroom, plain and bare, with a fireplace on one side. A single continuous line of desks, pine boards fastened to the wall, ran around the other three sides of the room. The benches, slabs on wooden legs, also formed a continuous line in front of the desks. When writing or studying, the children faced the wall with their backs to the teacher. To recite, they stepped over the benches and faced the teacher. In the middle of the room on high backless benches, the younger children sat primly and uncomfortably, their little feet dangling or struggling to touch the floor. Describing these school days, in later years, Emma Hart, then Mrs. Willard, wrote:

The school house was a place of rude structure; but be it remembered, it was fully as good as the dwelling houses. The children were not enervated by luxuries at home. They came of a cold winter morning, trooping along, with the ruddy glow of health and exercise. The boys had fed the cattle, and the girls had milked the cows, and made the beds in rooms which no fireplace or stove had ever disturbed; and now the bounding pulse of life beat high and strong in their veins; and they minded little the unwarmed condition of the meeting house on Sunday, or the whistling of the wind through the crevices of the schoolhouse on week days. They had learned 'to endure hardness as good soldiers.' Even the little children had begun to learn the same lesson. If no backs were provided for their seats in school, neither were there any at home to the blocks in the ample chimney corners upon which these favored ones were privileged to sit.

Emma trudged to school on cold winter days with her older brothers and sisters. Her short woven coat, the small white woolen shawl folded over her short cropped hair and pinned at her throat, the blue and white wool stockings and mittens which her grandmother had knit, the heavy leather shoes — all kept her warm. She sat on the backless benches patiently for hours with other little girls in long plain straight dresses, just like hers, of dark homespun, without ruffles, and covered with a blue and white checked apron tied at the waist.

The winter school was conducted by men, the summer school by women. Reading, writing, spelling, and some arithmetic were taught. When the school assembled, the children 'made their manners,' the boys bowing and the girls curtsying to the teacher. Reading from the New Testament by the pupils from the oldest class down to the 'ABC' children was always the first exercise of the morning. Then, while the older scholars studied, the younger ones said their letters. They had no books, and when they recited, they stood by the teacher's desk while he pointed out with his quill the letters in Webster's Spelling Book. The older pupils had their spelling lesson later. The blue-backed Spelling Book was also used as a reader. Besides the alphabet, many long columns of words, Roman and Arabic numerals, days of the week, months of the year, and so forth, it contained 'Lessons of easy Words, to teach Children to read and to know their Duty,' such as, 'Love not the world, nor the things that are in the world; for they are sin.' Its 'Proverbs, Counsels, and Maxims in Words of One Syllable' read, 'Haste makes waste, and waste brings want'; or, less cheerfully but more piously, 'The time will come when we must all be laid in the dust.'

Next in order was a writing lesson. The children all had copy-books, made at home from large sheets of paper folded and sewn into a brown paper cover. With a ruler and plummet, they lined the pages. The plummets were made at home by pouring molten lead into small grooves or cracks in the kitchen floor, and then smoothing off the hardened lead and sharpening it. The children brought home-made ink to school and goose quills which the schoolmaster made into pens for them.

Across the top of each page in the older pupils' copy-books, the teacher wrote a sentence, usually some edify-ing religious or moral sentiment which was painstak-ingly copied. The younger children practiced making curved and straight lines, then letters, words, and finally sentences. In the ciphering-books, which were similar to the copy-books, the pupils copied rules, dictated by the teacher, and problems which they had already solved, thus making their own arithmetic textbooks.

There was a short recess in the middle of the morning, first for the girls, then for the boys. During the noon hour, school was dismissed, the children ate the lunches which they had brought with them, and then played hard at games until the sharp rapping of the teacher's ruler brought them back into the schoolroom. The after-noon's work was similar to the morning's except that the older pupils used a reader which contained extracts from standard authors and from speeches of British statesmen.

These same subjects were pursued as long as the chil-dren were able to profit from them. Gradually grammar and geography were introduced. The Catechism of course was thoroughly learned. During the summer ses-sion when the teacher was a woman, the young chil-dren brought patchwork and knitting to school, and this helped to keep them quiet and amused. The older girls hemmed towels and tablecloths and made samplers. They were very proud of their samplers, worked in fine stitches of colored silk, which, when finished, would hang in the front room at home and be used as patterns for letters in marking household linen.

The best-educated farmers in the community taught during the winter months from a sense of duty to the younger generation as well as for pay. Often, the teachers were lawyers and physicians. The clergymen took a great interest in the schools, visiting them regularly and making suggestions. The awe and reverence with which the children regarded them is shown by the following recollections of Emma Hart, written many years later: 'But well do I remember when a child at school, during our play it was said, "Mr. Fenn is coming!" "There is Mr. Upson!" Every urchin of us stopt short in our play, and immediately repaired to the roadside to make a double file for him to pass between, and as he passed, we made in heart as well as in gesture profound obeisance.'

That puritanical influence which persecuted Captain Hart after he withdrew from the church also found its way into the schoolroom. The Hart children were made to pay the penalty for their father's opposition to orthodoxy, and often were unfairly treated by their Puritan schoolmasters. This aroused in Emma a lack of respect for their opinions, and an ambition to accomplish something which would bring honor to the family. 'None of my teachers,' she wrote later, 'so understood me as to awaken my powers or gain much influence over me.' This ambition to accomplish something led her to attempt to conquer by herself such subjects as geometry, which girls were deemed incapable of comprehending.

While the methods of teaching in the district schools were better than no teaching at all, there was great room for improvement. The difference in the ages of the pupils, the tendency to teach by rote, and the general monotony and somber religious tone of the instruction did not make the work highly interesting nor inspirational.

It was during these school days that Emma's father exerted such a steadying, progressive influence over her, interesting her in worth-while books and training her to use her mind. He delighted in reading and discussing metaphysics, particularly the philosophies of Locke and Berkeley, and early awakened in Emma a capability for metaphysical speculation. She described this relationship, years later, contrasting him with Milton, whose attitude toward women, characteristic of the age, was such that he made his daughter read Latin to him day after day without allowing her to learn it. Emma said of her father: 'He was fifty years my senior — he had descended of a long lived race by slow generations from the early Pilgrims, and I have known no man who more retained their gravity and simplicity of manner; yet would he often call me when at the age of fourteen from household duties by my mother's side, to enjoy with him some passage of an author which pleased him, or to read over to me some essay which he had amused himself in writing.'

The opening of an academy, less than a mile from Emma's home, when she was fifteen, made a great change in the course of her life. This was one of the first academies in Connecticut incorporated by the General Assembly, and pupils came not only from Worthington, but from Kensington, New Britain, and adjoining towns. The Principal, Thomas Miner, a graduate of Yale and a teacher of ability, understood Emma and brought out her latent powers. She herself described this formative period of her life very interestingly:

Before the opening of the Academy, my mother's children had each received a small dividend from the estate of a deceased brother. My sister Nancy ... determined, as our parents approved, to spend this in being taught at the new school; but having at that time a special desire to make a visit among my married brothers and sisters in Kensington (whose children were of my own age), I stood one evening, candle in hand, and made to the parents, who had retired for the night, what they considered a most sensible oration, on the folly of people's seeking to be educated above their means and prescribed duties in life. So Nancy went to school, and I to Kensington. A fortnight after, one Friday evening, I returned. Nancy showed me her books and told me of her lessons. 'Mother,' said I, 'I am going to school to-morrow.' 'Why, I thought you had made up your mind not to be educated, and besides, your clothes are not in order, and it will appear odd for you to enter school Saturday.' But Saturday morning I went, and received my lessons in Webster's Grammar and Morse's Geography. Mr. Miner was to hear me recite by myself until I overtook the class, in which were a dozen fine girls, including my elder sister. Monday, Mr. Miner called on me to recite. He began with Webster's Grammar, went on and on, and still as he questioned received from me a ready answer, until he said, 'I will hear the remainder of your lesson tomorrow.' The same thing occurred with the Geography lesson. I was pleased, and thought, 'you never shall get to the end of my lesson.' That hard chapter on the planets, with their diameters, distances, and periodic revolutions, was among the first of Morse's Geography. The evening I wished to learn it, my sister Lydia . . . had a party. The house was full of bustle, and above all rose the song-singing, which always fascinated me. The moon was at the full, and snow was on the ground. I wrapt my cloak around me, and out of doors of a cold winter evening, seated on a horseblock, I learned that lesson. Lessons so learnt are not easily forgotten. The third day Mr. Miner admitted me to my sister's class. He used to require daily compositions. I never failed, the only one of my class who did not; but I also improved the opportunities which these afforded, to pay him off for any criticism by which he had (intentionally though indirectly) hit me — with some parody or rhyme, at which, though sometimes pointed enough, Mr. Miner would heartily laugh — never forgetting, however, at some time or other, to retort with interest. Thus my mind was stimulated, and my progress rapid. For two successive years, 1802–03, I enjoyed the advantages of Dr. Miner's school, and I believe that no better instruction was given to girls in any school, at that time, in our country.

CHAPTER IV
THE YOUNG SCHOOLMISTRESS

Books and school were not the only interests of Emma Hart's girlhood. Full of life, enthusiastic, affectionate, understanding, and intensely interested in people, she made friends readily. Nor were her friendships of the moment only. They meant a great deal to her and she cherished them throughout her life. Nancy Wadsworth, the daughter of Dr. Wadsworth, of Southington, was Emma's most intimate school friend. One of the joys of their friendship was the writing of frequent letters filled with assurances of devotion and affection, confiding their secret ambitions, discussing their studies and the books they read, and often romancing. Letters, such as these, were characteristic of that period among educated women, perhaps because writing in those days was such a novelty for women that they indulged in letters for the pure joy of self-expression, just as to-day women enter other new fields with enthusiasm.

'Emma,' wrote Nancy in 1803, 'I do think you are a pretty girl and always did; and I like you better and better. I need not give you any advice, except to follow the impulses of your heart, and you will do perfectly right.'

Nancy was not prejudiced when she called Emma a pretty girl. She was handsome with her well-proportioned, well-rounded figure, her blue eyes, fair hair, and high coloring, her agile movements, and animated conversation.

Emma was curious, too, and daring, and when there was talk of a haunted house, near Lower Lane, where mysterious lights were seen at midnight, she determined to see for herself. One dark rainy night, she and a friend disguised themselves and hurried off on their adventure. Soon the house was in view. Lights shone from the windows. Full of excitement, their hearts beating rapidly, the girls cautiously crept toward a window. Would they see ghosts? They peered in only to find men playing cards by candlelight.

Another very dear friend, who exerted considerable influence over Emma's girlhood, was Mrs. Peck, a woman of forty. Emma described their friendship in these words, 'When we were first thrown together, it was for several days, and she treated me not as a child, but an equal — confiding to me much of that secret history which every heart sacredly cherishes; and I, on my part, opened to her my whole inner life, my secret feelings, anxieties, and aspirations.'

It was Mrs. Peck who urged Emma to teach when she was seventeen and suggested that a children's school in the village be put in her charge. In later years, Emma's recollections of this first teaching experience were very vivid and she wrote:

The schoolhouse was situated in Worthington street, on the great Hartford and New Haven turnpike; and was surrounded on the other three sides by a mulberry grove, towards which the windows were in summer kept open.

At nine o'clock, on that first morning, I seated myself among the children to begin a profession which I little thought was to last with slight interruption for forty years. That morning was the longest of my life. I began my work by trying to discover the several capacities and degrees of advancement of the children, so as to arrange them in classes; but they having been, under my predecessor, accustomed to the greatest license, would, at their option, go to the street door to look at a passing carriage, or stepping on to a bench in the rear, dash out of a window, and take a lively turn in the mulberry grove. Talking did no good. Reasoning and pathetic appeals were alike unavailing. Thus the morning slowly wore away. At noon I explained this first great perplexity of my teacher-life to my friend Mrs. Peck, who decidedly advised sound and summary chastisement. 'I cannot,' I replied; 'I never struck a child in my life.' 'It is,' she said, 'the only way, and you must.' I left her for the afternoon school with a heavy heart, still hoping I might find some way of avoiding what I could not deliberately resolve to do. I found the school a scene of uproar and confusion, which I vainly endeavored to quell. Just then, Jesse Peck, my friend's little son, entered with a bundle of five nice rods. As he laid them on the table before me, my courage rose; and, in the temporary silence which ensued, I laid down a few laws, the breaking of which would be followed with immediate chastisement. For a few moments the children were silent; but they had been used to threatening, and soon a boy rose from his seat, and, as he was stepping to the door, I took one of the sticks and gave him a moderate flogging; then with a grip upon his arm which made him feel that I was in earnest, put him into his seat. Hoping to make this chastisement answer for the whole school, I then told them in the most endearing manner I could command, that I was there to do them good — to make them such fine boys and girls that their parents and friends would be delighted with them, and they be growing up happy and useful; but in order to [do] this I must and would have their obedience. If I had occasion to punish again it would be more and more severely, until they yielded, and were trying to be good. But the children still lacked faith in my words, and if my recollection serves me, I spent most of the afternoon in alternate whippings and exhortations, the former always increasing in intensity, until at last, finding the difference between capricious anger and steadfast determination, they submitted. This was the first and last of corporeal punishment in that school. The next morning, and ever after, I had docile and orderly scholars. I was careful duly to send them out for recreation, to make their studies pleasant and interesting, and to praise them when they did well, and mention to their parents their good behavior.

Our school was soon the admiration of the neighborhood.

Some of the literati of the region heard of the marvelous progress the children made, and of classes formed ... and instruction given in higher branches; and coming to visit us, they encouraged me in my school, and gave me valuable commendation.

Emma Hart was not satisfied to follow in the beaten path of routine teaching, realizing, as she did, that education was more than book learning. She took a personal interest in her pupils, inspiring them with a desire for self-improvement. In this first school, she also began that practice which she followed continuously throughout her teaching career — the forming of new classes and the introduction of higher studies. Among her first pupils was her younger sister, Almira, and here began their common interest in education.

During her first teaching experience, Emma began to feel the need of further study to fit herself for future work. She was particularly eager for lessons in drawing and painting. Her father, at this time, was in straightened circumstances and unable to pay for her schooling, but fortunately, her brother Theodore, who had become a prosperous merchant in Petersburg, Virginia, was willing to send her money with which to continue her education.

That winter, she attended the school taught by the Misses Patten in Hartford. The school had been opened in 1786 and gave instructions in 'primary and essential branches,' in 'needlework, both lace and embroidery.' Mrs. Ruth Patten, mother of the Misses Patten and highly respected in the community for her piety, advised the girls and directed them in 'behaviour' and 'moral and religious duty.' It was said that the females in the school were 'entirely free from affectation and exhibiting a delicacy and propriety in their manners; with an improved mind and amiable disposition.'

Returning to Berlin the following summer, she taught a select school for older boys and girls in an upper room of her father's house. She was then asked to take charge of the winter school in Berlin — the very same school which she had attended under Dr. Miner. Now, it was she who taught from Morse's 'Geography' and remembered the lesson that she had learned that cold winter evening on the horse block under the stars. 'Elements of Geography,' the title read, 'A concise and comprehensive View of that useful Science, As divided into Astronomical, Physical or Natural, and Political Geography; Adapted to the Capacities of Children and Youth; and designed, from its Cheapness, for a Reading and Classical Book in Common Schools, and as a useful Winter Evening's Entertainment for Young People in Private Families.'

Of this school, she wrote:

I had the uncommon honor (uncommon at that time for a female) to keep the winter school, in what was then the southwest district of this parish. Whether it was four or five shillings a week which I received on that occasion, as a reward for my labors, I have forgotten. . . . Mr. and Mrs. Botsford gave me good board, (and such kind attentions as money cannot measure) for three shillings a week; such was their public spirit in favor of the school. At the close of the term, for which I had engaged, I held a public examination, which parents with encouraging zeal attended.

Now at nineteen she was engaged in teaching both winter and summer, but found time during the spring and autumn to attend Mrs. Royse's school in Hartford as a day scholar, making her home in the family of her cousin, Dr. Sylvester Wells, who had lately moved from Kensington to Hartford. This school, established by

Mrs. Lydia Bull Royse about 1800, was a celebrated institution and was said by some to be 'far ahead of the Misses Patten's.' Not only did the best families of Hartford send their daughters here, but pupils came from a distance, from states other than Connecticut. As room for boarders was limited, most of the pupils occupied quarters in town, as did Emma. Reading, writing, arithmetic, geography, French, dancing, drawing, painting, and needlework — subjects highly suited to young females — made up the curriculum. Among the teachers were several French émigrés. Mrs. Royse herself gave instructions in drawing, painting, and needlework, the subjects which Emma particularly wished to pursue. Some of the paintings supervised by Mrs. Royse are still in existence — one of Ruth and Naomi, one of Cybele, and the Parting of Hector and Andromache worked in embroidery with the faces painted in. Tuition for fourteen weeks was $7.62, with extras for drawing and needlework materials.

To be at school in Hartford was a wonderful experience for Emma, gratifying both her interest in people and her zeal for knowledge. Compared with the small quiet town of Berlin, Hartford with its brick mansions, its many shops, and numerous churches was very impressive. Living in the home of Dr. Sylvester Wells, who was keenly alive to political issues and the liberal thought of his day, she had much to think and talk about. Dr. Wells was a brilliant man, extreme in his views on religion and medicine, and an ardent Anti-Federalist. His move to Hartford had been made at the instigation of political friends to help in the fight against the 'Standing Order.' Later, as a member of the State Constitutional Convention, a State Senator, a Fellow of the Corporation of Yale College, and a candidate for Congress, he proved

his abilities. A firm friendship grew up between him and
Emma. They had many stimulating discussions, and
he thoroughly enjoyed her keen mind and conversational ability. Eunice, his wife, was Emma's ideal, and
she always thought of her as one of the most beautiful,
refined, and interesting women that she had known.

Dr. Wells's extreme religious views left their impression on Emma. Prejudiced against orthodox religion
because of the intolerance shown her father, she was
ready to consider new forms of belief. French philosophy with its appeal to reason had its advocates in America as well as in Europe. Its theories had appealed to
Emma's brothers and now she found it fashioning Dr.
Wells's religious opinions. Her own views, while sympathetic to these new ideas, were still in a state of flux.
Her father, in spite of his investigative turn of mind and
his withdrawal from the Congregational Church, was
distinctly religious, as was his wife, and the atmosphere
of the home was far from agnostic. The children had
always received religious instruction. In a letter to one
of his sons, on Christian belief, Captain Hart warned
him not to dwell too much in the region of dark speculation. 'I do not object,' he wrote, 'to a modest, candid
inquiry, and Search after Truth, but remember our chief
business is with our own Hearts.' Religion to him was
a 'Right Temper of Mind.' He continued: 'As Religion
is a matter of the Greatest Importance of any Thing
which concerns us, let me entreat you with all the
tenderness of Parental affection, and as you value your
own best Interests, to give your Earnest attention to
this Subject. ... Be willing that God should keep His
Throne, subject yourself to His disposal, cast yourself
entirely upon Him for Protection and Safety and never
question the Wisdom and Equity of His Government

and then ... whatever may be your outward Circumstances, you will feel Calmness and Serenity within your
own Breast, for none ever trusted in Him and was con-
founded — while on the other hand, none ever hardened
their heart against God and Prospered.' With this sane,
wholesome background Emma could not be led very
far into the realms of skepticism.

In the light of to-day, Emma Hart's girlhood seems
highly peaceful and proper, but against the background
of the early nineteenth century, it stood out in decided
contrast to the generally accepted idea of what was
proper for young women. While education then was far
better than it had been a generation before, and women,
whose mothers and grandmothers were unable to write,
wrote good letters and read some books besides the
Bible, nevertheless public opinion stood firmly against
broadening and enlarging the educational opportunities
for women. No college in the world admitted women.
There were no high schools for girls. Boarding-schools,
which only daughters of the well-to-do were able to
attend, taught the mere rudiments and stressed the accomplishments then thought so necessary for women,
such as painting, embroidery, French, a song or two for
company, playing on the harpsichord, and the making
of wax or shell ornaments. For poor girls, there was no
education beyond the district school. Rousseau's idea
was still generally accepted: 'The education of women
should be always relative to the men. To please, to
be useful to us, to make us love and esteem them, to
educate us when young and to take care of us when
grown up, to advise, to console us, to render our lives
easy and agreeable; these are the duties of women at all
times.'

Women had been taught that it was unwomanly to

hold opinions on serious subjects, that men admired
weak, clinging, innocent women. Their one ambition
was to attract men and gain husbands. The average woman did little thinking for herself, and was
distrustful of her abilities. A woman who discussed
politics or government, who held unorthodox views on
religion or presumed to enter the educational sphere of
men, was ridiculed as unwomanly, as aping men, and
was at once scheduled for moral shipwreck. The unfortunate, tragic life of Mary Wollstonecraft, who in
England had so strongly advocated education for
women, was held up as an example of the pernicious
influence of higher learning upon the morals of women.
For a woman of the middle or upper classes to earn
money was a disgrace. Her place was always in the
home of her nearest male relative.

The books of the day published particularly for the
edification and improvement of females impressed them
with their inferiority and the virtue of cultivating that
inferiority. They reminded them of the Biblical authority for the domination of man, of Saint Paul's words regarding the duties of women, and as women in general
were distinctly orthodox in their religious beliefs, they
accepted these statements without protest. Among
the favorite quotations in these books were the lines
by Milton, purporting to give his opinion on woman's
sphere:

'To whom thus Eve with perfect beauty adorned:
My Author and Disposer, what thou bidst
Unargued I obey; so God ordains;
God is thy law, thou mine; to know no more
Is woman's happiest knowledge and her praise.'

Hannah More, that model of female virtue, who willingly acknowledged the superiority of man, was also

freely quoted, eulogized, and upheld as an example for every woman to emulate. On the very proper pages of 'The Female Friend' were these words: 'a female politician is only less disgusting than a female infidel — but a female patriot is what Hannah More was and what every American woman should study to be.'

Although Emma Hart stepped out from all of these conventional ideas and binding theories regarding women, she did it naturally and easily, apparently with no sense of bitterness or of doing anything spectacular. This was undoubtedly due to the broad-minded, harmonious atmosphere of her home. Her father and all of her family encouraged her in every effort for progress. Her friendships with older men were most fortunate. Dr. Miner, Dr. Todd, and Dr. Wells, all appreciated her fine mind, conversed with her on equal terms, and helped her in her quest for knowledge.

Her normal happy girlhood stands out in vivid contrast to the sordid, tumultuous girlhood of Mary Wollstonecraft, whose bitter struggle against poverty, and whose contact with the brutality of men and their tyranny over the lives of women left their mark on her life. Little wonder that Mary Wollstonecraft was the tragic victim of circumstances, while Emma Hart, in a newer, freer country, was able to forge ahead, surmount obstacles, and actually work out a system of rational education for girls. Mary Wollstonecraft had prepared the thought of the world at least in a degree for the work of Emma Hart, but even Emma Hart with her vision and her open mind was unable to see beyond Mary Wollstonecraft's immorality, or to appreciate her struggle and her sincere, though apparently futile attempt to better the conditions of women. Instead, she felt only condemnation, thinking Mary Wollstonecraft had by her conduct hindered the advancement of her sex.

Thus, Emma Hart, while gradually forging ahead into new fields, satisfied the conventional minds of the age by her perfect conduct and her zeal for virtue.

CHAPTER V

EMMA HART, PRECEPTRESS

EMMA HART's unusual teaching ability and high qualifications of character gradually became known outside
of Connecticut. Soon after her twentieth birthday,
while she had charge of the Berlin winter school, she
was invited to teach in Westfield, Massachusetts, in
Middlebury, Vermont, and in Hudson, New York. All
three offers were good and presented opportunities for
progress in the teaching profession. She chose Westfield
because it was nearest home, and in the spring, became
an assistant in the well-known Westfield Academy.

Westfield then was the largest town in western Massachusetts, larger than Pittsfield or Springfield. The
Academy, established seven years before in 1800, was
housed in a pretentious building, the first floor of which
was used for classrooms, the upper story for an assembly hall. Two hundred was the average enrollment;
tuition, three dollars per quarter with twenty-five cents
extra during the fall, winter, and spring, for fuel, sweep-
ing, bell-ringing, and so forth. Pupils were received in
the homes of the best families as boarders; such was
the friendly interest of Westfield in its new school.
'Youths of both sexes who can read and write in a
decent manner, and only such, may be admitted to the
Academy,' read a by-law. The high purpose of the
institution was expressed, it is said, in the text of a
sermon preached on the opening day: 'That our sons
may be as plants grown up in their youth; that our
daughters may be as corner stones polished after the
similitude of a palace.' (Psalms 144:12.) It was one of

the few schools in the country that did not resort to
corporeal punishment in disciplining pupils.

The successive preceptors of the Academy, most of
whom were graduates of Williams College, were assisted
half of the year by a 'female.' It was this position of
female assistant that Emma Hart filled when she came
to Westfield in 1807. But Westfield did not satisfy her.
Heretofore in her short teaching experience, she had
always had full charge of her schools, and could develop
them at will. Westfield cramped her abilities. She
knew she deserved more salary, and could do more and
better work elsewhere. Middlebury's offer giving her a
chance to take full charge of a female academy was still
open, and after a few months, the trustees of Westfield
Academy unwillingly consented to her leaving to accept
this position. She had been so well liked in Westfield
that the next spring she was asked to return and make
her own terms as to salary. Good teachers were hard to
find in those days. Emma, however, did not leave Middlebury, for life there was too interesting.

The prosperous, influential town of Middlebury with
its wealth, culture, and fascinating social life introduced
Emma to a manner of living entirely new to her. The
leading families of the town with their luxurious homes,
their fine horses, their parties and balls, formed a little
aristocracy very dazzling to the young schoolmistress
from Berlin. She wrote in a letter to her parents: 'I find
society in a high state of cultivation — much more than
any other place I was ever in. The beaux here are, the
greater part of them, men of collegiate education. . . .
Among the older ladies, there are some whose manners
and conversation would dignify duchesses.'

As Emma said, many of the citizens of Middlebury
were college men, graduates of Yale, Dartmouth, and

WESTFIELD ACADEMY

Brown, and they prided themselves on their interest in education. For a long time, Middlebury had had a boys' academy. Middlebury College was established in 1800. Nor was education for girls neglected. That same year, the Honorable Horatio Seymour had invited Miss Ida Strong to open a school similar to Miss Pierce's celebrated school in Litchfield, Connecticut, which she had attended. Its first sessions were held in the Court House, but soon it attracted such favorable notice and was so well attended that funds were raised to erect a two-story building on land given by Mr. Seymour. So great was the enthusiasm over the undertaking that young men who were not able to contribute money offered their services in various ways, such as, laying board walks across the muddy ground in front of the building. This was one of the very first schools in the country built especially for the use of girls. Pupils came from all parts of the state and from New York. After a few years, Miss Strong was obliged to give up the school because of ill health and as there was no one to take her place, it was closed until the summer of 1807 when Emma Hart was called to reopen it. Meanwhile, the boys' grammar school had occupied the lower floor, and Emma began her school in one large room in the upper story with thirty-seven pupils. Having full charge of the school, she assumed considerable responsibility for a girl of twenty, but she was equal to it, and made a great success of the work.

Her busy days and some of her problems are described in a letter written to her parents in August, 1807:

I go to school generally before nine, and stay till one; come home, snatch my dinner, go again, and stay till almost sundown; come home, and dress in a great hurry to go abroad; get home about ten, fatigued enough to go to bed, and lie till seven the next morning, with hardly time enough to mend my stockings. Sunday I attend four meetings. My situation is a very trying one, in some respects. It will be difficult, perhaps impossible, to avoid making enemies. To please all is impossible — as much so as it would be for a person going two different ways at the same time. To please the greatest number of people, I must attend all the meetings Sunday, go to conference one or two afternoons in a week, profess to believe, among other articles of the creed, that mankind, generally speaking, will be damned. To please another set of people, I must speak in the most contemptible manner of conferences, and ridicule many of the notions of religionists, and praise many things that are disagreeable, such as dancing, playing cards, etc. In this situation I know of no better way than to follow the dictates of my conscience. This would direct me not to ridicule what others hold to be sacred; to endeavor not to treat any in such a manner as that they may have reason to be personally my enemies; to have no idea of pretending to believe what I do not believe.

In the family of Dr. Tudor, Emma enjoyed a pleasant home life. Dr. Tudor was a physician of high reputation, who had had a course of lectures with Dr. Rush of Philadelphia, an unusual advantage for medical men in those days. As Emma sauntered back from school on mellow autumn days in her fetching bonnet and Empire dress of soft muslin with a light cloak thrown about her shoulders, there was much to think about and dream about. Perhaps a flaming maple at the end of the street stirred to life some lines of poetry, or the memory of a conversation brought a smile of satisfaction to her face. On snowy winter days, wrapped in her fur-trimmed cloak, she braced herself against the cold north wind and hurried back and forth to school. Looking back in later years over the experiences of her first winter in Middlebury, Vermont, she wrote:

The winter of 1807–08 was one of exceeding hardship for me.

Although the weather was very cold, with frequent storms and much snow, I had to walk from Dr. Tudor's, where I boarded, to the academy and when there to keep my school in a large long room, formed like an ordinary ball room, occupying the whole upper story, while the only means of gaining warmth was from an open fire, in a small fireplace in the north end. Yet that winter I had an increased and very pleasant school. When it was so cold that we could live no longer, I called all my girls on to the floor, and arranged them two and two in a long row for a country dance; and while those who could sing would strike up some stirring tune, I with one of the girls for a partner, would lead down the dance, and soon have them all in rapid motion. After which we went to our school exercises again. The school had quite an increase in the spring from different parts of the state, and amounted to sixty. Among them and from the village was a remarkable band of maidens, ranging from about twelve to fifteen. I remained in this school two years from the time I commenced.

Teaching school or attending school during the cold winter months was not always comfortable nor easy, but when the teacher was as ingenious as Emma Hart and willing to interrupt the periods of study with dancing for warmth, exercise, and relaxation, the pupils were indeed fortunate. This introduction of dancing was just one example of Emma's natural exuberance which was so stimulating to her pupils. Enthusiastic about her work, she inspired her pupils with the same enthusiasm. Even in these early years, she deviated surprisingly from the stiff, routine methods of teaching which were then so common.

In her diary, Emma chronicled the events of those days in Middlebury, and always fond of philosophizing about life, commented upon the events in her characteristic moralizing manner. There were observations on friendship, on matrimony, on the relations between husband and wife, on religion. She criticized sermons, of course. This was a habit in journals in 1807. But her interest in sermons and moralizing did not keep her from enjoying to the full many parties and balls. Conversations with prominent men and women of Middlebury were recorded with a certain pride natural to hero-worshiping youth. A sensitiveness that made criticism and slights cut deep, a dread of misrepresentation, an excessive enthusiasm which often led to disappointment, an inherent kindness and practicality ran through the pages of her journal. She was studious, continuing her study of history and painting, and commenting on her progress. She had literary aspirations and wrote poetry, just as her father before her had written poetry, because she felt the need of expressing herself in verse, but she was very modest about these poetical attempts. While teaching interested her, there are no indications that she had any particular ambitions in this line or that she was evolving any definite plans for the improvement of woman's education.

After one very successful year at Middlebury, Emma became cognizant of an effort to break down the school. While she realized, when she first came to Middlebury, that her position would be difficult because of the religious differences among the townspeople, she did not expect that denominational jealousy would work aggressively against the school, for she had tried to be fair and tolerant and to offend no one. As she had given of her best, it hurt her deeply to be misunderstood. There is no definite record of what the trouble was, but whatever it was, it was soon cleared away, and although it caused Emma many unhappy, anxious moments, it gained for her the staunch support of friends and the friendship of one of the leading men of Middlebury, Dr. John Willard. As soon as Dr. Willard heard of the school

MIDDLEBURY FEMALE ACADEMY

difficulty, his sense of fair play was aroused, and he at once championed the young schoolmistress.

Emma was very much attracted to Dr. Willard. She was essentially a hero-worshiper. It was flattering indeed to have a man of education, wealth, and social prominence come to her defense, particularly in an age when men in general had little sympathy with independent young schoolmistresses. Then, besides, Dr. Willard was a physician, and some of the most highly respected friends of her girlhood had been members of that profession. He was a man of influence in politics, a Republican, and Emma, always interested in history and in politics, always Republican in sympathy because that party had opposed her father's religious persecutors, discovered much common ground for conversation and interest. Dr. Willard, instead of being disturbed, as many men might have been, by Emma's interest in government and politics and by her keen, inquiring mind, found her a stimulating companion and was charmed by her enthusiasm.

Those were proud joyous days of courtship for the young schoolmistress. Never had spring in Middlebury come with such a burst of blossoms; never had the hills been so blue. Middlebury, always full of interest, took on a meaning of supreme importance in her life. The young beaux looked so insignificant beside this older, more experienced man. Why had he singled her out? It was like a fairy tale, a thrilling novel. For Dr. Willard, these were days of happy companionship with Emma, whose irresistible beauty and freshness of youth held a depth of intellect and understanding that he had never before encountered. They were married on August 10, 1809, when Emma was twenty-two.

Although Dr. Willard was twenty-eight years older

than Emma, the difference in their ages was not markedly apparent. Dr. Willard was vigorous, active, in the prime of life. Emma, in spite of her youthful appearance, was mature mentally. It seemed very natural for her to marry a man so much older than herself. A younger man would not have satisfied her. She must necessarily marry a man whom she could look up to, a man who had accomplished something, whose mind and interests would make an appeal.

Dr. Willard had also come to Middlebury from Connecticut. He was born in East Guilford, where his father, Captain John Willard, was a shipmaster. Still a young child when his father died, he was brought up by his mother on a small farm. Farm work was drudgery to him and he escaped it by going to sea. During the last years of the Revolution, he was taken prisoner by the British and confined in a Jersey prison ship. When he finally was released and had recovered his strength, he was made quartermaster of a Connecticut regiment of volunteers. After the war was over, he began the study of medicine under the direction of a physician of East Guilford, and as he was fond of study, he took up, at the same time, a course of classical studies with the clergyman of the parish. Soon after his marriage with Esther Wilcox, he moved to Middlebury, where he began the practice of medicine. Middlebury then was still almost a wilderness, and the few roads that had been opened were practically impassable at certain seasons of the year on account of the mud. He was the first physician in the town and soon built up an extensive practice. He had only been in Middlebury about a year when his wife died, leaving a baby boy whom they had named Gustavus Vasa Willard. Some years later, he married Mindwell Meiggs, the widow of Thaddeus

Frisbie. Three children were born to them, William Tell Willard, Benjamin Franklin Willard, and a daughter, Laura. Then his second wife died, leaving him with a family of four children to look after.

Dr. Willard had gradually become more and more interested in politics. Appointed Marshal of the District of Vermont under Jefferson's administration, he discontinued the active practice of medicine, although his reputation as a physician had been high. He disapproved of the common medical practice of the day, especially the methods of country doctors, and that is possibly why he turned his attention to politics, which developed his abilities to a greater degree. He was very enthusiastic about Vermont and considered its constitution better than that of any other State. A power in the Republican organization of Vermont, he exerted more influence over party measures than any other man. When he married Emma Hart, he still held the position of Marshal of Vermont, was supervisor of the direct tax imposed by the Federal Government, was paymaster of pensions, chairman of the Republican organization of Vermont, and a director of the Vermont State Bank; he owned several farms near Middlebury and had just built a pretentious brick house on Main Street. Everything pointed to a prosperous married life for young Mrs. Willard.

CHAPTER VI
MORE MIDDLEBURY DAYS

EMMA entered into her married life with that enthusiasm so characteristic of her. She did nothing by halves. She loved and respected John Willard with all the strength of her being and was not to be disappointed in him, for he loved her devotedly and was sympathetic to all her interests. There are no indications that she regretted giving up teaching in spite of her marked abilities in that line. Like all girls of that period, her highest ambition was for happy married life, and possibly her personal ambitions were superseded by dreams of Dr. Willard's political advancement. Her patriotism and love for the new Republic would naturally lead her to wish for her husband an ever-increasing part in its government.

There was, however, one cloud over the otherwise happy married life of the Willards — the attitude of Dr. Willard's children toward their young stepmother. Emma, entering the family with a great desire to mother and befriend the children, found only antagonism. Repeated rebuffs and continued suspicion in return for her kindness wounded her so deeply that, as she herself said, her health was undermined. Remembering the affection in the Hart family toward her mother, who was the stepmother of seven, Emma could not understand this unjust treatment. Misrepresentation was a cross for her to bear.

The oldest of the family, Gustavus, was the same age as his stepmother. He had studied at Middlebury College in the class of 1805, and later, feeling the urge to go West, moved to Ohio. William Tell was thirteen,

DR. JOHN WILLARD

Benjamin Franklin eleven, and Laura a few years younger. It took years of patience, tact, and kindness to overcome their prejudice even in a degree. In a letter to her stepson Benjamin Franklin, written twelve years later, Mrs. Willard recalls these trying days:

I confess I am more easily irritated by you than by any other person. The reason of this is that, what comes from you, falls upon a wound which once was so deep that it undermined my health, and all but destroyed my reason. I allude to the treatment which I received from your father's family after I entered it. In the sacred presence of that God before whom we must all appear, I sincerely declare that I forgive you, and allude to it only to say I do not think you are yet wholly free from certain false opinions upon which that conduct proceeded. One of these is that I married your father from motives of interest rather than affection. I have heard from many sources that such was your belief. I have felt that I could never stoop to vindicate myself from such a charge; but, Frank, my mind is softened in regard to you. I will stoop to any thing that shall make you live as you ought, or die, if die you must, forgiving and forgiven. I therefore tell you that you are mistaken in the supposition that I married your father without affection for his person. A little candid reflection upon my conduct soon after our marriage — for you were old enough to remember it — would, I should think, satisfy you that, though it might be strange that so young a woman should love a man so much older than herself, yet love him I did with uncommon ardor of affection. Can you not remember how I wept at his departure? how I watched and counted the days till he should return? For his sake I gave up my literary ambition, and became a domestic drudge. . . . It is true I was young when I married, but, my mind in some respects outstripping my years, I had for a long time before my marriage formed my intimacies among people of nearly your father's age. Dr. Todd and Dr. Wells were among my intimate friends at this season. And why should I have married your father from other than pure motives? My standing in society was as good as his. My income arising from the exercise of my talents, of which I was fond, was more than sufficient for my support. My brothers in Virginia were wealthy, and anxious I should live with them. Your father was not rich, and he always told me so. Perhaps if all the men in the world had stood before me at my disposal, I might have loved some one else, but in youth one must love, and was there any one in Middlebury that I should so likely to love as your father? Indeed, Frank, I often think you undervalue your father. In several respects he is a man peculiarly calculated to gain a woman's affection, and he certainly deserves and possesses mine.

Dr. Willard's work kept him away from home a great deal. During these absences, Emma buried herself in his library, studying dry medical volumes, so that she might be able to discuss medicine and physiology intelligently with him. Dr. Willard was delighted with her interest and ability. Instead of crushing that interest, as practically every man of that day would have done, for the study of physiology was considered most unseemly for a woman, he encouraged her in her studies, and their days together were filled with happy, intelligent companionship. A great deal of credit is due Dr. Willard for his broad-mindedness. Many an older man would have dominated and stifled the personality of his young wife. He, however, appreciated Emma's rare personality, and with the wealth of his experience brought out the very best in her.

Emma's disappointment in her stepchildren was somewhat alleviated by the thought of the coming of her own child. As she busied herself with household tasks in the large, 'elegant' brick house on Main Street, or sat by the window sewing, looking out across the wide valley toward the encircling hills, which brought back memories of her Connecticut home, she treasured the thought that her own child would love her and crave her affection. On the twenty-eighth day of September, 1810, she held her own baby boy in her arms. She named him John Hart Willard.

The Willard home faced Middlebury College, and daily the chapel bell and calls to recitations rang out across the campus. The bells told time for Emma, and often she watched the boys hurrying to and from classes, envying them a little their college education. One of the boys, John Willard, her husband's nephew, lived with them for four years while he attended Middlebury College. This opened up another avenue of interest for Emma. It brought her in close touch with the workings of a man's college. John gave her full accounts of his class work; she read his textbooks, and thus became familiar with his course of study. Geometry attracted her, as it had when she was a girl of twelve, and again she began to study it by herself. When she felt that she had mastered everything in John's textbook, she asked him to give her a thorough examination in the subject. She wanted to be absolutely sure that she understood it, because people in general so firmly believed it to be beyond the grasp of the female mind. John found her very proficient in geometry, and encouraged by his verdict, she next undertook the study of Paley's 'Moral Philosophy' and Locke's 'Essay Concerning Moral Understanding.'

This close contact with the course of study in a man's college opened Emma Willard's eyes to the disadvantages under which women labored to obtain an education. She had never before realized so fully what women were being deprived of. Heretofore, she had been interested in knowledge for its own sake, for the pure joy of study, and as she had never been thwarted nor discouraged in any of her efforts for higher learning, she had not grasped the situation of the average woman. She had not realized how girls were taught mere smatterings while their brothers had every educational advantage. She had proved for herself that women were able to pursue higher studies. Now, aroused by the inequality of educational opportunity and man's assumption of superiority, she began to ponder over these things and grope for a solution of the problem.

After three years of prosperity, the Willards were suddenly faced with serious financial reverses. The Vermont State Bank, of which Dr. Willard was a director, was entered by a false key and robbed. The public suspected the directors of being implicated in the robbery and called upon them to make up the loss. The Supreme Court rendered a judgment against them for twenty-eight thousand dollars. The greater part of this claim was later remitted by the Legislature, and the discovery of the false key in an attic, years afterward, completely vindicated the directors. Nevertheless, the general feeling toward them for some time was one of suspicion and distrust, and as a result, Dr. Willard not only lost his prestige in the community, but was obliged to put heavy mortgages on all his land to make good the loss.

Throughout these difficulties Emma was very loyal to her husband. She calmed his fears, encouraged and comforted him. Never was there a complaint on her part, nor any sign of unhappiness because of their changed circumstances. A letter written to him at this time shows how bravely she did her part:

I regret that your absence from home must be prolonged, but, much as I feel the want of your society, and much as we need your care, I am not weak enough to request you to return while exertions remain unmade to relieve you from your embarrassments.

MIDDLEBURY COLLEGE

Your affairs at home have, I believe, suffered less by your absence than could have been expected. Godenow has, I believe, prosecuted the farming business, with great zeal and attention. The winter-apples are gathered; the cider is made — twenty-three barrels; the potatoes are nearly all in; the buckwheat is gathered, but lies on the barn-floor unthreshed, which, by the way, places us in a predicament about the wheat; the cows and hogs have been fed according to your directions; the carrots and garden vegetables are out yet, but will be gathered immediately; no injury has been done to the farm by unruly cattle; Wilcox has let us have a quarter of beef.

As respects myself, I have not been five rods from the house since you left, and it is not probable I shall exceed those bounds until you return. I have seen no company at home, so you can see I have been a widow indeed, and, I can add in haste, I count the days when I may expect you home.

The unexpected financial misfortunes of the Willards came at a time when the whole country was in a state of dissatisfaction and indecision. For years, both England and France had made continued attacks on American shipping, France confiscating American cargoes and ships, and England impressing American seamen on the ground that they were deserters from the English navy. This finally led to the War of 1812, which was entered into half-heartedly by the North and East, especially New England. There were men who considered America inferior to foreign powers, and felt that all that had been gained in the past would be lost by another war. There were some who preferred a war with France to war with England. All these things, Dr. Willard and Emma discussed by their fireside, when Dr. Willard came home from his long trips into the country. Benjamin Franklin Willard was a lieutenant in the militia. News of the war was awaited eagerly, and great was the rejoicing over the victories of the frigate Constitution un-

der the command of Commodore Isaac Hull. From the
western frontier, reports were discouraging until the
romantic story of Perry's capture of the British fleet on
Lake Erie came through, and his report, 'We have met
the enemy and they are ours,' passed with truly American pride from lip to lip. There was talk of Henry Clay
from Kentucky, the eloquent young Speaker of the
House, a representative of the virile, growing West.
There was talk of other young men who had entered
Congress, Calhoun, of South Carolina, and Daniel
Webster. All three were of a new generation, vigorous,
intensely American, with unbounded pride in the Republic. Naval victories brought confidence to the
country and united it as nothing else had done. England now had a rival on the seas. Then the burning
of Washington stirred the country. Key wrote 'The
Star-Spangled Banner' during the attack on Baltimore;
and spasmodic warfare continued until the signing of
the Treaty of Ghent in December, 1814.

All of these things interested Emma, as the stories
of the Revolution and the formation of the Republic had
interested her when a child. History was being made,
and history was almost a passion with her. She was an
insatiable reader. Locke, Paley, and the huge volumes
in her husband's medical library did not continually
claim her attention, for she had a decided taste for
romance. Scott was her favorite, and she spent many
hours engrossed in 'Marmion' and 'The Lady of the
Lake.'

As always, Emma carried on an extensive correspondence. Her friends were many and an essential part of
her life. Her affection for her dearest friends was very
deep. The following extract from a letter gives some idea
of what friendship meant to her:

You make a particular request that I shall write on the *first* leaf of a book which you devote to friendship. With solemnity of thought, fully aware of what I do, I write on the leaf. There — it is done! What is done? The league of friendship, existing before in the spirit, is now in the letter also. You are set apart from the world as respects me — I as it respects you. If I am in need, sickness, or adversity, the world may pity, but it is for you to relieve. If you are the victim of misfortune, then it must be me to bring you relief and consolation. This is not marriage; but it is something like it. Mutually to love, to trust, to rejoice, to mourn together — such is the relation which subsists between Julia Pierpont Werne and Emma Willard.

Many letters passed between Emma and her father during these years. He had been happy over the successful marriage of his daughter and over his new grandchild, and just as he had called Emma to him for a talk when she was a child at home, so now he wrote her letters filled with good advice and religious reflections. The news of his death in August, 1813, caused Emma great sorrow, for they had been very close — the thoughtful, dignified, old man with his progressive views and the impulsive young woman, eager for knowledge, who had as yet barely glimpsed the fullness of her ability. She comforted herself in a poem, 'To the Memory of Samuel Hart,' one verse of which emphasized his most outstanding trait:

> He held, it was a right which free-born man
> Possessed, to freely think, and freely speak;
> Nor deemed it good inquiry to repress,
> And with authorities to silence reason;
> Nor e'er would he, dishonest to himself,
> Permit his reason thus to be subdued.

It continued with lines about the graveyard, the mourning widow, the 'daughter afar' who could not mingle her tears with her mother's or soothe her woes, and ended with this effort at comfort:

Yet let us rather look beyond this life
When, reunited, we may all rejoice.

Emma's generosity and fairness regarding the settlement of her father's estate are especially worthy of notice in view of the fact that she was in financial difficulties at this time. She wrote to her brother:

DEAR BROTHER: In the settlement of our father's estate it is an object most desirable that such an understanding be kept up between us as in the end we shall all be satisfied. To effect this it is necessary that we frequently commune together, believing, in a spirit of charity and brotherly love, that there are none of the heirs who do not intend to do right. I am much pleased with the proposal to settle the estate without resorting to law. If it is settled according to equity, that is sufficient. And, if we lay prejudice aside, we surely can be better judges of that than strangers can. In the first place, I think it ought to be considered that, with regard to the property our father left, we children have not, in justice, any claim; because none of us, except, perhaps, yourself, helped either to acquire or preserve it; and I believe our father thought he gave you compensation, and I never heard but what you were satisfied. We received our existence in the old mansion. We were nursed in our infancy, and the wants of our childhood were supplied. This, surely, does not give us any claim. But, with mother, the case is different. She entered the family at an age when she was capable of rendering assistance instead of requiring it. She has spent more than forty years of hard labor, care, and anxiety, in it, and to her care it is owing that our large family have been brought up, and so much of the property remains. So, to what is left, after paying the debts, it follows that she has the superior right — enough to support her, even if that should comprehend the whole.

During these years when the Willards were confronted with reverses, Emma was looking for a way to help her husband. She was filled with a great desire to help not merely by comforting and encouraging him, but in some tangible way which would pay off the many mortgages. Her mind naturally turned to teaching. Her plan was to open a boarding school for girls in her own home. When she first suggested this to Dr. Willard, he objected, but his scruples were finally overcome by her earnestness, and putting aside his pride, he coöperated with her in every way. Without his assistance and wide experience, it would have been very difficult for her to carry out the work which evolved during the next years. Emma Willard was being turned again to the cause of education, her life work, which was to prove of such inestimable value to the women of America.

CHAPTER VII

MIDDLEBURY FEMALE SEMINARY

IN the spring of 1814, when her little boy was four years old, Emma Willard opened a boarding school in her home. 'My leading motive,' she wrote, 'was to relieve my husband from financial difficulties. I had also the further motive of keeping a better school than those about me.' At first, she taught the light, superficial studies which were then considered suitable for girls, but gradually introduced higher subjects. Her plan was not to allow any pupil to study more than three so-called higher subjects at a time; for example, mathematics, history, and a language. The rest of the school day was to be filled with music, drawing, penmanship, and lighter studies. Eager to disprove the popular fallacy that education undermined the health of young women, she arranged the hours of study, exercise, and sleep according to her ideas of what was best for the health of the girls. She believed heartily in training both the mind and the hands, feeling that woman's sphere demanded skill in handwork. Her pupils were daughters of some of the best families of the surrounding country — all enthusiastic over their work and eager to learn. They had a happy social life at the school, just as if they were one large family. Mrs. Willard with her rare conversational ability and her interest in literature made the evening sewing circle highly interesting. She read to the girls from Wordsworth, Coleridge, and Southey; sometimes a play was read or acted by the girls; there were always discussions. It goes without saying that Mrs. Willard used these discussions as opportunities to give her pupils good advice and to inspire them with high ideals.

This tendency to pass on good advice was no particular priggishness on the part of Mrs. Willard. It was characteristic of the age. A certain zeal for virtue was very becoming in a woman. Letters were weighed down with good advice, and not only letters from parents to children, but letters of friendship written by one girl to another. Emma Willard, a married woman and a teacher, felt she had much to impart from her experience, and delighted in giving friendly counsel. These few lines, written to her sister Almira, are typical of her sermonizing:

As I have but a few moments to write, I believe it would be most profitable to spend that time in endeavoring to give you some good advice. In the first place, refrain from pampering your imagination too much with novels. You and I ought rather to consult our understanding. A person who has the voyage of life before her, with too much imagination for her understanding, is a vessel on a boisterous ocean, with too much sail, exposed to a thousand accidents. In the next place, be economical both of your time and your money. True, the sun shines today; but it may storm tomorrow. Thirdly, in intercourse with the world, seek rather to avoid censure than to attract attention.

Emma and Almira had much in common — a love for study, a special aptitude for teaching, and a great desire to progress and improve the intellectual status of women. Almira was six years younger than Emma and looked up to her as a model of virtuous, progressive womanhood. She, too, had taught in the Berlin schools at an early age and in the towns near by. She had visited Emma in Middlebury, and they had talked over woman's meager educational opportunities, her disadvantages, and her possibilities. She had studied at

the Academy in Pittsfield conducted by her cousin
Nancy Hinsdale, and later came to Middlebury again,
when Emma had opened her school in her own home.
Here she was impressed by her sister's work in the more
solid subjects, and when she took charge of a female
academy in Sand Hill, New York, she likewise introduced higher studies. Emma's interest and solicitude
followed Almira wherever she went, and when, a few
years later, word came that she was engaged to Simeon
Lincoln, the editor of 'The Connecticut Mirror,' published in Hartford, Emma, in the midst of arduous school
duties, took time to write her lengthy letters of advice
on matrimony. She warned her not to let 'those tender
and delicious sensations which accompany successful
love' soften or enervate her mind. She must prepare for
a life of vicissitude. She suggested that her husband
might not always appear as devoted as she expected him
to be, that he might be engrossed in his work, that his
business might worry him and make him appear disinterested and gloomy, that he might sometimes be
impatient. Emma wanted her sister prepared for the
worst, for, as she explained, 'If you enter the marriage
state believing such things to be absolutely impossible,
if you should meet them, they would come upon you
with double force. We should endeavor to make a just
estimate of our future prospects, and consider what
evils, peculiar situations in which we may be placed, are
most likely to beset us, and endeavor to avert them if
we can; or if we must suffer them, to do it with fortitude,
and not magnify them by imagination, and think that,
because we cannot enjoy all that a glowing fancy can
paint, there is no enjoyment left.'

Emma had learned something about human nature
during the first six years of her married life, and they

had been happy years, with Dr. Willard. Dissatisfied
stepchildren and financial reverses had only made her
wiser, and oh, the joy of passing that wisdom on to
another!

Emma closed one of her letters to Almira with this
glimpse of her life:

> I am involved in care. There are forty in our family and
> seventy in the school. I have, however, an excellent house-
> keeper and a very good assistant in my school. . . .
> Little John says I must tell you he has learned a great deal.
> He goes to a little children's school, and is doing very well.
> Doctor has not gone to Pittsfield after mother, but expects to
> set out this week. We both feel very unpleasantly that he
> could not have gone before, but a succession of engagements
> made it impossible.

Mrs. Willard's school proved to be a great success in
every way. The girls took up the higher subjects with
ease and great interest. Parents were pleased with the
results of the school. They found their daughters as
refined and ladylike as ever, and intelligent as well.
None of the much-prophesied dire effects of education
were noticeable. All this spurred Mrs. Willard on to
work for a fairer, better system of education for girls.
Not only did she feel the injustice of depriving girls of
a good education, but she was impressed by the short-
sightedness of the men. She was convinced that married
life would be happier and on a higher plane if the wife
was the intellectual companion of her husband. She
knew that mothers whose minds and ideals had been
strengthened by education would give the world better
sons. She longed to share these views with the world,
but first she must be able to furnish concrete proofs
by continually improving her own school. In this, she
encountered difficulties. She could not afford to employ

professors to teach the higher subjects. She could not
ask fathers to pay too highly for their daughters' education. She appealed to Middlebury College, hoping her
pupils would be allowed to sit as listeners in some of the
classes, but this was refused. She asked if she might attend the boys' examinations to become familiar with
college methods and the standard of scholarship. This
too was refused on the grounds that it would be unbecoming for her to attend and might create an unfortunate precedent. Otherwise, the President and the
Professors of the College took a friendly interest in her
plans. There was nothing left for Mrs. Willard to do but
to evolve her own methods, to train her own teachers,
to study new subjects, and to teach them herself. In a
sketch written for a friend some twenty-six years later,
Mrs. Willard described her efforts:

My exertions meanwhile, became unremitted and intense.
My school grew to seventy pupils. I spent from ten to twelve
hours a day in teaching, and on extraordinary occasions, as
preparing for examination, fifteen; besides, always having
under investigation some one new subject which, as I studied,
I simultaneously taught to a class of my ablest pupils. Hence
every new term some new study was introduced; and in all
their studies, my pupils were very thoroughly trained. In
classing my school for the term of study, which was then about
three months, I gave to each her course (being careful not
to give too much), with the certain expectation, that she must
be examined on it at the close of the term. Then I was wont
to consider that my first duty as a teacher, required of me
that I should labor to make my pupils by explanation and il-
lustration *understand* their subject, and get them warmed into
it, by making them see its beauties and its advantages. During this first part of the process, I talked much more than the
pupils were required to do, keeping their attention awake by
frequent questions, requiring short answers from the whole
class — for it was ever my maxim, if attention fails, the

teacher fails. Then in the *second* stage of my teaching, I made each scholar recite, in order that she might *remember* — paying special attention to the meaning of words, and to discern whether the subject was indeed understood without mistake. Then the *third* process was to make the pupil capable of *communicating*. And doing this in a right manner, was to prepare her for examination. At this time I personally examined all my classes.

This thorough teaching added rapidly to my reputation. Another important feature of a system, thus requiring careful drill and correct enunciation, was manifested by the examinations. The pupils there acquired character and confidence. Scholars thus instructed were soon capable of teaching; and here were now forming my future teachers; and some were soon capable of aiding me in arranging the new studies, which I was constantly engaged in introducing.

Here I began a series of improvements in geography — separating and first teaching what could be learned from maps — then treating the various subjects of population, extent, length of rivers, etc., by comparing country with country, river with river, and city with city — making out with the assistance of my pupils, those tables which afterwards appeared in Woodbridge and Willard's Geographies. Here also began improvements in educational history. Moral Philosophy came next, with Paley for the author . . . ; and then the Philosophy of the Mind — Locke the author. . . .

Mrs. Willard also taught mathematics in her Middlebury School, and it was here, as she says, that 'the stream of lady-mathematicians took its rise.'

As Mrs. Willard had no model to follow, she evolved her own examinations and fearlessly conducted them, making a great deal of them and inviting the Professors of Middlebury College as well as many prominent citizens to attend. In this way, she felt she could best bring to the notice of the public the fact that the female mind could comprehend collegiate studies.

An extract from a letter, written in 1815, to a friend,

the wife of Governor Skinner, shows what thoughts and reasonings were constantly passing through her mind:

I thank you for your favorable opinion of my exertions in my school, and I am not so modest as to say that I do not think I have in some degree deserved them. Certainly, when I compare what I have done with my ideas of perfection, I have much cause to be humbled; but, when I compare my labors with what are generally done in schools of a similar kind, I feel some cause to be satisfied with my own. I am gratified with your sentiments on female education; and I wish legislators thought as you do and I do. They can expend thousands for the education of male youths, but when was anything ever done by the public to promote that of females? And what is the reason of it? It is not because the expense is valued, nor because fathers do not love their daughters as well as their sons. It is partly from inattention to the subject, and partly from the absurd prejudice that, if women's minds were cultivated, they would forget their own sphere, and intrude themselves into that of men. And whence arises this? Not from a liberal and candid investigation of the organization of the female mind in general, but because a few individuals of masculine minds have forcibly broken through every impediment, and rivalled the men even in their own department. These, however, do not constitute the rule, but the exception. They might as well reason that, because there is now and then a brawny woman who can lift a barrel of cider, her whole sex should be kept constantly within-doors and not allowed to exercise, lest, if they should attain the full perfection of their bodily strength, they would contest the prize upon the wrestling ground, or attempt to take the scythe and the hoe from the hands of men, and turn them into the kitchen. The truth is that, when men suffer from mortification in being rivalled by women in point of strength either of body or mind, they suffer a thousand times from their weakness. How many a man has lived straitened and depressed in his circumstances, or been absolutely ruined as to his property, because his wife had a childish partiality to this place or that; and she chose it because she chose it; or because his wife wanted to appear as her neighbors appeared, without considering whether her husband's purse might compare with her neighbor's; or whether her neighbors were not indulging their vanity to their ruin! What boots it, to a man who has so weak a thing for a wife, how many elegant pieces of embroidery she may have wrought in her youth, or how bright a red or green she may have produced upon paper, or even that she possessed the most cultivated manners, and all those soft attractions that are capable of dissolving his soul in fondness? Untaught to form any extended views, destitute of any strength of reason, they are in her hands but a delicious poison, or it may be a lure to destruction. I have taken a view of woman merely as a wife; but, taking also the view as a mother, the importance of her character rises almost infinitely. When we consider that the character of the next generation will be formed by the mothers of this, how important does it become that their reason should be strengthened to overcome their insignificant vanities and prejudices, otherwise the minds of their sons, as well as of their daughters, will be tinctured by them!

Emma Willard was roused to action. She had found her mission. Just as her father's convictions had led him to advocate tolerance and freedom of thought in an age of religious intolerance and bigotry, just so Emma Willard was being driven by her convictions to take her stand fearlessly in the face of bitter prejudice for the education of women. Her father had instilled her with idealism and courage. Her mother's influence had developed practicality and executive ability. With these qualities at her command, Emma Willard was well equipped for the contest.

CHAPTER VIII

THE PLAN FOR IMPROVING FEMALE EDUCATION

WHEN Mrs. Willard had proved to her entire satisfaction her own ability and the capacity of her pupils to master difficult so-called masculine subjects, she began to write out a plan of education which she hoped to present to the public. At first she kept this even from her husband, although she knew that he had always been sympathetic with her views. Her dream was to head an institution indorsed by prominent men, an endowed institution which would receive regular appropriations from the state, as did many men's colleges. As she planned, she searched for a name for her ideal institution. She did not dare call it a college, because a college for women would have been considered entirely too absurd. In this way she found the name: 'I heard Dr. Merrill pray for "our seminaries of learning." I said I have it — I will call it a Female Seminary. That word, while it is as high as the highest, is also as low as the lowest, and will not create a jealousy that we mean to intrude upon the province of the men.' The title, Female Seminary, coined by Emma Willard, gradually came into general use as a name for higher institutions of learning for girls.

Mrs. Willard had been so accustomed to discuss her plans and ambitions with her husband that she could not keep these from him for very long. To her great relief and joy, he encouraged her. Her intellectual progress and experiments in teaching had shown him the fallacy of the man-made supposition that women's minds were inferior, and he too became eager to help

the sex which he now believed had been outrageously
neglected. Mrs. Willard was deeply touched by her
husband's whole-souled coöperation. She said of him,
'With an affection more generous and disinterested than
ever man before felt, he, in his later life, sought my elevation indifferent to his own. Possessing on the whole
an opinion of me more favorable than any other human
being ever will have — and thus encouraging me to
dare much — he yet knew my weaknesses and fortified
me against them.'

For several years she worked on her 'Plan for Improving Female Education,' telling no one but her
husband about it until a year after the manuscript was
completed, for, as she said, 'I knew that I should be regarded as visionary almost to insanity, should I utter
the expectations which I secretly entertained in connection with it. But it was not merely on the strength
of my arguments that I relied. I determined to inform
myself and increase my personal influence and fame as
a teacher, calculating that in this way I might be sought
for in other places, where influential men would carry
my project before some legislature, for the sake of
obtaining a good school.'

Mrs. Willard was correct in her assumptions. She
soon had offers to go elsewhere. Governor Van Ness suggested her going to Burlington, Vermont, as principal of
a female seminary which was to be opened in the college
buildings. As these plans did not materialize, she turned
her thoughts toward New York State, realizing that the
ideal situation for a seminary would be in the Hudson
River Valley, near the head of navigation. The coming
of several pupils from Waterford, New York, to Middlebury Female Seminary gained for her the friendship of
General Van Schoonhoven, who was greatly interested

in her views on education and offered to show the manuscript of her 'Plan' to the Honorable J. Cramer of Waterford and to De Witt Clinton, who was then Governor of New York.

This was the opportunity for which Mrs. Willard had been waiting. She copied the manuscript with great care and sent it to Governor Clinton with the following letter:

To his Excellency, De Witt Clinton:

SIR: Mr. Southwick will present to you a manuscript, containing a plan for improving the education of females, by instituting public seminaries for their use. Its authoress has presumed to offer it to your Excellency, because she believed you would consider the subject as worthy of your attention, and because she wished to submit her scheme to those exalted characters, whose guide is reason, and whose objects are the happiness and improvement of mankind; and among these characters where can plans to promote those objects hope for countenance, if not from Mr. Clinton.

The manuscript is addressed to a legislature, although not intended for present publication. The authoress believed she could communicate her ideas with less circumlocution in this than in any other manner; and besides, should the approbation of distinguished citizens, in any of the larger and wealthier states, give hopes that such an application would be attended with success, a publication might then be proper, and the manuscript would need less alteration.

Possibly your Excellency may consider this plan as better deserving your attention, to know that its authoress is not a visionary enthusiast, who has speculated in solitude without practical knowledge of her subject. For ten years she has been intimately conversant with female schools, and nearly all of that time she has herself been a preceptress. Nor has she written for the sake of writing, but merely to communicate a plan of which she fully believes that it is practicable; that, if realized, it would form a new and happy era in the history of her sex, and if of her sex, why not of her country, and of mankind? Nor would she shrink from any trial of this faith; for such is her conviction of the utility of her scheme, that could its execution be forwarded, by any exertion or any sacrifice of her own, neither the love of domestic ease, or the dread of responsibility, would prevent her embarking her reputation on its success.

If Mr. Clinton should not view this plan as its authoress hopes he may, but should think the time devoted to its perusal was sacrificed, let him not consider its presentation to him as the intrusion of an individual ignorant of the worth of his time, and the importance of his high avocations, but as the enthusiasm of a projector, misjudging of her project, and overrating its value.

With sentiments of the deepest respect, I am, Sir,
Your Obedient Servant
EMMA WILLARD

MIDDLEBURY, VT., *February 5*, 1818

Both the manuscript and the letter were perfect specimens of penmanship. The 'Plan' with its many pages was handwritten in fine clear script as legible as print, with not a word erased or interlined. Mrs. Willard was very proud of her beautiful penmanship, which she considered an inheritance from her father, and had made a special effort to perfect it, believing it to be an important asset in her educational work.

She awaited Governor Clinton's reply with great eagerness. When it finally came, it assured her of his interest in her views. He had already shown his sympathy with education by serving as the first president of the Free School Society, organized in New York City in 1805. He wrote her as follows:

ALBANY, 31*st Dec.*, 1818
MADAM:
I have read your manuscript with equal pleasure and instruction. Its views of the present defective plan of female education, and of the beneficial effects and tendencies of the proposed system, are often original and always ingenious, and

are conveyed in perspicuous and elegant language; and independently of the conclusive considerations which you urge in favor of the claim and capacity of your sex for high intellectual cultivation, the *very fact* of such a production from a female pen, must dissipate all doubts on the subject.

I shall be gratified to see this work in print, and still more pleased to see you at the head of the proposed institution, enlightening it by your talents, guiding it by your experience, and practically illustrating its merits and its blessings.

The favorable opinion of me, not only implied by the submission of the manuscript to my judgment, but expressed in the polite letter accompanying it, is highly flattering; and, in any other case, I would say that it was both the reward and the evidence of merit.

.I have the honor to be with perfect respect,
Your most obedient servant
DE WITT CLINTON

MRS. E. WILLARD

In his next message to the Legislature, Governor Clinton referred to Mrs. Willard's 'Plan' without mentioning her name and recommended legislative action to improve women's education.

Mrs. Willard's friends from Waterford arranged to present her 'Plan' to the Legislature and thought it best that Dr. and Mrs. Willard spend some time in Albany during the session. This they did, and the experience was a momentous one for Mrs. Willard, then just thirty-two years old. To be in the legislative center of New York State, to be called upon by the Governor and his friends and by various legislators, to discuss with them the plan so dear to her heart — all this moved her deeply. She idealized legislators far beyond their merit; for, to serve the country in an official capacity seemed to her one of the highest, noblest ambitions of man. She read her manuscript by request several times to influential members of the Legislature and once before a large group of people. For a woman to do this was quite out of keeping with the conventions of the day. Still, that did not seem to occur to Mrs. Willard, so filled was she with enthusiasm for her purpose. Nor did her friends among the legislators look upon her less favorably because of such presumptuous proceedings. Governor Clinton was very agreeably impressed by her, by her appearance, by her ability, and the soundness of her views. She was a woman to arouse admiration and respect. Well-dressed, handsome, with the bearing of a queen, intelligent and yet womanly, she impressed them not as the much-scorned female politician, but as a noble woman inspired by a great ideal. And yet, Mrs. Willard in Albany, disseminating her views on education, was probably the first woman lobbyist.

Governor Clinton suggested that Mrs. Willard move her school to New York State, and several prominent citizens of Waterford urged her to come there. Day after day she hoped for action from the Legislature. Finally, an act was passed granting a charter to the 'Waterford Academy for Young Ladies,' said to be the first legislative measure recognizing woman's right to higher education. The Legislature also voted to include Waterford Academy in the list of institutions to receive a share of the 'literary fund' of the state, which had hitherto been divided exclusively among schools for boys. In addition, an endowment of five thousand dollars for Waterford Academy was recommended by the Committee, but this was unfavorably acted upon by the Legislature.

Back at her school in Middlebury, Mrs. Willard, drilling her girls in the population of cities, the length of rivers, the capitals of nations, was dreaming of success. She was dreaming of the ideal institution of learning which she would found with the aid of noble men. She was ready, eager to be the saviour of womankind, whatever the sacrifice. 'Once,' she said, 'I had almost determined to go in person before the legislature, and plead at their bar with my living voice; believing that I should throw forth my whole soul in the effort for my sex, and then sink down and die from the exertion, and that my death might thus effect what my life had failed to accomplish.'

Meanwhile, she had published her 'Plan' in pamphlet form at her own expense under the title, 'An Address to the Public; Particularly to the Members of the Legislature of New York, Proposing a Plan for Improving Female Education,' and had sent it to prominent men throughout the country with the hope of arousing general interest. It received the approval of many noted men, among them President Monroe, John Adams, Thomas Jefferson, and various members of Congress. John Adams wrote her regarding it:

QUINCY, MONTEZILLO, *Dec.* 9, 1819

DEAR MADAM:

I am deeply indebted to you for your polite and obliging letter, and much more for the elegant, sentimental, and most amiable volume that attended it. The female moiety of mankind deserve as much honor, esteem and respect as the male, the duties of allegiance and obedience are reciprocal in a family as well as in the State, and similar limitations and restrictions are applicable to both. Whenever I hear of a great man, I always inquire who was his mother, and I believe there have been very few extraordinary men who have not been cherished and guided in their morals, and their studies in their infancy, by extraordinary mothers, from the Gracchi and their mother to this time.

I rejoice that the experiment has been made under the Legislature of New-York, who have done, no less honor to themselves than to you by their patronage of your University.

Accept, Madam, the kindest respects and warmest wishes of your sincere friend, and most obedient humble servant,

JOHN ADAMS

The Honorable Duncan Campbell, a member of the Georgia Legislature, was so interested in her 'Plan' that he recommended its principles to his legislature. It was also widely circulated in Europe. George Combe, then at the height of his fame, published the entire 'Plan' in his 'Phrenological Journal.'

The literary aspirations which the young preceptress, Emma Hart, had recorded in her diary some ten years before, were being gratified not through the publication of poetry as she had dreamed, but by the publication and wide circulation of a comprehensive plan for the education of women — a work so original, so able, so worthy of approbation that it demanded attention and support, broke down the superficial barriers which had deprived women of adequate education, and paved the way for all higher schools and colleges for women. The 'Plan' has been called the 'Magna Charta of the rights of woman in matters of education.'

Mrs. Willard concentrated all the fruits of her experience, all her theories of education, and many of her views regarding the advancement of her sex in her 'Plan for Improving Female Education.' It was a concise, sane document, and proved that the female mind could evolve a thesis, logical and clear, worthy of a legal mind. One can well imagine that Mrs. Willard rewrote it seven times, polishing and impersonalizing it, and omitting much that was in her first draft. None of the impulsive arguments that must first have come to her are there. No bitterness, no rebellion is apparent, but there is instead remarkable tact and a supreme effort to placate those whom the idea of female education might antagonize.

In contrast with Mary Wollstonecraft's passionate appeal for education in her 'Vindication of the Rights of Woman,' written twenty-seven years before, Emma Willard's 'Plan for Improving Female Education' reads like a lawyer's brief. It is the work of a woman who could control her emotions and direct them to the accomplishment of a purpose, who in a scientific spirit had tested the ability of her sex and was now presenting her case.

'The object of this address,' she began, 'is to convince the public that a reform, with respect to female education, is necessary; that it cannot be effected by individual exertion, but that it requires the aid of the Legislature: and further, by showing the justice, the policy, and the magnanimity of such an undertaking, to persuade that body to endow a seminary for females, as the commencement of such reformation.'

Then she at once assured her readers that she was not advocating a college for young ladies, but a seminary which would be as different from a man's college 'as female character and duties are from the male.'

She drew up her 'Plan' in four parts: first, pointing out the defects of the present system of education, then, considering the principles which should regulate education, next, describing a well-planned female seminary, and lastly, showing what benefits society would reap from such seminaries.

She called attention to the fact that the present schools for girls were conducted by individuals whose object was a desire to make money and who were unable in most instances to provide suitable living quarters for the girls or adequate libraries or other apparatus. As they were interested primarily in obtaining pupils, they taught such subjects as would attract the greatest number, and naturally clung to the superficial, showy, so-called accomplishments. Since qualifications for entrance, the course of study, and the school term were not regulated, as in boys' academies, girls' schools were not efficiently managed, and parents interfered in the course of study, choosing what they wished their daughters to learn. Often preceptresses were not the right type to guide young girls during their impressionable years, but as they were accountable to no one, they continued their harmful influence unmolested.

Mrs. Willard's illustrations of the faulty education of girls were graphic. She pictured the daughters of the rich being hurried through the routine of superficial boarding-school studies and then being introduced into the gay world with only one object in life, amusement. While these girls were 'gliding through the mazes of the midnight dance,' their brothers employed the lamp 'to treasure up for future use the riches of ancient wisdom, or to gather strength and expansion of mind in exploring the wonderful paths of philosophy.' She maintained that such a difference in education resulted in a difference in character and explained why women were looked upon as 'the pampered wayward babies of society.' Another mistake was making the taste and the pleasure of men, whether good or bad, the standard for the formation of female character. She insisted that women as well as men were independent beings, or, as she expressed it, primary existences. 'A system of education,' she said, 'which leads one class of human beings to consider the approbation of another as their highest object, teaches that the rule of their conduct should be the will of beings imperfect and erring like themselves, rather than the will of God, which is the only standard of perfection.'

After these frank statements, she again hastened to placate those who might be offended by her unconventional views. She wrote:

I would not be understood to insinuate that we are not, in particular situations, to yield obedience to the other sex. Submission and obedience belong to every being in the universe, except the great Master of the whole. Nor is it a degrading peculiarity to our sex to be under human authority. Whenever one class of human beings derive from another the benefit of support and protection, they must pay its equivalent — obedience. . . . Neither would I be understood to mean that our sex should not seek to make themselves agreeable to the other.

Mrs. Willard's definition of education stands to-day as wholly adequate, well-chosen, and comprehensive:

Education should seek to bring its subjects to the perfection of their moral, intellectual, and physical nature, in order that they may be of the greatest possible use to themselves and others; or, to use a different expression, that they may be the means of the greatest possible happiness of which they are capable, both as to what they enjoy and what they communicate.

All of Mrs. Willard's educational theories were brought to a focus in her description of an ideal seminary. As the enterprise was too large and too expensive to be carried on by an individual, she urged State aid, and recommended that the management be put in the hands of a board of trustees. For the institution, she required a large building with rooms for lodging and recitations, a well-equipped library, a laboratory, and rooms for philosophical apparatus and the domestic department. She wanted maps, globes, musical instruments, and some good paintings which would cultivate the artistic taste of her pupils and could be used as models. A large staff of teachers was essential. The course of study which she advocated, she divided under four heads — Religious and Moral, Literary, Domestic, and Ornamental. She especially emphasized religious and moral instruction, mentioning tactfully that 'it would be desirable that the young ladies should spend part of their Sabbaths in hearing discourses relative to the peculiar duties of their sex.' She did not describe her plans for literary instruction in detail, because 'such enumeration would be tedious.' She did, however, strongly recommend those studies which would lead women to understand the operations of the human mind. She felt this to be extremely important in view of the fact that mothers exerted such an influence over the impressionable minds of their children. She believed that mothers could be taught to mould their children's minds aright. She also urged the teaching of natural philosophy, so that mothers would be able to answer their children's questions about natural phenomena intelligently. She advocated domestic instruction, believing that such a department would prevent 'estrangement from domestic duties.' Her views on this subject entitle her to be called the originator of Domestic Science in girls' schools. She said: 'It is believed that housewifery might be greatly improved by being taught, not only in practice, but in theory. Why may it not be reduced to a system as well as other arts? There are right ways of performing its various operations; and there are reasons why those ways are right; and why may not rules be formed, their reasons collected, and the whole be digested into a system to guide the learner's practice?'

The ornamental studies which she recommended for a seminary were music, drawing, painting, 'elegant penmanship' and 'the grace of motion.' She did not include needlework which, in its most ornate phases, was considered an essential part of the curriculum of a girls' school. In defense of this omission, she said that she considered the use of the needle for other purposes than 'the decoration of a lady's person or the convenience or neatness of her family' a waste of time, since it was of so little value in the formation of character. Music, drawing, and painting, she advocated because of their refining influence. 'The grace of motion' would be learned chiefly from dancing, and dancing would also provide exercise and that recreation which was essential for the 'cheerfulness and contentment of youth.'

Mrs. Willard also summarized the benefits which would result from the establishment of female seminaries. Most important among these was the great improvement that she expected to see in the common schools, as many young ladies trained in the seminaries would become teachers, and release from that service men whom the country needed for other work. Women, she contended, would be able to give all their time to teaching, whereas men looked upon it as a temporary occupation. She felt that well-trained women would not only make better teachers than men, but could afford to accept lower salaries. 'Equal pay for equal work' was not to be thought of in those days, or if it ever was thought of, it became unimportant in the face of the more urgent need of enlarging woman's sphere. As a result, women to-day are still combating the injustice and unreasonableness of that compromise made so many years ago.

Then Mrs. Willard advanced her most telling argument — her pet theory — that for the sake of the Republic women must be educated. She reminded her readers of that all-too-general opinion that the Republic could not last, that other republics had failed, that the Republic of America would also speedily decline and fall. Women, she maintained, gave society its tone, and the women of America could with the proper education save their country from destruction. Higher education for women would preserve the country from enervating luxuries, follies, and vices, and would build up an intelligent womanhood which would be the bulwark of society. Women of education and character would bear nobler sons and would train them for useful citizenship.

Again at the close of her address, Mrs. Willard showed her supreme tact by appealing to the pride and superiority of American men, and she did this with all the eloquence of which she was capable:

In calling upon my patriotic countrymen to effect so noble an object, the consideration of national glory should not be overlooked. . . . Where is that wise and heroic country which has considered that our rights are sacred, though we cannot defend them? that though a weaker, we are an essential part of the body politic, whose corruption or improvement must affect the whole; and which, having thus considered, has sought to give us, by education, that rank in the scale of being to which our importance entitles us? History shows not that country. It shows many whose Legislatures have sought to improve their various vegetable productions and their breeds of useful brutes; but none whose public councils have made it an object of their deliberations to improve the character of their women. Yet, though history lifts not her finger to such a one, anticipation does. She points to a nation which, having thrown off the shackles of authority and precedent, shrinks not from schemes of improvement because other nations have not attempted them, but which, in its pride of independence, would rather lead than follow in the march of improvement — a nation wise and magnanimous to plan, enterprising to undertake, and rich in resources to execute. Does not every American exult that this country is his own? And who knows how great and good a race of men may yet arise from the

forming hand of mothers enlightened by the bounty of that
beloved country — to defend her liberties — to plan her
future improvement — and to raise her to unparalleled
glory?

The 'Plan' of course aroused opposition. The title
in itself was startling — 'An Address to the Public;
Particularly to the Members of the Legislature of New
York, Proposing a Plan for the Improvement of Female
Education.' Any move for the improvement of female
education was looked upon with suspicion, but for a
woman to address the public on this subject, particularly to address a legislature, was an unheard-of audac-
ity. Although a considerable number of broad-minded
men approved of Mrs. Willard's efforts for education
and a few worked actively to aid her, the general
opinion, even among her sympathizers, was the usual
one — that the public was not ready for such a step.
Consequently, although prominent men were flattering
and pleasant, nothing happened. Nor did Mrs. Willard
escape the ridicule and the annoyances which come to
all women who pioneer for the progress of their sex.
Such remarks as that of the indignant farmer, 'They'll
be educating the cows next,' were frequent. Dissenting
legislators argued that book learning would not help
women knit stockings or make puddings. Some maintained that masculine studies, such as mathematics,
the sciences, the classics, and philosophy, would rob
women of their delicacy, refinement, and charm. Others
hotly insisted that these studies would encourage women
to rival men and thus upset the established order, would
so impair their health that the race would be enfeebled
and the population decreased.

Although Mrs. Willard's appeal to the Legislature
may have been premature, and although the general

public was indifferent, underneath the surface, particularly among women, there was a strong movement for education. Women were awakening. They were beginning to realize their abilities. The descendants of Revolutionary patriots were eager for education so that they might serve the Republic by training better citizens. The first faint signs of the Woman's Rights movement were also appearing. Throughout the country, other women who, like Mrs. Willard, felt the urge for education were in a small way attempting to establish schools and were preparing younger women for the improvements in education which were soon to appear.

In this movement for the higher education of women, Emma Willard must be given first place. No other woman had made such definite experiments in education; no other woman had so daringly stepped into the limelight to wage her fight for education; nor was there anything at the time which compared in influence with her 'Plan for Improving Female Education.'

Fifty years later her 'Plan' was still considered so able and so applicable that it was printed in full in the proceedings of the convocation of officers of colleges and academies at Albany, New York. In 1893, in an article published in 'Harper's Bazar,' Thomas Wentworth Higginson wrote, 'When in 1819, Mrs. Willard published her address to the public, particularly to the members of the Legislature of New York, introducing a plan for improved female education and establishing her school under State patronage at Waterford, she laid the foundation upon which every woman's college may now be said to rest.'

CHAPTER IX

In the spring of 1819, as soon as the stagecoach and wagons could make the trip over the muddy roads, Mrs. Willard moved her school from Middlebury, Vermont, to Waterford, New York. Even in this, she had the consent and support of her husband, who willingly left his home in Middlebury to further her educational work. A board of trustees, appointed by the citizens of Waterford, had leased the 'Mansion House' for the school, a large three-story brick building known as the finest in Saratoga County. Although no financial assistance had yet been forthcoming from the Legislature, Mrs. Willard and the trustees hoped the matter would be reconsidered favorably during the year. As the school was moved during a vacation, its sessions were uninterrupted, and many of the pupils who attended in Middlebury were again enrolled. By this time, Mrs. Willard had trained several of her Middlebury pupils to act as teachers and to assist her in her work.

Mrs. Willard at once began to enlarge the course of study. She made higher mathematics a permanent part of the curriculum, and regarded this step as a most important one in the progress of woman's education. She called geometry the ploughshare of the mind, and believed that mathematics more than any other subject would develop and train the minds of women, clarify and steady their thinking, and be the means of equipping them for greater usefulness.

After taking two or three lessons in algebra from a teacher in Waterford, and finding that he could not

CATALOGUE

OF THE

WATERFORD FEMALE ACADEMY.

FOR THE TERM ENDING SEPTEMBER 13th, 1820.

Officers.

EMMA WILLARD,   PRINCIPAL.
E. SHERRILL,
F. GREGG, }
J. GILBERT, } *ASSISTANT TEACHERS.*
M. HEYWOOD. }

STUDENTS.

Mary C Adams,	Waterford, N. Y.	Catharine L. Morris	Cambridge N. Y.
Miranda M. Aldis	St. Albans, Vt.	Fanny C. Mower	Montreal L. Cana.
Hannah Mary Aldrich	Ballston, Spa. N. Y.	Sarah C. Mower	" " "
Ann Bailey	New York.	Margaret Myers	Waterford N. Y.
Susan Clark	Sandy Hill, N. Y.	Catharine Mott	Newtown N. Y.
Julia Frances Converse	Troy, N. Y.	Harriet Newel	Charlotte Vt.
Elizabeth Cotheal	New York.	Lucretia Paine	Troy N. Y.
Mary Cramer	Waterford, N. Y.	Grace Phillips	Cherry Vally N. Y.
Frances V. S. Davis	"	Harriet Platt	Waterford N. Y.
Ann Fanning	New York.	Belinda Porter	Prattsburgh N. Y.
Mary B. Fanning	"	Laura Porter	Waterford N. Y.
Mary Field	New Fane, Vt.	Mary Porter	" N. Y.
Sarah Augusta T. Frothingham	Sand Lake, N. Y.	" " "	" N. Y.
Susan Fullerton	Chester Vt.	Sarah M. Radcliff	" N. Y.
Lydia Gardner.	Troy, N. Y.	Sarah Jane Ross	Albany N. Y.
Lydia Garrison.	Putnam N. Y.	Ann Russel	" N. Y.
Augusta Gates.	Waterford, N. Y.	Ricca Satterlee	Middlebury Vt.
Jane Gates.	" N. Y.	Jane Eliza Scott	Waterford N. Y.
Maria Haines	Hoosack N. Y.	Jane Maria Scott	" N. Y.
Ann Jane Hill	Lansingburg N. Y.	Caroline Sherwood	" N. Y.
Sarah W. Hinsdale	Middletown, Con.	Mary Sims	Troy N. Y.
Cornelia Hoag	Chatham, N. Y.	Fanny Smith	Schaghticoke N. Y.
Eliza Holmes	Waterford, N. Y.	Ann Stillwell	Albany N. Y.
Lucretia Hudson	" N. Y.	Sarah Jane Taylor	Ballston Springs N. Y.
Theodosia Hudson	" N. Y.	Caroline Thorn	Saratoga N. Y.
Sarah S Huntington	" N. Y.	Margaret Thorn	" N. Y.
Maria Hurd	Augusta, U. Cana.	Margaret Tracy	W Etesborough N. Y.
Mary Ketchum	New York	Eliza Van Schoonhoven	Saratoga Springs N. Y.
Elizabeth Knickerbacker	Schaghticoke N. Y.	Elizabeth Van Schoonhoven	Waterford N. Y.
Rebecca Knickerbacker	Waterford N. Y.	Elizabeth Van Veghten	Schaghticoke N. Y.
Eleanor Leverson	Watervliet N. Y.	Hester Van Zandt	Albany N. Y.
Caroline Adelia Lewis	Saratoga Springs N. Y.	Ann Eliza Vibbard	Waterford N. Y.
Louisa Abigail Masters	Schaughticoke N. Y.	Caroline Vibbard	" N. Y.
Elizabeth Melick	Waterford N. Y.	Mary Vibbard	" N. Y.
Maria Jane Melick	" N. Y.	Louisa Viclie	" N. Y.
Magdalene Melick	" N. Y.	Phebe Warren	Troy N. Y.
Laura Merril	Castleton Vt.	Catharine Wendell	Cambridge N. Y.
Angeline Morrel	Johnstown N. Y.	Maria Wendell	" N. Y.
		Emily Williams	Salem N. Y.
			Total :7

understand nor explain many of the problems, she studied by herself. Her knowledge of geometry had been acquired when, as a girl of twelve, she had worked out theorems on the hearthstone, and later, during the first years of her married life in Middlebury when she had mastered her nephew's textbook.

She now taught geometry, and eager to make her pupils understand, cut out paper triangles for concrete illustrations. For her solid geometry class, she carved cones and pyramids out of potatoes and turnips. As geometry textbooks were very hard to get, the pupils were dependent entirely upon Mrs. Willard's oral teaching and these figures of turnip, potato, and paper. Mrs. Willard also studied by herself trigonometry, conic sections, and Enfield's 'Natural Philosophy,' and as she mastered these subjects, began to teach them. The introduction of mathematics to such a degree aroused a great deal of criticism and ridicule, and when one of the pupils, Mary Cramer, was publicly examined in geometry, it caused as great a stir as did woman's entry into the fields of medicine and law, years later. In fact, many insisted that Mary Cramer's examination was pure memory work, for no woman ever had or ever would be able to understand geometry.

Mrs. Willard also continued to improve her methods of teaching geography. There were few textbooks available and those few were highly unsatisfactory. In many of the geographies, the principal cities were located by giving their distances from London; for example, 'Pekin, the capital of China, stands 8052 miles, southeasterly from London.' There were many questions such as this: 'What curiosities are there in France?' Each question had its answer which was to be memorized. Geography taught in this way was a dry, mechanical process, and no wonder the following verse was often written by pupils upon the fly-leaves of their geographies:

If there should be another flood
Then to this book I'd fly;
If all the earth should be submerged,
This book would still be dry.

Such methods of teaching geography gave pupils little idea of the various countries or peoples. Mrs. Willard aimed to remedy this by using maps and charts, which appealed to the eye rather than to the memory. At a glance the location, relative position, and population of a country or city could be seen. Map drawing was an essential part of her course. Finding that these new methods produced better results and aroused the interest of her pupils, she began work on a geography textbook and was assisted in this by one of her pupils, Elizabeth Sherrill.

Elizabeth's mother had been given a position in the Middlebury Female Seminary when Elizabeth was still a child. Mrs. Willard, who loved little girls, grew very fond of her, and cared for and educated her as if she had been her own daughter. Elizabeth thrived under Mrs. Willard's training and when she was only fourteen taught a few classes and drew many of the maps for Mrs. Willard's geography.

In the fall of that first year in Waterford, Mrs. Willard wrote her brother Asahel Hart that she had twenty-two boarders in her school — more than she had had in Vermont at that season. Her mother spent the winter in Waterford with her, quite at home in the large household and happy with her little grandson John, who was then nine years old.

Mrs. Willard described her school further in a letter, written in 1820, to her cousin John Hinsdale:

That this school affords advantages superior, in proportion to the expense, to any other school in our country is, I think, evident from the fact that the pupils are not expected to pay the whole expense of the institution. A part is defrayed by *subscription*, and a part by the literary fund.

What I conceive to be the superior advantages of the school are these: we have a very large building, which affords a good accommodation as to room, and we have a sufficient number of instructors, who each have their peculiar branches to teach; and we have a highly-respectable board of trustees, who, while they afford the instructors some security against the caprice of individual opinion, also stand committed to the public that no deception shall be practised by the instructors.

From these advantages we are enabled to make many useful recitations which otherwise we could not; but perhaps I can in no way give you a more definite idea of our proceedings than by describing the ordinary routine of business for the day. We rise at five or six in the morning, then assemble for devotions, and then spend nearly an hour in recitations. From half-past seven to half-past eight our domestic teacher takes charge of those who are to be instructed in matters likely to increase their domestic knowledge, taking care that they write receipts of whatever cooking they do. Though not required, all my pupils belong to this department. Our study-hours are from nine till twelve, and from two till five in the afternoon, and from eight till nine in the evening. The young ladies who board with me study in their rooms; but they are not permitted to have loud talking, or any disorder, or to pass from room to room in school-hours. As our house is large, we are enabled to have different recitation-rooms for the different classes. One of our teachers is wholly devoted to the ornamental branches. Our terms are forty-two dollars per quarter for board and tuition in all the branches taught, except music and dancing. Music is ten dollars extra per quarter. The pupils furnish their own bed and bedding; we wish them also to furnish their own spoons, knives and forks, and candle-sticks.

While Mrs. Willard's thoughts were first and foremost on the building-up of her school and the working-out of her 'Plan for Improving Female Education,' she also kept up her interest in history and world affairs. Hers was a mind of international scope, never satisfied with provincialism. Her work in geography and her constant study of the Bible led her to reflect upon the Bible prophecies which heralded universal peace and the gathering of the nations in Jerusalem. She wrote out her ideas on this subject, and in 1820 published them under the title, 'Universal Peace to Be Introduced by a Confederacy of Nations, Meeting at Jerusalem.' Forty-four years later she developed this thesis more fully and seriously, but she did not dare advance this first effort except as a work of imagination.

After Waterford Academy had been in session for about a year, Governor Clinton again appealed to the Legislature in its behalf:

While on this important subject of instruction, I cannot omit to call your attention to the academy for female education, which was incorporated last session, at Waterford, and which, under the superintendence of distinguished teachers, has already attained great usefulness and prosperity. As this is the only attempt ever made in this country to promote the education of the female sex by the patronage of government; as our first and best impressions are derived from maternal affection; and as the elevation of the female character is inseparably connected with the happiness of home, and respectability abroad, I trust you will not be deterred by common-place ridicule from extending your munificence to this meritorious institution.

Governor Clinton's appeal, however, was not sufficient to break down the general feeling against education for women. Although a bill granting the school two thousand dollars was passed in the Senate, it failed in the Lower House; and the Regents of the University decided that no part of the 'literary fund' should go to the Female Academy. This was not only a bitter disappointment to Mrs. Willard but alarming as well, for so confident had she been of financial assistance from the State that she had let the expenses of the school exceed its income. Convinced, as she was, that no one person could carry on such a school as she had established, without State aid, she felt that her work had been a complete failure, and it was with a heavy heart that she listened to her girls prove the theorems of Euclid. In those days of defeat and thwarted ambition, she did not realize that she was to accomplish the impossible. Weighed down with discouragement, she wrote:

To have had it decently rejected, would have given me comparatively but little pain, but its consideration was delayed and delayed until the session passed away. The malice of open enemies, the advice of false friends, and the neglect of others, placed me in a situation mortifying in the extreme. I felt it almost to frenzy; and even now, though the dream is long past, I cannot recall it without agitation. Could I have died a martyr in the cause, and thus have insured its success, I should have blessed the fagot and hugged the stake.

It was by the loss of respect for others that I gained tranquillity for myself. Once I was proud of speaking of the Legislature as the 'Fathers of the State.' Perhaps a vision of the Roman Senate played about my fancy, and mingled with the enthusiastic respect in which I held the institutions of my country. I knew nothing of the maneuvers of politicians. This winter has served to disenchant me. My present impression is, that my cause is better rested with the people than with their rulers. I do not regret bringing it before the Legislature, because in no other way could it have come so fairly before the public. But when the people shall become convinced of the justice and expediency of placing both sexes more nearly on an equality, with respect to privilege of education, then Legislators will find it their interest to make the proper provision.

In 1821, the trustees of the Academy again petitioned the Legislature for funds and again were unsuccessful. Then, Mrs. Willard began to listen to offers from influential citizens of Troy, New York, who were urging her to move her school there and were promising her financial assistance. The lease of the school building was to expire in May. Neither the citizens of Waterford nor the Legislature had provided the funds necessary for the renewal of the lease, and Dr. and Mrs. Willard were unable to meet this expense alone. The overtures from Troy were a godsend. In a letter to her mother, telling of her plans to move her school to Troy, she wrote: 'It seems now as if Providence had opened the way for the permanent establishment of the school on the plan which I wish to execute. I believe, if Troy will give the building, the Legislature will grant the endowment.'

CHAPTER X

THE FOUNDING OF THE TROY FEMALE SEMINARY

TROY, in 1821, with a population of about five thousand, was a thriving prosperous city, one of the most enterprising cities outside of New England. Because of its cotton mills, its nail factory, paper mill, soap factory, its tanneries and potteries, it was looked upon as one of the manufacturing centers of the country. Its situation as an inland port on the Upper Hudson River was a tremendous asset commercially in the days before the coming of the railroad. The Erie Canal, then in the process of construction, promised further opportunities for commercial development, since it would connect Troy with the vast unsettled territory to the west. The citizens of Troy were awake to the possibilities of building up their city and realized the importance of encouraging education and the arts as well as business. A school, such as Mrs. Willard proposed, appealed to their progressive spirit. It was something new. There was no school like it in the country. Troy must have it. While few of Troy's citizens were moved by any great sympathy for the education of women or for Mrs. Willard's plans for the improvement of her sex, they were far-seeing enough to read the signs of the times, and sufficiently discerning to appreciate Mrs. Willard's business and executive ability. They were confident that a school carried on by a woman of her caliber must be a success. They made her generous offers and she accepted them. Never before had financial assistance come to her so spontaneously. Never had her sponsors performed their part with such alacrity nor in such a business-like manner.

On March 26, 1821, the Common Council of Troy passed a resolution to raise four thousand dollars by special tax for the purchase or erection of a suitable building for a Female Academy. Moulton's Coffee House on Second Street opposite the Court House was purchased in April. It was a three-story wooden building with twenty-two rooms and a large ballroom. Centrally located and near the churches and public buildings, it was well situated for the school. The additional money needed for the purchase and for repairs was raised by subscription. The Common Council of Troy then appointed a board of trustees and they in turn appointed a committee of ladies who were occasionally to confer with Mrs. Willard regarding the school. This was a progressive step which vitally interested the women of Troy in educational matters. The work of remodeling the building began at once. The old building was stripped of its weatherboarding and bricked, and the interior rearranged and repaired according to Mrs. Willard's suggestions. She said to the trustees, 'I want you to make me a building which will suit my trade; and then I will not complain provided you finish it so that we do not get slivers into our fingers, from rough boards. I expect the life of the school will be on the inside, and not on the out; and when the school wants to grow, you must enlarge its shell.' Although the school was Mrs. Willard's, the legal status of married women made it necessary to lease all of the property to Dr. Willard. The rent stipulated was four hundred dollars a year, which was to be used by the trustees for paying interest on loans and for making repairs.

That spring, Mrs. Willard moved her school to Troy, but as the building was not finished, she found temporary quarters in two houses near by and began teach-

ing in the lecture room of the Troy Lyceum of Natural
History. The school building was finished in September
and the Troy Female Seminary established in permanent quarters. Ninety young ladies representing the
leading families of New York State, Massachusetts,
Vermont, Connecticut, Ohio, South Carolina, and
Georgia attended the opening session. Twenty-nine
were residents of Troy.

Mrs. Willard was thirty-four years old when she
opened her school in Troy and embarked upon a venture
which no woman before had tried. Beautiful, vigorous,
earnest, and highly intellectual, she was eminently fitted
for the task. Parents were favorably impressed by her
charming manner and her ability. Pupils idealized her
and were fired with ambition by her enthusiasm. The
first years in Troy brought the annoyances, difficulties,
and misrepresentations which usually attend every progressive enterprise, but these faded into insignificance
as Mrs. Willard saw her school grow in numbers and in
popular favor.

In repeated petitions to the Legislature, which
brought forth no financial assistance, Mrs. Willard
stated the facts plainly: 'Heretofore the claims of their
daughters have been merely overlooked by the fathers
of State: the time has now arrived, when, if they are
not granted, they must be refused.' They were refused,
much to Mrs. Willard's disappointment, but the interest
of the citizens of Troy and the excellence and immediate popularity of the Seminary enabled her to succeed
without State aid.

Through all these new experiences, Mrs. Willard's
domestic life was increasingly happy. Dr. Willard, never
jealous of her success, aided her in every possible way
and made himself indispensable as business manager and

school physician. Their son John, now twelve years old, was sent to Hadley, Massachusetts, to begin his studies with the Reverend Mr. Huntington.

Mrs. Willard was now assisted by a professor who taught the modern languages, painting, and music, and by a number of teachers, most of whom she had trained herself. To have employed educated men as professors in all the branches would have been a prohibitive expense, and besides, Mrs. Willard felt that teachers educated by her were better adapted to reach the untrained minds of young girls. Keeping her high ideal of woman's education always before her, she took definite steps to improve the curriculum. No girls' school in the country offered such a complete course of study. She added more advanced courses in history and natural philosophy. She continued her system of studying and teaching mathematics, staying a few lessons ahead of the classes she taught. Her favorite time for the study of algebra was early in the morning when she took her daily exercise, a walk through the streets of Troy. Proud of the ability of her pupils, she often told how one or two of them, who had more time for study than she, got ahead of her occasionally in the solution of an algebra problem. Her methods of teaching geography were decidedly original, and she tested her theories as she taught. Well satisfied with her results, she resumed work on the geography textbook which she had begun in Waterford, New York.

Meanwhile, William Channing Woodbridge was also preparing a geography and heard of Mrs. Willard's undertaking just as his book was ready for publication. Their theories and methods of teaching proved to be so similar that they decided to collaborate and in 1822 published 'A System of Universal Geography on the

WEST WILLAGE SEMINARY

Principles of Comparison and Classification.' Mrs. Willard's contribution to the book was the section on Ancient Geography 'accompanied with an atlas,' also problems on the globes, and rules for the construction of maps. In the Preface, Mrs. Willard pointed out the advantages of her new method of teaching geography, maintaining that facts were acquired with greater ease and were retained longer by appealing to the eye rather than to the memory, with maps and charts which compared and classified geographical data. This comparison and classification, she believed, disciplined the mind and also developed an enlarged understanding. She said, 'It is nearly eight years since I began to teach geography by this method. Intending to publish my plan of instruction, I carefully watched its operation in the minds of my pupils, while at the same time I studied it in the most approved system of the philosophy of the mind, and my success in teaching it far surpassed my expectation.'

Woodbridge and Willard's 'Geography' attracted a great deal of attention, was highly spoken of, and widely circulated, as it met a great need in the schools. It was by far the best geography available at the time, a great step ahead in that it made the subject much more interesting and attractive to pupils, but its presentation of facts in the stilted style of the period and its lack of pictures would repel a boy or girl of the twentieth century. The success of this book not only brought Mrs. Willard a substantial financial return but also increased her prestige as an educator. An article of hers entitled, 'Will Scientific Education Make Woman Lose Her Dependence on Man,' was also published at this time in the 'Literary Magazine' of New York.

To supervise the lives as well as the studies of such a

large number of young ladies as now attended the Troy
Female Seminary was considered a colossal undertaking
in those days, but here Mrs. Willard's executive ability
served her well. As it was one of her theories that girls
lived more naturally and normally two by two in small
rooms than in large dormitories, she had the building
arranged accordingly. The uncarpeted rooms were comfortably though simply furnished, each with a low-post
double bed, a painted bureau, two chairs, and a box
stove for wood. The girls were to regard their rooms
as their homes and keep them in perfect order. They lit
their fires from a pan of coals in the hall and filled their
water pitchers from the pump in the yard. Each room-
mate was responsible for the room for a week at a time,
and if the monitor in her hourly round found anything
out of place, a fault mark was recorded against the careless girl. The inspection of rooms was rigid. No gloves
were to be found on the bureau, nor books on the bed.
No girl in a thoughtless moment could sit on her bed or
leave a towel on a chair without a demerit.

The two upper stories of the building were divided
into forty lodging and study rooms for the girls and
teachers. On the second floor were the chapel, the large
examination room, and the rooms set aside for the Willard family. The dining-room which also served as a
dancing hall, the kitchen, the laundry, a room where the
pupils were taught pastry cooking, a lecture room, and
a few small rooms for musical instruments were all on
the first floor. It was an imposing institution.

Board including bed and bedding, furniture for room,
and light was furnished at $2.50 a week. Tuition varied
according to the studies pursued. 'If any should prefer
paying a stipulated sum by the year,' read the catalogue, 'they can be furnished with board including bed

and bedding, furniture for the room, fuel, light, room
rent, washing, and tuition in the first and second class
of English studies at $200. . . . Boarders are to furnish
themselves with a table spoon, a tea spoon, and towels.'

Life at the Troy Female Seminary was strictly regulated. The rising bell sounded every morning at six-
thirty in the summer, in the winter at seven. The girls
then assembled for half an hour of study, and half an
hour of exercise in the dormitory or park. Breakfast
was at eight. Study hours and recitations followed until
twelve when a substantial dinner was served. At four,
school was dismissed with a prayer offered by Mrs. Willard, and then the girls had two free hours which they
spent walking, visiting, or attending to their wardrobes.
After their six-o'clock supper and before commencing
their evening studies, the girls danced for an hour, their
curls bobbing in the frolic of a contredance, their swiftly
moving slippered feet peeping modestly from beneath
the long, full skirts of their plain, high-waisted muslin
dresses. Mrs. Willard, looking on, beamed with satisfaction at the graceful movements of her rosy-cheeked
girls, more firmly convinced than ever that dancing was
a most useful exercise and relaxation. Her girls proved
that intensive study did not undermine the health.
They were vigorous in an age when weak, fainting,
delicate women were the fashion.

Because she felt that her school should prepare for
life, Mrs. Willard instituted a form of self-government,
appointing various girls as monitors. They made regular
tours of inspection through the rooms and reported their
findings to the Officer of the Week. Each teacher took
her turn as Officer of the Week and at the Teachers'
Friday Evening Meeting gave Mrs. Willard a report of
the pupils' conduct, of their fault and credit marks, thus

summarizing the reports of the various monitors. This plan worked very well in spite of the prophecies that the girls would band together and deceive the teachers.

Simplicity of dress was another of Mrs. Willard's rules for her girls. The school catalogue made that clear. It read: 'Mrs. Willard wishes the dress of her pupils during school hours to consist of calico, gingham, or crape, made in plain style. Parents and guardians are earnestly requested not to furnish their daughters or wards with expensive laces, jewelry, or any other needless articles of apparel, nor to leave with them the control of money.' Any girl who attempted to overdress received a demerit. Mrs. Willard had no patience with so-called fashionable schools that encouraged luxury and interest in furbelows. Her girls were to be sensible and intelligent, a credit to their sex. This did not mean that they were to pay no attention to their looks. She laid particular stress on good manners and personal appearance.

It was her firm belief that it was every woman's duty to be as beautiful as possible, not to satisfy her vanity or to please man, but 'to glorify her Maker,' to be a pleasure to her friends, and to increase her influence. Because she was convinced that beauty in woman was a source of power, she encouraged simple, tasteful dress, insisted on exercise, proper food, and regular hours of sleep, and aimed to cultivate cheerful dispositions. She taught the girls how to enter and leave a room properly, how to rise and be seated gracefully. She watched their table manners. She was very patient with awkward girls and gave them private instructions. In well-planned lectures, she impressed the girls with their social duties. She sought to cultivate in her pupils whatever would make them attractive, interesting, and influential. These ideas were already formulated when she

taught her first school in Berlin, and she advocated them
all through her life. Even when she was a very old lady,
she said to her eight-year-old grand-niece, shaking her
forefinger at her for emphasis, 'It is every woman's duty
to look as well as she can.' She, herself, always lived up
to these theories, dressing in plain, elegant black with a
white surplice. Her manners and her bearing aroused
the admiration of the girls.

As Mrs. Willard regarded religious teaching as the
basis of all education, she endeavored to instill in her
pupils a love of God and a desire to be guided by His
laws. All religious instruction in the school was non-
sectarian, and while church attendance was compulsory,
parents selected the church which their daughters attended. Mrs. Willard had become a member of the
Episcopal Church, because that church more than any
other met her religious needs. She had outgrown the
religious doubts and questionings of her youth, and although still sufficiently liberal to be regarded by some
as unorthodox, she was deeply religious. She was very
careful, however, not to force her own particular church
upon her pupils and was firmly resolved that the school
should always be wholly non-sectarian. Her views on
this subject were well expressed in a letter to Dr. Be-
man, a Presbyterian clergyman of Troy:

I am confident that you, sir, will agree with me in opinion
that it is not proper for a person keeping a school — profes-
sedly not for any particular religious sect — to suffer the religious education of that school to become sectarian. Yet,
that religious instruction should be faithfully given to every
assemblage of young persons, you, sir, cannot believe more
sincerely or more feelingly than myself. Two courses there are
before the principal of an institution like mine: the one, to
invite clergymen of every Christian denomination to claim
alternately the attention of my pupils; the other, which I

have adopted, of faithfully endeavoring to furnish the pupils with instruction in the fundamental truths of natural and revealed religion, being careful to stop at these points where different Christian sects divide, and referring them on these points to such religious instruction as the parents of each individual shall choose for their child. On this plan no parent has, I think, a right to complain; but, on the other, every one would by turns be dissatisfied. I apprehend that the general opinion of the Christian community would be against presenting to young minds a diversity of religious sentiments by a frequent change of religious teachers, as no judicious Christian would advise any one, especially a young female, to be frequently changing in her place of attending public worship from one religious denomination to another.

Every morning or evening, the girls read a chapter in the Bible, and Sunday mornings, as they filed in to prayers, each girl handed Mrs. Willard a slip of paper on which she had written a Bible verse selected from her reading. In speaking to the girls about reading the Bible, Mrs. Willard once said, 'You must read it as a special letter from God to yourself.' Her praise of the twelfth chapter of Romans led them to memorize it in full. Sunday afternoons, the girls gathered for further religious instruction and recited lessons from the Bible or from Paley's 'Evidences of Christianity.' Young ladies of 1823 were distinctly religious. The somber tone of Paley did not oppress them. There were exceptions, of course — girls who preferred enjoyment in this present life to preparation for future bliss, but such rebellious opinions were not expressed at the Troy Female Seminary.

The girls assembled every Saturday noon for the weekly lecture given by Mrs. Willard, in which she touched on their manners and general behavior, on their religious duties, and on the 'peculiar duties' of their sex. It was a discourse on practical Christianity. Referring to this lecture, Mrs. Willard said, 'This duty which I perform myself, I consider more arduous, and more important, than any other one which belongs to my place; for it is here the opinions of our little public are more formed and guided than anywhere else.'

CHAPTER XI

EMMA WILLARD'S 'DAUGHTERS'

MRS. WILLARD loved her girls. They were all her 'daughters,' and she was vitally interested in their development and their plans for the future. The girls of 1823, like the girls of to-day, played their pranks, looked forward to Wednesday's lunch of fresh gingerbread and Friday's applesauce, had their fads and fashions, smuggled in forbidden delicacies, and feigned terror over the Friday evening teachers' meetings, which they called the 'Inquisition'; but Mrs. Willard, in spite of her zeal for scholarship and organization, understood this side of their lives. Her courtly bearing and her dignity might at first seem to hold her aloof from them, but she felt near them, and always won their confidence and affection. The girls looked up to her as if she were a queen or a goddess, and imitated her studied, finished manners. Any girl who received special attention from Mrs. Willard was looked upon with envy, and she who was chosen to walk to church with her was sublimely happy and proud.

Many of her girls were far from home, some from the South, some 'western girls' from the interior of New York State and Ohio, who made the long journey by stage and canal boat; and in those days, when travel was so arduous, it seemed best for them to spend their vacations at the Seminary. Often they lived there several years before returning home. They needed a principal who would be a mother to them, and this office Mrs. Willard filled naturally and sympathetically. One day, a very young girl who had just lost her mother came to

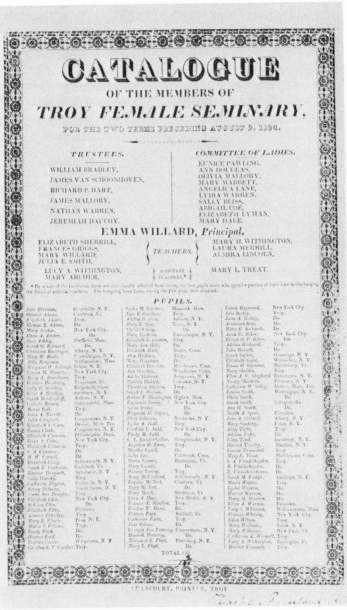

CATALOGUE
OF THE MEMBERS OF
TROY FEMALE SEMINARY,
FOR THE TWO TERMS PRECEDING AUGUST 9, 1834.

TRUSTEES.	COMMITTEE OF LADIES.
WILLIAM BRADLEY,	EUNICE PAWLING,
	ANN DOUGLAS,
JAMES VAN SCHOONHOVEN,	OLIVIA MALLORY,
	MARY MABBETT,
RICHARD P. HART,	ANGELICA LANE,
	LYDIA WARREN,
JAMES MALLORY,	SALLY BLISS,
	ABIGAIL COE,
NATHAN WARREN,	ELIZABETH LYMAN,
JEREMIAH DAUCHY.	MARY HALE.

EMMA WILLARD, *Principal.*

ELIZABETH SHERRILL,		MARY H. WITHINGTON,
FRANCES GRIGGS,		LAURA MERRILL,
MARY WILLARD,	*TEACHERS.*	ALMIRA LINCOLN,
JULIA E. SMITH,		
LUCY A. WITHINGTON,	*ASSISTANT TEACHERS.*	MARY L. TREAT.
MARY ARCHER,		

* By a rule of the Institution there are occasionally selected from among the best pupils some who spend a portion of their time in discharging the duties of assistant teachers. The foregoing have been, among the past year, thus selected.

PUPILS.

TOTAL 175.

DANCOURT, PRINTER, TROY.

the Seminary. Forlorn and heartbroken, she struggled to adjust herself to her new life. Mrs. Willard, sensing her grief and homesickness, asked her to share her living quarters, and mothered her until the sharp edge of her sorrow had worn off. There were countless such examples of her human interest and kindness.

When the girls needed reprimanding, Mrs. Willard sent for them singly; and instead of condemning them or rebuking them sternly, she talked quietly with them, emphasizing their good qualities, pointing out the possibilities in their characters, and arousing in them a determination to do better. This method of bringing out the best in her pupils was the result of her unusual understanding of human nature. She anticipated the psychology of to-day. 'Do your best and your best will be growing better' was one of her favorite maxims. To a pupil who complained that unkind things were being said about her, she quoted these lines from Pope:

> Trust not yourself, but your defects to know,
> Make use of every friend and every foe.

She was always ready to give her girls good counsel and her interest followed them out into the world. It was one of her greatest joys to visit them in their homes, or to hear from them after they had become teachers or were married and established in homes of their own.

Emma Willard's 'daughters' were of various types — rich and poor, frivolous and serious, young and old, some destined for society, others eager to become teachers. The Troy Female Seminary had become celebrated, and attracted not only daughters of wealthy and prominent families, but girls from frontier settlements, and poor girls who had struggled and economized to attend at least one term. The average age of the students was seventeen, but there were also many older girls, some teachers, some young widows who wished to add to their meager education. Daughters of Troy clergymen were given free instruction and daughters of other clergymen received a large reduction in tuition, as did many girls who were studying to become teachers.

Mrs. Willard was proud, and could well be, of the prominent names among her pupils. The daughters of many governors were enrolled, daughters of Governor Van Ness of Vermont, Governor Cass of Michigan, Governor Worthington of Ohio, and Governor Skinner of Georgia. Effie, Catherine, and Sarah Irving, nieces of Washington Irving, spent several years at the Seminary. Aaron Burr brought his nieces to visit, and Mary Wollstonecraft, niece of the famous Mary Wollstonecraft, the wife of William Godwin, spent a few years at the Seminary after a very tragic girlhood. Her father, Captain Wollstonecraft, had come to this country in 1812, had settled and then married at West Point. He took his five-year-old daughter with him on a journey to New Orleans, contracted yellow fever, and died, leaving her helpless among strangers. She was bound to a Baptist minister and his wife who treated her cruelly and would not allow her to learn to read. Finally, through an advertisement in a New Orleans paper, offering a large reward, her mother recovered her, took her back to West Point, and later sent her to the Troy Female Seminary, where she tried to regain some of the education of which she had been so unfortunately deprived. How fitting it was for a niece of the author of the 'Vindication of the Rights of Woman' to be a pupil in one of the first female seminaries founded to further the higher education of women!

Many of Mrs. Willard's nieces were given a home in

the Seminary, for she wanted the girls of her family to have the very best educational advantages. She delighted in mothering all her younger relatives. Mary Lydia Treat, the daughter of Mrs. Willard's sister, Lydia, came to Troy to make her home with the Willards in 1822, when she was twelve years old, and was adopted by Mrs. Willard, who was devoted to her. Later, when Emma Willard Hart, the daughter of Mrs. Willard's half-brother, Jesse, was left without a mother, Mrs. Willard adopted her too. Both girls eventually became teachers at the Seminary.

From the very first year of the Troy Female Seminary, Mrs. Willard took a special interest in the training of teachers. She knew that there was a crying need throughout the country for efficient teachers and felt it her duty to provide as many as possible. Many girls who would otherwise have spent their days after leaving the Seminary in idleness or in society, she encouraged to enter the teaching profession, a profession which she considered highly proper for young ladies and well-suited to their abilities. She urged others in moderate circumstances, who would always be dependent upon male relatives, to support themselves by teaching, and thus not only benefit society but improve their own status.

She received numerous applications from girls who could not afford to pay their tuition, but who longed to study and become teachers. Many of them were accepted at the Seminary and given free instruction. Some were even provided with suitable clothing, and sometimes with traveling expenses. The girls in turn contracted to repay their tuition gradually when they became teachers, as this would enable other girls to have similar opportunities for study. Although it was one of

Mrs. Willard's greatest joys to help girls who craved an education, her judgment was very keen and she seldom chose an applicant who proved disappointing. A girl who sent her a careless, poorly written letter was at once rejected. No one ever knew which girls received free tuition. Rich and poor were treated alike. During her connection with the Seminary, Mrs. Willard loaned approximately seventy-five thousand dollars to girls for their education, but she was business-like enough to see that the number of non-paying pupils did not assume too large a proportion and put a strain on the finances of the school. She was probably the first woman to provide scholarships for girls.

Mrs. Willard was also one of the first educators in the country who took definite steps to train teachers. As early as 1814, when she opened her school in Middlebury, she began to train girls to assist her in teaching, and this phase of her work gradually developed to such an extent in the Troy Female Seminary that she furnished teachers for schools in all parts of the country. A school certificate signed 'Emma Willard' was considered the highest recommendation a teacher could have. The Troy Female Seminary may well be called the forerunner of the normal school. In fact, Mrs. Willard considered it the first normal school. She said: 'I continued to educate and send forth teachers, until two hundred had gone from the Troy Seminary before one was educated in any public normal school in the United States. Thus early was my system of female education carried to every part of the country, and the school which, in 1814, was begun in Middlebury is fairly entitled to the honor of being the first normal school in the United States.'

The following lines from a poem, written by Mrs.

Willard, show her sentiment about sending her pupils
out from the Seminary as teachers:

TO A YOUNG LADY

About to Leave Me, to Take Charge of a Female Academy

And thou dost leave me, Julia, and thy course
Wend far away? Go, in the name of God.
Prosper, and prove a pillar in the cause
Of woman. Lend thy aid to waken her
From the long trance of ages. Make her feel
She too hath God's own image, and the fount
Of the mind's grand and beautiful, is hers.
She, too, should learn her Maker's works and will;
Her first, best homage and obedience, His.

Although Mrs. Willard was primarily concerned in
training and developing the minds of her girls, she
wanted them to be skillful and happy in the so-called
womanly tasks. To this end, she provided instruction
in pastry cooking. Maids did not tidy the girls' rooms
nor make their beds. The girls did this themselves and
it was considered an important part of the day's work.
Rich Southern girls who had never before touched a
broom or a duster, now took great pride in cleaning their
rooms. There was no hurried bedmaking at the Troy
Female Seminary. Every bed must be smooth and trim.
The girls often told how Mrs. Willard taught them to
make a bed, advising the use of a broom handle to
smooth it toward the top, in case ordinary methods
failed to make it smooth enough. Their womanly interest in handwork was also encouraged. They created
marvelous workboxes covered with floral decorations
and painted mourning pictures in memory of departed
relatives and friends. These pretentious mourning pictures, painted in water colors on China silk, not only

portrayed the likeness of the departed, but often depicted the death scene itself. Such uncheerful occupation did not seem to fill the girls with gloom, so occupied were they with the workmanship. Most of their religious training centered their thoughts on death and they seemed to enjoy the contemplation of it, or perhaps it was a comfort to them to relieve their feelings in funereal poetry and mourning pictures.

Mrs. Willard heartily disapproved of the hours spent in fashionable schools on useless painting, embroidery, and the making of shell ornaments, but evidently the usefulness of workboxes and the solemnity of mourning pictures justified them. She was willing to yield in a degree to the popular demand for such accomplishments and considered the time spent on them relaxation after the higher studies.

Even in those days, girls were interested in presidential elections, although they were not supposed to be. During the campaign of Adams and Jackson, when the feelings of the nation were at a high pitch, some of the Seminary girls held a secret meeting, made dramatic speeches, and stirred up considerable political animosity. Some were staunch supporters of the safe, refined, scholarly John Quincy Adams. Others were swept away with enthusiasm for their picturesque western hero from Tennessee, who was the friend of the plain people. When Mrs. Willard heard of this indiscretion among the girls, she at once felt called upon to remind them of the duties of their sex and to point out to them the differences in the duties of men and women. She was not going to have her girls called 'hyenas in petticoats,' nor was her school to encourage that much-scorned movement for women's rights. She could not let such things creep in to endanger the cause of woman's education.

She agreed with the sentiments of 'The Female Friend,' that little book so widely recommended for young ladies, that 'a female politician is only less disgusting than a female infidel — but a female patriot is what Hannah More was and what every American woman should study to be.' She explained the situation by comparing man to the oak and woman to the apple tree. The oak could never be the apple tree nor the apple tree the oak, but each could be beautiful and useful as a tree.

Thus, a woman with remarkable vision and zeal for the advancement of her sex, closed the door of her mind to the consideration of women's political rights. Doubtless, her mind was so filled with the cause of woman's education, that no other movement seemed important in comparison. She was convinced that education must come first, that nothing must be done to cast the higher education of women into disrepute. She read the signs of the times accurately. The world was not ready to hand women their freedom all at once; nor were women as a whole willing or ready to accept it. She had faced bitterness, scorn, and opposition from women as well as from men, in her fight for education. She knew that the emancipation of women must come gradually, step by step. Women, so long in bondage, must be prepared for the freedom that was bound to come to them in this new country, the Republic of America, as she loved to call it. Women needed a practical idealist to lead them, and they found her in Emma Willard.

So, Emma Willard's 'daughters' were taught to be apple trees, not oaks, to improve their minds, to be beautiful, influential, and useful, to follow the example of Hannah More, and to stay virtuously in the distinct and separate sphere which their Maker had ordained for them.

CHAPTER XII

LAFAYETTE'S WELCOME

WHILE 'female politicians' were scorned at the Troy Female Seminary, 'female patriots' were nurtured there. So ardent a patriot and hero-worshiper as Emma Willard naturally instilled these same qualities in her pupils. When in the fall of 1824, Lafayette began his triumphal tour of the United States, Mrs. Willard's enthusiasm for him was revived. All her life, she had heard of Lafayette and idealized him. As a child on her father's knee, she had listened spellbound to stories of the Revolution, of young Lafayette's dramatic, gallant part in it, of his friendship with Washington. She had listened to stories of the French soldiers on their march through Connecticut, of their camps at Hartford, Farmington, and Southington, of the gratitude and enthusiasm of the Americans as they greeted their allies. All the childhood glamour remained. Later, her interest in history and current events led her to follow his career in France — his share in the French Revolution, his efforts for constitutional liberty, his sufferings in an Austrian prison. Now, this same Lafayette, this apostle of liberty, this saviour of America, was coming to Troy. Mrs. Willard was moved to express her feelings in verse. Then she planned to invite him to visit the Seminary, to show him that unique American institution. The girls were prepared for his visit. Their history classes retold his achievements, but most romantic of all to them was the tale of his flight to America, when still a boy of nineteen, to champion the cause of liberty.

At last, the day came when Lafayette was to honor Troy. The girls had rehearsed their part in the celebration; and dressed in white with blue sashes, each wearing a satin badge upon which the face of Lafayette was painted, they breathlessly awaited his arrival. Across the park in front of the Seminary, an arbor had been constructed and covered with evergreens and flowers by the ladies of Troy. This inscription was emblazoned over its entrance,

AMERICA COMMANDS HER DAUGHTERS TO WELCOME
THEIR DELIVERER, LAFAYETTE

Over the doorway of the Seminary was an arch of evergreens and flowers bearing the motto,

WE OWE OUR SCHOOLS TO FREEDOM;
FREEDOM TO LAFAYETTE

About noon, the guns boomed, announcing the arrival of the General on the canal boat Schenectady Packet. Loud continuous cheering and the rousing strains of military bands told of his triumphal ride through the streets to the Troy House, where he was to be received by the common council of Troy and the Royal Arch Masons.

While he was at luncheon, the following note was presented to him:

To GENERAL LAFAYETTE: The Ladies of Troy, having assembled at the Female Seminary, have selected from this their number a committee to request General Lafayette that he would grant them an opportunity of beholding in his person, their own, and their country's generous and beloved benefactor.

He accepted this invitation with eagerness and was escorted by Colonel Lane to the arbor of evergreens in front of the Seminary. Here he was met by a committee of ladies headed by Mrs. Albert Pawling, who welcomed him:

RESPECTED AND DEAR SIR:

The ladies of Troy rejoice in the opportunity of meeting the illustrious friend and early benefactor of their much loved country — and through me, tender to you, sir, their most affectionate respects and cordial welcome to this now peaceful and happy land.

The ladies are also proud in being able to present, in the pupils of the adjoining seminary, a living testimony of the blessings conferred by that independence, which you, sir, so essentially contributed to establish, and in which our sex enjoy a prominent share.

Permit me, sir, the pleasure of introducing you to the principal and assistant teachers of 'The Troy Female Seminary,' — an institution which we consider an honor to our city and country.

The General, after expressing his joy at being so cordially received by the ladies of Troy, was escorted through the arbor of evergreens to the steps of the Seminary where he was presented to Mrs. Willard by Mrs. Pawling. In front of him in the hallway stood the pupils of the Seminary, who greeted him with a song of welcome, written by Mrs. Willard. The instructress of music, Miss Eliza Smith, sang the verses and the girls enthusiastically joined in the chorus:

> And art thou, then, dear Hero come?
> And do our eyes behold the man,
>   Who nerved his arm and bared his breast
> For us, ere yet our life began?
>   For us and for our native land,
> Thy youthful valor dared the war;
>   And now, in winter of thine age,
> Thou'st come and left thy lov'd ones far.

> CHORUS
> Then deep and dear thy welcome be;
> Nor think thy daughters far from thee:
> Columbia's daughters, lo! we bend,
> And claim to call thee Father, Friend!

But was't our country's rights alone
Impell'd Fayette to Freedom's van!
No! 'twas the love of human kind —
It was the sacred cause of man —
It was benevolence sublime,
Like that which sways the Eternal mind!
And benefactor of the world,
He shed his blood for all mankind!

CHORUS

Then deep and dear thy welcome be;
Nor think thy daughters far from thee:
Daughters of human kind we bend,
And claim to call thee Father, Friend!

At the close of the song, two of the girls, the daughters of Governor Cass of Michigan and Governor Van Ness of Vermont, stepped forward and presented him with a copy of Mrs. Willard's 'Plan for Improving Female Education' and with a copy of the verses just sung, beautifully printed on a sheet of embossed paper, bordered with blue.

General Lafayette was deeply moved, and with tears in his eyes said to Mrs. Willard, 'I cannot express what I feel on this occasion; but will you, Madam, present me with three copies of those lines, to be given by me, as from you, to my three daughters.'

Then he greeted the pupils individually. One of them, recalling the event in later years, said, 'I remember his looks perfectly. He was tall and had a smiling face. He shook hands cordially, and said a kind word to every one.'

When it was time for his departure, he was conducted down the steps and through the arbor by Mrs. Willard and the Committee of Ladies, followed by the girls 'harmoniously raising to heaven their grateful voices,' as a contemporary expressed it. At the outer gate, they took leave of him, while several thousand spectators looked on — silent with reverence.

On July 1, 1825, Lafayette again passed through Troy and called at the Troy Female Seminary. The report of his visit in the Troy 'Sentinel' read in part:

> He was received with great propriety by the respectable lady principal of that valuable institution and after gratifying the amiable members of the school with another sight of the friend of their country, he returned to the Troy House, where a delegation from Albany met him and took him into their carriage as he bid farewell to Troy.

Lafayette's visits not only brought great personal joy to Mrs. Willard, but widened the Seminary's sphere of influence. The news of his visit spread quickly and gave the Seminary a certain fame and prestige. Lafayette, always interested in everything which tended to improve society, was greatly impressed by this unique venture in female education and spoke enthusiastically about it in France. So touched was he by his welcome at the Seminary, that he sent Mrs. Willard a most cordial invitation to visit his family. A very friendly correspondence ensued, which developed into a firm friendship. The following letter shows his interest in the Seminary and its Principal:

LA GRANGE, *October* 29, 1827

DEAR AND RESPECTED MADAM:

Your kind letter, July 5th, has afforded me the double gratification I shall ever find in the testimonies of your friendship and of your confidence.

I feel the great importance of the commission intrusted to my care. As a warm and grateful admirer of the Female Seminary of Troy, as a respectful and affectionate friend of Mrs. Willard, I have, I confess, a very exalted notion of the requisite qualities to be associated with such an institution and its directress.

My first application has been to Mlle. S——n, an intimate friend of ours, who herself directs a seminary of the highest order in Paris, whose principles, sentiments, and talents, render her the fittest person I know, to find and to guarantee what we want. The result of a late conversation with my daughter-in-law has been that, though it has often happened that she has had it in her power to procure the object of our inquiries, she knew no one at the present who would fully answer the purpose. But she will endeavor to discover it.

My researches will not be limited to one source of information. I shall seek everywhere; and, should I be so happy as to meet your views, shall not lose time to advise you by the regular packets. We remain in the country until January, making some occasional calls in town: one of them will be next month, to the marriage of my son's eldest daughter to a most amiable young man. No opportunity will be neglected to execute my confidential and much-valued charge.

My three daughters have been highly sensible of your goodness in the affectionate wish you have been pleased to express. Should it be possible to part with the young women, there is no person on either side of the Atlantic from whom such a proposal would be more welcome and highly appreciated. I wish, dear madam, we could receive you under our friendly roof of La Grange, where my daughters love to recall the happy memories of Troy, and singing what has been my delight to hear from my amiable young friends, to whom I beg you to offer my best regards and good wishes. My son begs to be respectfully remembered to you, in which sentiments the whole American colony of La Grange join most cordially.

Your affectionate and grateful friend,

LAFAYETTE

A letter from Lafayette was always a great event at the Seminary. The girls assembled and listened eagerly while Mrs. Willard, enthroned before them, regal in her black silk, read it aloud with great dignity and feeling. Then they in turn reverently transcribed it.

Mrs. Willard carried on a wide correspondence with prominent men. So enthusiastic was she about her educational projects that she never hesitated to enlist the interest of any one whose influence might aid her in her work. She craved the confidence, respect, and approval of great men. There was nothing bold or presuming in this correspondence. It was the natural impulse of an enthusiastic nature and it won her many friends.

CHAPTER XIII

THE WIDENING INFLUENCE OF THE TROY FEMALE SEMINARY

A MAN of great influence in whom Mrs. Willard found a staunch friend and helper was Professor Amos B. Eaton, whose popular lectures and field work in botany, geology, and mineralogy had aroused such an interest in the natural sciences. He had been called from Williams College in 1818 by Governor Clinton of New York to give a course of scientific lectures before the Legislature in Albany. His subsequent lectures in Troy led to the establishment of the Lyceum of Natural History, where Mrs. Willard held classes before her school building was ready for occupancy. Professor Eaton was as enthusiastic about his work and the cause of natural science as Mrs. Willard was about female education. Both were indefatigable. Professor Eaton felt extremely friendly toward the education of women and was the first man to accept women as students of science. Mrs. Willard naturally turned to him to increase her knowledge of the sciences and took lessons from him in a great variety of subjects. He was amazed at her capacity for study, her earnestness, her mental keenness, her memory, and her ability to turn from one subject to another. Their methods of teaching were similar. Both strove to get away from pure memory work, to encourage reasoning and experimentation, and to make education applicable to life. Their evenings of study together must have been highly profitable to both, Professor Eaton eagerly watching the aptitude and progress of a brilliant woman, Mrs. Willard stimulated by the vigorous personality of the enthusiastic scientist. Their exchange of opinions, scholar to scholar, not as man to woman, inferior mentally, meant a great deal to Mrs. Willard. She called him 'the republican philosopher,' because of his simple tastes and habits and his vast fund of knowledge.

At Professor Eaton's suggestion, Mrs. Willard introduced into the curriculum of the Troy Female Seminary courses in science which were in advance of those in most men's colleges. He took charge of this new department and taught at the Seminary until women had been trained to teach the sciences. In 1822, he published a 'Zoölogical Syllabus' especially for the Troy Female Seminary, and also dedicated his 'Chemical Instructor' to Mrs. Willard and Dr. Beck. When, early in 1825, Stephen van Rensselaer, who had been greatly impressed by Professor Eaton's work and ability, established the Rensselaer School, later the Rensselaer Polytechnic Institute, and made Professor Eaton its Senior Professor, Mrs. Willard's opportunities for study with him increased.

It was about this time that Mary Lyon, whose interest in science had been aroused by Professor Eaton's lectures at Amherst, spent a summer in Troy with his family, continuing her studies. It was here that she met Mrs. Willard, but unfortunately no records of the impression which these two pioneer educators made upon each other have been found.

Mrs. Willard's sister, Mrs. Almira Hart Lincoln, who came to Troy in 1824 to teach at the Seminary, also became a pupil of Amos Eaton. In fact, she became one of his outstanding pupils, contributing more to science than any other woman of that period in America. Her progress was rapid, and she was soon teaching botany at the Seminary, and later, chemistry and geology. Under her guidance, these subjects became favorites among the girls.

Mrs. Lincoln had come to the Troy Female Seminary with her two young daughters, Jane and Emma, shortly after her husband had passed away. Eager to have something to occupy her mind and to enable her to support her children, she began teaching, and at the same time studied French, Latin, mathematics, botany, geology, and chemistry. Her love of teaching and her years of success in it before her marriage now served her well, as more and more work opened up for her at the Seminary. The two sisters, Emma and Almira, always drawn to each other by their love of study, their interest in teaching, and their desire for progress, worked well together. Mrs. Willard grew very fond of her two small nieces, and became especially devoted to Jane. During Dr. Willard's long illness, Mrs. Lincoln was a great comfort to her sister, and took over much of her work.

Dr. Willard passed away May 29, 1825, leaving Mrs. Willard with the full responsibility of the school. He had done his share of the work so quietly and unobtrusively, in such an orderly systematic manner, calling so little attention to himself, that few realized what a factor he had been in building up the school. The comments of the Troy 'Sentinel' show with what high regard he was looked upon in the city in which he had made his home for the past four years:

We are not sufficiently acquainted with the events of Dr. Willard's life to attempt even a sketch of it. We can, however, bear unhesitating testimony to the respectability of his character, and the esteem in which he was held by the community. His life must have been regulated by sound principles, for it was accompanied by the good opinion of society and the confidence of his friends. . . .

Dr. Willard bequeathed to his wife all of his household furniture, all of his books, manuscripts, charts, maps, prints, paintings, pictures, musical instruments, and one third of his real and personal property. The copyrights of her geographies and her 'Plan for Improving Female Education,' which he, as her husband, had owned, now under his will were turned over to her. The rest of his property was divided equally between his sons, John Hart Willard, Gustavus Vasa Willard, and William Tell Willard. John was still a young boy, fourteen years old; Gustavus was living in Ohio; and William, now twenty-eight, was becoming interested in Lucretia Paine, one of Mrs. Willard's pupils, and married her in Troy a few years later. The other son, Benjamin Franklin Willard, had passed away at Matanzas, Cuba, two years before, while Laura, the only daughter, was not mentioned in her father's will.

Mrs. Willard was overwhelmed with grief for her husband. Their married life had been one of such sympathy and understanding, and she had so instinctively turned to him for encouragement in her hopes and plans, that she now seemed utterly alone in the world. Her pupils, filled with sympathy for their principal who had passed through such a great sorrow, made her a gift of a mourning ring, saying in the note of presentation, 'Will our dear Instructress accept the inclosed as a pledge of the tender regard of her affectionate pupils.' Such evidences of affection and esteem always moved Mrs. Willard deeply.

The amount of work to be done at the school carried her through this difficult experience. She took over a large share of Dr. Willard's duties, looking after the finances and keeping the books. The school property was now leased to her. The growth of the Seminary made a larger building necessary, and when, in 1826, the city of Troy lengthened it forty feet, Mrs. Willard's rent was raised to seven hundred dollars a year.

The responsibility for her son's future now also confronted Mrs. Willard and she wrote to the Speaker of the House of Representatives, asking him to obtain for John an appointment as cadet at West Point. Through the efforts of several influential friends, including Governor Clinton, John was able to enter West Point within a year. Many letters passed between mother and son, showing her great love for him and her interest in his welfare. In spite of her arduous duties at the Seminary, there was always time for a letter to John, filled with good advice, warning him against folly and pointing out the path of virtue. The following extract from a letter is characteristic:

My hopes for your future course are high. I think you have now seen so much of the operation of good and bad conduct, that an enlightened regard to self-interest would lead you of yourself about right. I hope you have both the love and fear of God before your eyes, to invite you to virtue and warn you from evil; and I hope you will never be ashamed or afraid to maintain in all companies all virtuous sentiments, and frown decidedly on vicious ones. Now, John, hear me prophesy: Have the courage to form yourself on the model of character which I propose to you, and it will not only be what your duty requires, but it will be setting you forward as a leader in society, and make you looked up to and admired by that class of females whose education and character and standing place them among the first. Let gentleness, and kindness, and sweetness of nature, accompany manly seriousness and graceful dignity. You have at times a fault which you came honestly by — that of a kind of gasconade — you have the appearance of affecting wit, but the affectation of gayety and frolicking does not become you. You are naturally serious and contemplative, and, if I may say it, something peculiarly manly about you; and hence dignity and grace, not jests and tricks and prettiness, should be your ambition.

It was about this time that Mrs. Willard corresponded with Elijah Burritt, the eminent mathematician and astronomer, who was then conducting a private school in New Britain, Connecticut. Their correspondence dealt principally with the admission of Mr. Burritt's daughter as a student at the Troy Female Seminary, but Mrs. Willard also took this opportunity to ask Mr. Burritt to use his influence in furthering that which was nearest her heart, equal educational rights for women. Mr. Burritt's 'Geography of the Heavens' was later used as a textbook at the Seminary.

A momentous event had occurred in October, 1825 — the opening of the Erie Canal. Celebrations in all of the towns along the Canal and the Hudson River made this a gala occasion. By special invitation from Governor Clinton, Mrs. Willard and the pupils of the Troy Female Seminary celebrated the event by a boat trip to 'the nine locks.' The opening of the Erie Canal, however, meant more than this to the Troy Female Seminary. It meant growth and an ever-widening opportunity for service. It meant that all the newly opened western territory could now more readily send its daughters to Troy for an education, while the Seminary in turn could send more teachers out through the West. To Mrs. Willard, always an eager student of contemporary history, it meant the growth and expansion of her beloved country. She sensed its significance. East and West were being linked together. Now, throughout that wide expanse of wilderness included in the Louisiana Purchase of 1803, settlers would be pushing farther and farther west. The thirteen poverty-stricken, war-racked colonies, which at the time of Mrs. Willard's birth in 1787 were struggling to come to terms in the Constitutional Convention, had developed and expanded so that in 1825 the Republic of America was beginning to assume the proportions of a vast empire.

The Canal brought prosperity to Troy. Since 1820, Troy had more than doubled in population, and within three years after the opening of the Canal, had added three thousand to its population. Oil lamps now lighted its streets; door numbers were used to mark houses; River Street, the principal business thoroughfare of the city, was paved. An 'elegant and secure' steamboat, the Chief Justice Marshall, now plied between Troy and New York two or three times a week, while not so many years before, the voyage was made by sloop and often took a week, although sometimes with favorable winds the round trip could be made in four days. These sloops, propelled by oars or floating with the tide when there was no wind, had traveled at the rate of fourteen miles a day. Robert Fulton's epoch-making trip up the Hudson from New York to Albany on his steamboat, the Clermont, in 1807, had so revolutionized river traffic that by 1830 eighty-six steamboats were operating on the Hudson River. Stagecoaches made regular trips between Troy and Boston, to Schenectady and Saratoga. Troy was in the hum of commercial development.

The Female Seminary also gave Troy a certain fame, and kept pace with the growth of the city, attracting pupils from every part of the country. In 1828, it became necessary to erect an additional building; a few years later, more land was purchased and the main building was again enlarged. Mrs. Willard was receiving a substantial income from the sale of her geographies and was able to live very comfortably. Distinguished visitors came to the Seminary to investigate that distinctly American experiment in female education.

In a letter to Maria Edgeworth, written about this

time, Mrs. Willard commented upon the observations of
one of these visitors:

An English traveller attended for a time upon my last
examination. He said to me, on leaving: 'Madam, you are
making a grand experiment here; we have nothing to compare
with it on our side of the water; but I fear you are educating
girls too highly, and that they will not be willing to marry.'
But I have never experienced any difficulty of this sort. The
young men sought them so resolutely for wives that I could
not keep them for teachers.

For many years, Mrs. Willard had looked up to Maria
Edgeworth, not only because of the fame that she had
attained as an author, but because she stood for the education of women in a country where women's safety and
virtue were considered synonymous with ignorance.
Maria Edgeworth had proved that a woman could be
well-educated, succeed as an author, receive praise and
adulation, and still remain virtuous. It was only natural that Mrs. Willard's enthusiasm for such a woman
should lead her to open up a correspondence for the exchange of views on the subject of woman's education.

Mrs. Willard was always looking for opportunities
to spread her message of higher education for women.
Consequently, after she became acquainted with the
Colombian minister, she sent through him to Bolivar a
copy of her 'Plan for Improving Female Education' and
a letter pleading for her sex, with the result that a female
seminary was established in Bogota. Her influence was
being felt throughout the world.

CHAPTER XIV

THE AWAKENING OF AMERICAN WOMEN

LITTLE did Mrs. Willard dream when she presented her 'Plan for Improving Female Education' to the Legislature of New York in 1819 that, within ten years and without State aid, the cause of woman's education would receive such an impetus. The success of her Seminary in Troy did much to change public opinion regarding the propriety of education for women, especially since her pupils emerged from the Seminary after several years of higher education as ladylike, if not more ladylike, than before they took up their studies, and did not rush out into the world demanding to usurp man's sphere. The teachers sent out every year from the Seminary spread the message of woman's education in an ever-widening circle.

But the Troy Female Seminary was not the only school that was paving the way for the higher education of girls; nor was Mrs. Willard the only woman giving her life for the cause of woman's education. Academies and seminaries were being founded throughout the country. The South was especially friendly toward the education of women, and it was there that the majority of Mrs. Willard's young teachers found positions. Southerners were not afraid to use the word 'college' in connection with woman's education. Elizabeth Academy in Old Washington, Mississippi, founded in 1817, was chartered as a college in 1819, but its course of study did not rank with that of later women's colleges. Dr. Mark's School at Barhamville, South Carolina, established in 1815 and incorporated as a college in 1832, grew each year in

numbers and influence. In Lexington, Kentucky, Lafayette Seminary, founded in 1821, shared the honors
with the Troy Female Seminary in receiving a visit from
Lafayette, and at that time had one hundred and thirty-
five pupils and nine instructors. Many of these schools,
like the Troy Female Seminary, were introducing higher
subjects and were working toward a standard of education for women more nearly equal to that for young men.

Mary Lyon, in the hills of Massachusetts, was becoming known for her ability and zeal as a teacher. At
Londonderry, New Hampshire, and then at Ipswich,
Massachusetts, with Zilpah P. Grant, she was experi-
menting, adding new subjects to the curriculum, and
planting the seeds for her endowed seminary at Mount
Holyoke.

In Hartford, Connecticut, in 1823, Catherine Beecher,
with the aid of her sister, had opened a select school for
fifteen young ladies in a room over a store. During the
next few years, so many pupils flocked to her seminary
that she was obliged to call upon the prominent men of
Hartford to subscribe money for the erection of a more
adequate school building. Through the influence of the
women of Hartford, this was accomplished, and the
Hartford Female Seminary prospered, enrolling one
hundred to two hundred pupils. Catherine Beecher,
acting as Principal with eight teachers to assist her,
held yearly exhibitions to show what progress was being
made. The girls wrote Latin compositions and versified
their translations of Virgil and Ovid. In spite of her
many duties, Catherine Beecher found time to prepare
an arithmetic for use in her school and also to write a
textbook on mental philosophy, entitled 'Mental and
Moral Philosophy, Founded on Reason, Observation,
and the Bible.' She finally managed to have every pupil

of the Hartford Female Seminary study geography, arithmetic, and grammar. She found that most parents desired a 'finishing' school with superficial studies, for their daughters, and was convinced that only schools with established reputations could introduce higher subjects. In 1829, she published 'Suggestions on Education,' which was widely read and focused attention on the Hartford Female Seminary. It described the work done there and emphasized the inequalities in the provisions for the education of men and women.

Writing to Catherine Beecher about this educational treatise, Mrs. Willard said, 'Accept, my dear madam, my thanks for the able work which you had the goodness to send me. I have perused it with deep interest. Every effort to advance the cause it advocates has my best wishes for its success.'

In 1826, the first public high schools for girls were established in Boston and New York. So great was the popularity of the Boston school that the self-constituted protectors of woman's sphere were alarmed and stirred up such feeling against it that it was closed two years later. The New York school was closed because it lacked an efficient head. Yet, in spite of critics and calamity criers, the cause of woman's education pressed steadily forward.

Still hoping to gain an endowment for her Seminary from the New York Legislature, and by this act to receive their public endorsement of female education, Mrs. Willard, in 1826, wrote a very frank letter to Francis Granger, one of her friends among the legislators. It read:

To Mr. Granger,

DEAR SIR: Shall I draw too heavily on your friendship to me, your liberality of feeling, and generous zeal in the service of the ladies, if I tell you that I want you as an *active* friend in our cause. Will you have the goodness to stir up your friends to help us. Tell those among them who have any regard for the feelings and opinions of the ladies, that the trial of this question this year will cause a great sensation among us; that we shall set our marks on our friends, and on our — enemies shall I say — I think tyrants the better word. What better appellation can a woman of spirit give to a man who is unwilling her sex should share with the other in the means of intellectual light? — This view of our subject may have some weight with the younger cavaliers of your corps, and you may depend that it is true — but what shall we say that will have any effect on the stubborn sour old 'habitans' who think that every thing must be, precisely as it has been, and that because their wives are ignorant that it is better that all women should be so? Are there many of that stamp in the legislature this year? I never expect that complete justice will be done to our sex until this old set are chiefly with their fathers. But I am confident that our cause is a righteous one, and I believe that from year to year it is growing.

Yours with the most cordial esteem

EMMA WILLARD

TROY FEMALE SEMINARY
March 4th, 1826

Meanwhile, women were beginning to think about their rights, and some advanced thinkers realized that education was but a step toward a sphere of greater freedom and usefulness. The anti-slavery movement appealed to their sense of justice, and a few women in the face of bitter abuse asserted their right to speak and work for that reform. Among them were the Grimke sisters of South Carolina who freed their slaves, moved north, and began speaking for abolition. They were mobbed many times, ridiculed, insulted, denounced, not so much because they were speaking for the abolition of slavery as that they, as women, were publicly expressing themselves on a political question. But they continued;

other courageous, crusading women joined them; and as a result the National Female Anti-Slavery Society was formed in 1833.

Mrs. Willard, however, took no part in any of these new movements, fearing that the disapproval of the men would work ill for the cause of woman's education. When in 1829 Catherine Beecher wrote her asking her coöperation in a matter which Mrs. Willard considered too political for women, she replied: 'In reflecting on political subjects, my thoughts are apt to take this direction: the only natural government on earth is that of the family — the only natural sovereign, the husband and father. Other just governments are these sovereigns confederated. . . .' These sovereigns, according to Mrs. Willard, would consider the interference of women 'unwonted officiousness' and would say, 'The studies which you pursue have inflated and bewildered you; you are the worse for your knowledge; return to your ignorance.' Then she added, 'Such a sentence as this, my dear madam, you and I, as guardians of the interests of our sex's education, are alike desirous to avoid; and when the warm dictates of a generous benevolence shall have given place to sober reflection, I cannot but believe you will agree with me that we cannot, without endangering those interests, interfere with the affair in question.'

Although abolition, temperance, and political subjects were taboo, women were establishing themselves in the field of literature. 'Moral Pieces in Prose and Verse,' published in 1815 by a young girl, Lydia Huntley of Hartford, later Mrs. Sigourney, aroused interest and favorable comment. This was but the beginning of Mrs. Sigourney's prolific outpouring of poetry and prose which gained for her great popularity and the reputation of being the Hemans of America. Catherine Maria Sedgwick of Stockbridge, Massachusetts, encouraged by her brother to publish her 'New England Tale,' became the outstanding woman novelist in America, and her romances translated into foreign languages and reprinted in England were more widely read in Europe than either Irving or Poe. In 1828, Mrs. Sarah Josepha Hale became the editor of the 'American Ladies' Magazine,' published in Boston and afterwards consolidated with 'Godey's Lady's Book.' The aim of this magazine was 'to recommend to the hearts and minds of American ladies, with the pursuit of intellectual and elegant accomplishments, the practice of every feminine duty and Christian excellence that can adorn and dignify the name of woman.' In its pages, women were given the opportunity to plead for the education of their sex.

About this time, Mrs. Willard's sister, Almira Lincoln, fulfilled an ambition which she had cherished ever since she had heard of the publication of 'Moral Pieces in Prose and Verse' by Lydia Huntley. She published her first book, a botany textbook, which was to become famous as 'Lincoln's Botany.' Mrs. Lincoln had been studying botany with Professor Amos Eaton and teaching it at the Troy Female Seminary. Not finding a textbook that suited her, she wrote out her own lectures and on the advice of Professor Eaton published them. Up to this time, botany had been taught in very few schools, but the new textbook aroused such interest in the subject that in less than four years ten thousand copies had been sold. For many years, 'Lincoln's Botany' was the standard textbook in schools and colleges throughout the country. It was reprinted in England and translated into foreign languages. Such a wide sale not only brought Mrs. Lincoln fame, but provided her with a very comfortable income. The critics of the day considered the book written in attractive style and evidently agreed with Mrs. Lincoln's introductory remarks that 'the study of Botany seems peculiarly adapted to females; the objects of its investigation are beautiful and delicate; its pursuit leading to exercise in the open air is conducive to health and cheerfulness.' Throughout the book, interspersed with scientific data, were floral quotations from the poets, such as Chaucer's lines on the daisy, also accounts of the superstitions connected with various plants, and the inevitable moralizing which tempted every writer of that day. Mrs. Lincoln's 'Botany' was followed shortly after by the publication of the 'Dictionary of Chemistry,' translated from the French with additions.

Mrs. Willard had already become known as an authoress by the publication of her 'Plan for Improving Female Education,' her 'Ancient Geography,' and various poems. Her next book, 'Republic of America,' appeared in 1828. This book gave full play to her powers. Her love of history which was so marked even in childhood, her great affection for her native land, her enthusiasm for the republican form of government, her interest in contemporary events led her naturally to the writing of such a book. In the opinion of a contemporary, no other woman and few men in the United States were so well acquainted with the events and characters of the country. Mrs. Willard dedicated 'Republic of America' to her mother, Lydia Hart, in a poem fervid with sentiment toward her beloved country:

> Accept this offering of a daughter's love,
> Dear, only, widowed parent; on whose brow
> Time-honoured, have full eighty winters shed
> The crown of wisdom.

Mother, few are left,
Like thee, who felt the fire of freedom's holy time
Pervade and purify the patriot breast.
Thou wert within thy country's shattered bark,
When, trusting Heaven, she rode the raging seas,
And braved with dauntless, death-defying front
The storm of war. With me retrace the scene,
Then view her peace, her wealth, her liberty, and fame:
And like the mariner, who gains the port
Almost unhoped-for, from the dangerous waves,
Thou canst rejoice: — and thankful praise to God
The Great Deliverer, which perchance I speak —
Thou, in thy pious heart, wilt deeply feel.

Beginning with a chapter on the 'Aboriginal Inhabitants of America,' the book traced in minute detail the history of the country through 1826. As Mrs. Willard explained in her Preface, her method of teaching history was unique. She had arranged for her pupils a series of maps illustrating the history of various epochs. It finally became necessary for her to fit her maps to some one history, and with the assistance of a few of her advanced pupils, she began writing her own textbook. She laid out her plans, the pupils gathered material from standard authors of American history, and then she worked over the whole. From the War of 1812 on, her material was drawn from original sources, and she assured her readers that she had tried to be accurate and unprejudiced. In place of a table of contents, Mrs. Willard used an interesting chronological chart of several columns, which was another of her original devices for teaching history.

The suggestions to teachers in the Preface give a clear idea of the methods used in teaching history at the Troy Female Seminary. Each pupil brought her blackboard to class. On it she drew from memory a map relating to the history lesson of the day, marking the paths of navigators and explorers, and the march of armies. Then she explained her map. Mrs. Willard felt it was useless to make pupils commit many dates to memory and instead wished them to become familiar with the dates of epochs and be able to group events accordingly. She suggested that pupils connect events of history with the events of their own lives or of their families, for it was her theory that the more a pupil connected his knowledge with himself the better he would remember it and the more effectively he would use it in later life. Believing firmly that 'moral improvement is the true end of the intellectual,' she urged teachers to turn from the events of history to make such moral reflections as the events might suggest. The Constitution of the United States, the Declaration of Independence, and Washington's Farewell Address were given in full in the appendix, because Mrs. Willard felt they should be studied by the youth of the country as their 'political scriptures.'

'Republic of America' was extremely well received and was commented upon most favorably by educators, prominent men, and newspapers among which were the 'Boston Traveler,' the 'Cincinnati Gazette,' the 'United States Gazette,' and the 'Albany Evening Journal.' The 'Boston Traveler' reviewed it as follows:

We consider the work a remarkable one, in that it forms the best book for general reading and reference published, and at the same time has no equal, in our opinion, as a textbook. On this latter point, the profession which its author followed with such signal success, rendered her peculiarly a fitting person to prepare a textbook. None but a practical teacher is capable of preparing a good school-book; and as woman has so much to do in forming our early character, why should her influence cease at the fireside — why not encourage her to

exert her talents still in preparing school and other books for
after years?

The Ward School Teachers' Association of the City of
New York called it 'decidedly the best treatise on this
interesting subject' and added:

The student will learn, by reading a few pages, how much
reason he has to be proud of his country — of its institutions
— of its founders — of its heroes and statesmen: and by such
lessons are we not to hope that those who come after us will be
instructed in their duties as citizens, and their obligations as
patriots.

Your committee are anxious to see this work extensively
used in all the schools in the U.S.

A letter from Lafayette highly endorsed her account
of the Revolutionary War. Daniel Webster wrote her:

I cannot better express my sense of the value of your history of the United States than by saying I keep it near me as
a book of reference, accurate in facts and dates.

These comments brought joy to Mrs. Willard. She
loved fame and appreciation. In her struggle for the advancement of woman's education, she had continually
encountered ridicule and abuse. Now praise was very
sweet. She could justly be proud of her historical work.
For a woman to compile a history in those days was a
rare accomplishment and to have it looked upon favorably by prominent men and indorsed by newspapers
was a still greater triumph. Ten years before, newspapers would have scorned the idea of a woman historian. Now, the 'Boston Traveler' suggested that women
teachers be encouraged to write textbooks. Mrs. Willard could also be proud of her original contributions to
the methods of teaching history. She was a born teacher.
Never content to follow others slavishly and always

striving to get her pupils and teachers away from the deadening monotony of memorizing mere words and facts, she eagerly explored untried paths in education. She was one of the outstanding progressive educators of her day. Aside from all this, possibly more than all this, was the satisfaction of having done her country a great service. One of the great ambitions of her life was to see disproved all the prophecies of European statesmen regarding the inevitable fall of the Republic of America, and instead to see her country steadfast, prosperous, true to its ideals, an object lesson to Europe. This could be accomplished, she felt, only by the proper education of America's youth, the barometer of future generations. It warmed her heart to think what love of country and what zeal for noble citizenship her book would inspire in the youth of America.

CHAPTER XV

AN OCEAN VOYAGE IN 1830

AFTER sixteen years spent as Principal of an enterprising female seminary, Mrs. Willard began to long for a rest. Year in and year out, she had been supervising and teaching, and studying during her free hours at night. Added to all this, the strain of Dr. Willard's illness and death, her grief, increased responsibilities, and intensive work on 'Republic of America' had been too great a burden. It now seemed wise to call a halt for a time.

Mrs. Willard at once thought of a trip to Europe. This was something for which she had always longed, but which had always seemed far in the future — so far that it was more like a dream than a possibility. But the more she thought of it now, the more feasible it seemed. She could afford it, for the publication of her geography and history textbooks had made her financially independent. The Seminary was flourishing and could be left in charge of her sister, Almira, who had proved to be an admirable vice-principal. Such a journey as this, of course, could not properly be undertaken alone, but her son John, now a young man of twenty, would accompany her. Although the trip would mean a break in his work at Washington College, Hartford, where he had gone after two years at West Point, it would be a rich educational experience for him. Then, as she thought it all over, she began to feel that she owed it to her school and the cause of female education to investigate European educational methods. As a prominent American educator, she could travel with introductions which would assure her entrance into European educational circles. Lafayette's friendship would mean much to her in France. He had repeatedly urged her to make his country a visit.

In spite of the dangers and hardships involved, it was an opportunity not to be lost. Mrs. Willard had reflected upon the dangers and uncertainties of ocean travel, and she was prepared. Her affairs were in order. She busied herself to fulfill one last request of her pupils, the publication of a book of poems. They had written her:

DEAR MADAM:
Many of your affectionate pupils expecting to leave you in a short time, not to return, and wishing to possess some memorial of your kindness and affection, as well as of the many happy days they have passed beneath your roof, anxiously request you to fulfill the promise made them that you would have the poems published which you were so good as to read for them in April, accompanied with an engraving of yourself, and which promise subsequent melancholy occurrencies in your family have as yet prevented you from fulfilling.

The collection of poems, which Mrs. Willard prepared for the printer, was entitled: 'The Fulfilment of a Promise; by Which Poems by Emma Willard Are Published, and Affectionately Inscribed to Her Past and Present Pupils.'

In the Preface, she sentimentalized, as she loved to do and as the age loved to have her do: 'About to cross an ocean for the first time, I feel, no doubt, the possibility of never returning, more fully than those to whom voyaging is familiar. On this occasion, I have set myself to do, as far as possible, every thing which in case of sudden death it would be desirable that I had done; and in particular to leave upon my conscience, as far as may be, no obligation unfulfilled. Along with making my will,

I have gathered this little volume for the press; all but
the first article, which I have written in two days and
two nights, amidst the preparation for my departure,
which takes place to-morrow morning, the bustle of a
New York boarding-house, and the kind parting calls of
affectionate friends.'

In the first poem, 'Prophetic Strains,' she once more
bade farewell to her pupils:

> My children! ye, whose minds are born of mine,
> Whose hearts beat toward me with a filial pulse,
> I leave you, so I deem God wills, and go,
> A wanderer o'er the main, to foreign lands.
> Ye weep as I depart. Your fancy swells
> The dangers of the deep, and ye are griev'd; —
> Grieved most of all, that ye on earth may see
> My face no more.
>   The world knows not how dear
> Ye are to me, and I to you, my daughters!
> .   .   .   . Ye are to me
> The bodying forth of a long lov'd idea.
> I see in you the representatives
> Of future woman; of the cause I've served,
> Even with a martyr's zeal, and still will serve ...

The book contained a variety of poems, some very poor,
some with real merit. Some had the funereal touch so
characteristic of the period, and many had long ex-
planatory titles, truly Wordsworthian, such as, 'On the
Recovery of a Sister from a Melancholy Derangement'
and 'To My Adopted Daughter, About to Depart for
Georgia, Written May 29th, 1827, the Second Anniversary of the Death of My Husband.' Several hymns
were included, written for the pupils of the Seminary
and sung by them at the close of their examinations.
Contemporaries praised a short poem of two stanzas,
'The Eye':

Mystic source of wond'rous meaning!
Pleading herald of the heart,
Thou, with thousands intervening,
Keen sensations canst impart.

Whence hast thou thy power so killing,
That when words would fail to move,
Thy potent glance, the bosom thrilling,
Melts it to tumultuous love.

So many changes were made in the poems by the printer
that Mrs. Willard suppressed the edition as soon as she
was aware of what had happened. Some critics ranked
Mrs. Willard's poetry with that of Mrs. Sigourney, but
on the whole her poems were not received with enthusiasm. Nothing, however, could rob her of the joy of
composing them.

On October first, 1830, Mrs. Willard and her son John
embarked for France, on the sailing vessel Charlemagne,
one of the largest and fastest of the packets which were
then the pride of the port of New York. As their ship
carried them farther and farther out on the deep, Mrs.
Lincoln, at the Troy Female Seminary, was conducting
the Saturday morning lecture with great solemnity.
'Every receding wave,' she said, 'is now bearing her
from us, and her loved and cherished institution. The
affectionate and admonitory words which she spake at
parting, are yet fresh in our minds; and we, like the
Ephesians, when St. Paul tore himself from them, sorrow
most of all lest we see her face no more. But let us hope
that her life may be preserved, and that she may be
restored to us with renewed health, and a mind enriched
by the state of female education in foreign countries, and
with increased facilities for usefulness in her own.'

Most of the passengers on the Charlemagne were

Americans. Mrs. Willard shared the ladies' cabin with
Mary E——, a little girl of eight traveling alone from
Philadelphia to Geneva, where she was to be educated
by her grandmother, and Miss D——, a young lady
who was traveling with her father, and whom Mrs. Willard characterized as interesting, intelligent, and accomplished. The trip was long, and very rough, but
Mrs. Willard appeared to enjoy it all, even the dashing
waves and rolling ship. She wrote to her sister:

> Yet I have not been sea-sick, neither have I exercised as
> much on deck, owing to the roughness of the weather, as I
> could have wished: but the perpetual motion in which I am
> kept by the winds and waters; rocking, and rolling, and toss-
> ing; holding with might and main, by some fixed object during
> the day to keep from being shot across the cabin, and grasping
> the side of my berth at night for fear of being rolled over the
> side — all this, though not particularly diverting at the time,
> is yet very conducive to my health; and seems to put in mo-
> tion those vital functions, which want of suitable exercise for
> the body, or too much mental exercise had deranged.

She walked the deck on the arm of the stalwart Captain, whom she imagined to be like Captain John Paul
Jones, and with his assistance wrote a description of the
ship, illustrated with drawings, which she sent to her
pupils for their instruction.

The sight of land, after the long voyage of twenty-
four days, moved her deeply. She wrote, '... when I
realized that I was indeed beholding that ancient world
of which I had so often strained my fancy to give me an
idea — when I realized, that through a guardian Providence, my feet had escaped the dangers of the treacher-
ous ocean, and stood again on the lap of my mother
Earth — my joy was intense. I could have acted ex-
travagances, but we belong to a race, who seem cold,
because we suppress our feelings.'

Landing at Havre, Mrs. Willard began at once in her thorough manner to investigate everything and comment upon everything. She was as enthusiastic as a child about new experiences. The quaintness of the buildings, the dresses of the peasants, the customs of the people fascinated her. The hotel received a complete analysis. She described it in minute detail for her sister, from beds and candlesticks to table d'hôte and the deafening racket made by Frenchmen in their animated conversation during a meal.

On the long journey by diligence from Havre to Paris, through the countryside by moonlight and by day, she saw the moss-grown, thatched cottages of France and the ivy-covered walls about which she had so often read in poetry. The roses were in bloom; the fields were green. She was charmed by it all, and yet with truly American self-satisfaction, she considered 'the scenery of France as much less interesting than that of America.'

CHAPTER XVI

DAYS OF DISCOVERY IN PARIS

PARIS was filled with innumerable delights and discoveries for Mrs. Willard. She was ready for anything. The people, their customs, and their point of view interested her most of all. She went to the theater as much to see 'the dresses of the French ladies and the general outward appearance of genteel society' as to hear the celebrated actress, Madame Malibran. She was impressed by the numbers of well-dressed women, by the beauty, perfection, and style of their gowns, by their charming manners. The shops, public buildings, statues, art treasures, glimpses of royalty, and drilling of the soldiers were some of the many things, aside from politics and Lafayette, that kept her busy observing and philosophizing. She wrote long letters to her sister Almira and to her pupils, letters typical of a teacher, written with an idea to instruct, massed with details and moralizing. But dimensions and plans of famous buildings, bits of history, and the Puritanical viewpoint of an exemplary woman could not smother the natural enthusiasm, insatiable curiosity, good humor, and refreshing originality which would crop out in her letters. She loved nothing better than a turn of wit such as this, 'Here we see some of the greatest lions of Paris: — lions literally, *couchant*, on either side of the gate, which leads to the garden of the Tuileries. Fear not, but boldly advance; they have turned to stone, or rather stone has turned to lions; and though they grin frightfully, they are like many other "lions in the way," harmless to impede our entrance.'

Mrs. Willard and John continued their friendship
with Mr. and Miss D——, who had been companions
of their ocean voyage, and together they set out on
many sight-seeing expeditions. 'Mr. D——'s example
and conversation are precisely what I would wish for my
son,' wrote Mrs. Willard, 'and his daughter is to me,
everything that is polite and companionable. . . . In
order that our young folks may never be without staid
counsel and sober example, when we walk out all together, Mr. D—— always walks with his daughter, and
I with my son.'

To Mrs. Willard, however, Paris meant first and foremost, Lafayette. After she had been in the city a few
days, she sent him a note telling him of her arrival, and
he immediately called upon her. She cherished every
moment of that meeting and described it in detail to her
sister Almira:

He met me affectionately. His heart seemed to expand as
to a confidential sister, and he talked to me freely of his family, and of the most important political movements. He gave
me a sketch of the Revolution — detailed the part which he
himself had taken — spoke of the present state of affairs, and
of the hopes and fears of the liberal party. . . . His greatest
regret was, that such was the state of public affairs, and such
his relation to them, that he had not the time he could wish to
devote to his personal friends. I repeated that those who
loved him best, would best know how to appreciate his situation. Yes, but he spoke for himself. His friends might be
better reconciled to all this than he was.

He enquired about his Troy acquaintances — spoke of you,
my dear sister, and of his young friends, my pupils — of the
pleasure he enjoyed there; of the beauty of the place. . . . His
observations in speaking of political affairs, were such as often
gave to my patriotic feelings a thrill of pleasure. He said . . .
that he looked upon the government of the United States as
by far superior to any other existing. . . .

He asked me if I had been to the house of Deputies. I had
not. I must go — he would procure tickets, and one of his
daughters would call for me the next morning. Do not, I be-
seech you, General, embarrass yourself about me. 'I will,'
said he, 'embarrass myself about you; I will have that pleasure.' He then asked me if I had been to the Grand Opera. I
had not . . . he would have the pleasure to go some evening
with me. I did not utter a word, but bowed very low. I did
not feel like speaking. I was deeply grateful for the honor he
intended me.

When the General had departed, I sat some time to recall
his conversation, that it might not escape my memory. His
discourse on the late revolution, and on the condition of
France, is past and present history, drawn from its original
source; for La Fayette, more than any other man of the present day, is making history for others to write, and for posterity to read.

Emma Willard was in Paris and Lafayette had called
upon her — that very Lafayette who had been the hero
of her girlhood. Even her wildest girlhood dreams had
not aspired to this. Lafayette, the maker of history, had
once more bowed over the hand of Emma Willard. He
had talked to her with intellectual respect. He had
deemed her, a woman, worthy of sharing a conversation
on political matters. Her cup of joy was running over.
The visit to the House of Deputies required preparation. As Mrs. Willard wished to be suitably clothed,
Madame Maziau, her hostess, recommended a milliner
who chose a becoming hat for her to wear on this momentous occasion. When Lafayette's eldest daughter,
Madame Latour de Maubourg, called for her, she spoke
with pleasure of her father's reception at the Troy
Female Seminary and of how many times they had sung
the verses which Mrs. Willard had written and presented
to them. From the gallery of the House of Deputies,
they listened to the debates, watching for the arrival of

Lafayette. After he had entered the Chamber and greeted his friends, his eyes searched the galleries until he discovered Mrs. Willard and his daughter. Then, he bowed three times. That afternoon, Mrs. Willard met another of Lafayette's daughters and was invited to attend his soirée. This invitation was repeated the next morning by Lafayette's daughter-in-law, Madame George Lafayette, who called and carried on an hour's animated conversation with Mrs. Willard in French. They were charmed with each other.

A few days later at half past eight in the evening, Mrs. Willard, regally clad, arrived at the soirée of General Lafayette. She was cordially received by him and his family and introduced to Mrs. Opie and James Fenimore Cooper, who with his family was spending some time in Paris. Of Mrs. Opie, she said: 'She attracts your notice, first among the crowd, from her quaker costume, worn however with something of a modish air. She uses also the Quaker *thee* and *thou*; yet with her fine flow of thought, and occasionally ornamented style of expression, it can hardly be called the plain language. The other sex seem charmed with her conversation.'

From social pleasures with the Lafayettes, Mrs. Willard turned again to sightseeing. Equipped with heavy leather shoes, she tramped sturdily over cobblestones and braved the French mud. One of her favorite haunts was the bridge of Louis XVI. She loved it especially for the twelve white marble statues placed along its sides, statues of warriors and statesmen of other days. 'I am so fascinated,' she said, 'by the marble society of this bridge, that I am in danger of running against something that I should not ... I am never tired of the acquaintance of these sages and veterans; and should I meet their shades, I am confident I should know them.

... A people who erect statues to their great men, are more likely to know well, and intimately the history of their nation. And even strangers, sojourning among them, will better learn it.' The learning of history was always a passion with Mrs. Willard. She was gratified, too, that these statues were clad so as not 'to offend the eye of modesty' and hoped that this was evidence that decency and propriety were coming into their own. The immodesty of statues in France was a continual source of distress to her. In a letter to her pupils describing the garden of the Tuileries, she wrote: 'No — my dear girls, I shall not take you to examine those statues. If your mothers were here, I would leave you sitting on these shaded benches, and conduct them through the walks, and they would return, and bid you depart for our own America; where the eye of modesty is not publicly affronted; and where virgin delicacy can walk abroad without a blush.' The beauty of the garden, she told them, might at first lead them to believe that they had found Paradise itself, but the expression on the faces of the crowds would quickly dispel that delusion. 'Give me,' she added, 'for real, enduring happiness, the faces of the throng, who issue from the door of a New-England church, rather than those of the crowds I meet in the Tuileries. . . .'

At the Louvre, where because of her great fondness for paintings, she expected to be sublimely uplifted, her pure womanhood was again shocked. However, she was willing to find the wheat among the tares, to control her eyes and mind and ignore what to her seemed vulgar. The Titians and the Raphaels at first disappointed her. The paintings of Girodet and the 'wild sublimity' of Salvator Rosa aroused her admiration. The pictures of the Italian school fascinated her, and kept drawing her

back to them, until she knew she liked them best.
Rubens was a dreadful disappointment. 'His works
here,' she said, 'are full of faults, and the greatest of all
are moral ones.' She was never tired of gazing at the
landscapes, and no picture so haunted her as that of
Madelaine, 'clasping her hands, with upturned and
streaming eyes, and disheveled hair.' 'I am not ashamed
to say,' she wrote, 'I have not visited the statuary. . . .
I should rather be ashamed to say that I had.'

The paintings at Versailles also troubled her, especially those which with blasphemous effrontery attempted to portray God as a man. Of this she wrote, 'I
felt that my own spirit was debased and degraded by
the sight.' The many spouting fountains in the gardens
aroused her disapproval, because they were a 'disgusting and outrageous perversion' of nature. Versailles
brought forth still another pithy observation: 'The
world has but one Versailles, and it is to be hoped it will
never have another. Men now understand too well their
rights, and their strength, to allow one of their own
number, again to fancy himself the state; and to use its
united toil, and treasure, to uphold his personal vanity,
and gratify his luxurious pleasures.'

The trip to Versailles brought back to her forcibly
all that she had read and heard of the causes of the
French Revolution. She reflected upon the changes
which had taken place, how trade and commerce had
built up private fortunes so that bankers, merchants,
and manufacturers could live in grandeur as well as
kings, and how 'the increased facilities for intercourse
between mind and mind' had enlarged the influence of
the 'republic of letters.' In Paris, whenever she crossed
the Place Louis XV where the guillotine had stood, she
cringed at the thought of the tragic days of the Revolu-

tion. It was not Marie Antoinette who came to her
mind, but Charlotte Corday and Madame Roland,
whose dying exclamation, 'Oh, Liberty, how many excesses are committed in thy name!' rang in her ears.
The stormy history of France was much in her mind
these days, for Lafayette had spent an hour with her
telling her the details of the recent revolution in which
he had taken such a prominent part. Deeply moved as
she was by the political confidences of a great man, she
was even more impressed by the importance for a historian of being in the midst of events which promised to
be the turning point for the political destinies of France.

Lafayette had told her of the successive moves of
Charles X to reinstate the clergy and reimburse the
nobility for their losses; how he had issued a series of
ordinances which had utterly destroyed the last signs
of constitutional government, how the press had been
muzzled, the number of voters reduced, the newly
elected Chamber of Deputies dissolved, and the King
given the power of initiating all laws. Aroused by such
oppressive measures, the small republican party, which
still clung to the traditions of 1792, had started an insurrection, and Lafayette, hearing of this, had left La
Grange for Paris to assume whatever responsibilities
were waiting for him. He was then an old man of
seventy-three, but was still fired by the cause of liberty
and love for France. Mrs. Willard retold the story of his
arrival in Paris as she heard it from his own lips: 'When
he first appeared in the street, he was received with ac-
clamations. Directly there was a hush — "We endanger
his life!" was whispered from one to another, and in
profound silence, often greeted with tears, a way was
opened for him to move through the dense throng, which
crowded the streets.'

Placed at the head of the provisional government, Lafayette set to work to untangle the snarls. It was his aim to conduct this revolution without needless executions and shedding of blood. 'He would have preferred a republic,' recorded Mrs. Willard, 'but besides the odium, which former excesses committed in this name, had cast upon France, he knew that he should bring a host of foreign foes upon his country.' He knew that the French were still monarchical at heart and not yet ready for a republic. In searching for a possible successor to Charles X, his thoughts turned to Louis Philippe, Duke of Orléans, who was known as a liberal. Assured by him that he would support the principles of the Revolution, Lafayette agreed to make him king and promised, at his request, to remain at the head of the National Guard. After a satisfactory conference, Lafayette and Louis Philippe, in the truly dramatic manner of the French, stepped out on a balcony before the waiting crowds; Lafayette embraced Louis Philippe, and Louis Philippe waved the tricolored flag, which had not been displayed in Paris since the last days of Napoleon. In this way, the crowds were informed that Lafayette and Louis Philippe had come to an understanding and that Louis Philippe sympathized with the doctrines of the liberals. Now, Louis Philippe was king and still there were undercurrents of dissatisfaction and rebellion. Lafayette hoped for the best and so did Emma Willard as she thought over all that he had told her and meditated on the character of the French people.

The day finally came when Lafayette could take the time to go to the Opéra with Mrs. Willard. They went to the Opéra Français where they had a box next to the King's, and with them were two of Lafayette's granddaughters, Mrs. S—— of Baltimore, and an officer of his household. Lafayette had not attended the theater since the recent revolution. Determined not to be recognized by the audience, he came in citizen's clothes. Upon his insistence, Mrs. Willard occupied a seat in the front of the box. As she gazed out over the audience, she was dazzled by the beauty of the gowns and the splendor of the theater. She looked very lovely as she sat there, faultlessly gowned, her color heightened by the excitement of the evening. Now at forty-three, she was in the prime of her beauty. Experience and accomplishment had given her poise. Animated, intelligent, a rare conversationalist, she easily took her place with the Lafayette family and their friends. Lafayette was delighted with her. The vigorous, gray-haired hero, twenty years her senior, appreciated the Americanism which Emma Willard personified, that capable, intelligent, idealistic womanhood, which only America could produce.

In the midst of the first short opera, 'Le Dieu et la Bayadère,' Lafayette was summoned by the King, but he returned in time for the ballet pantomime of 'Manon Lescaut,' which pleased him very much because the scenery and costumes reminded him of his boyhood. Then, as Mrs. Willard told the story, 'I observed that the eyes of the people were ever and anon, turning toward our box; — and when at another interval, we rose from our seats, as everybody did, suddenly there was a short, "Vive La Fayette! Vive La Fayette!" It resounded again and again, and was echoed and re-echoed by the vaulted roof. In the enthusiasm of the moment, I exclaimed, "You are discovered — you must advance —" and I handed him over the seats, unconscious at the moment that I was making myself part of the spectacle. He advanced, bowed thrice, and

again retreated — but the cries continued. Then the
people called out "La Parisienne! La Parisienne!"'

In answer to this, the curtain rose, and an actor, who
too had been one of the heroes of the revolution, sang
'La Parisienne,' the popular song of the Revolution of
1830. As he sang, he waved the tricolored flag, and
when he sang the part which referred to Lafayette 'with
his white hairs, the hero of both worlds,' the audience
cheered. 'I looked at him [Lafayette],' said Mrs. Willard, 'and met his eye. There was precisely the same expression as I marked, when we sung to him in Troy; and
again I shared the sublime emotions of his soul, and
again they overpowered my own. My lips quivered, and
irrepressible tears started to my eyes. When the song
was over, the actor came and opened the door of the
box, and in his enthusiasm embraced him. "You sang
charmingly," said La Fayette. "Ah, General, you were
here to hear me!" was the reply.'

When, in leaving the theater, the party reached the
lower lobby, they found that the crowd had formed a
pathway for Lafayette. Mrs. Willard described their
triumphal exit:

There was that in this silent testimonial of their affection,
more touching, than the noisy acclaim of their shouts. There
was something too, remarkable in the well defined line which
bounded the way left open. A dense crowd beyond — not
even an intruding foot, within the space, which gratitude and
veneration had marked. I can scarcely describe my own feelings. I was with him, whom from my infancy I had venerated
as the best of men; whom for a long period of my life I had
never hoped even to see in this world. Now I read with him
his noble history, in the melting eyes of his ardent nation.
And I saw that he was regarded as he is, the father of France
— aye, and of America too. America! my own loved land! It
was for her sake I was thus honored, and it was for me to feel

her share in the common emotion. My spirit seemed to dilate, and for a moment, self-personified as the genius of my country, I enjoyed to the full his triumph, who is at once her father, and her adopted son.

The next evening Mrs. Willard and her son went to another of Lafayette's soirées. As they entered, Mr. Rives, the American Minister, joined them. 'The rooms were full,' wrote Mrs. Willard to her sister. 'We edged along, conversing together — expecting to find the General in the next room; when suddenly the countenance of the blessed patriot, full of benevolence, was beaming upon us. After answering his enquiries about my health, I told him I hoped he was none the worse, for the dissipation of the last evening. "Oh, no," said he, "I am all the better for having spent the evening with you!" This he said, not emphasizing *you*, but in just such a way that it might mean, "I am the better for having been amused last evening" — and I told him I was happy that he had been entertained. It may look like vanity for me to tell you of these things; but it is not my pride alone; it is my deeply filial affection, my reverential love, that is gratified thus to meet a return, where I had so little reason to expect it.'

CHAPTER XVII

A GLIMPSE OF COURT LIFE

MRS. WILLARD was soon to see Paris on the verge of an uprising. The trial of the ministers of Charles X was under way and all sorts of rumors filled the air. The populace demanded a death sentence and feeling ran high. The Royalists expected a repetition of the bloody scenes of the former revolution, but there were others who believed that Lafayette could hold the mob in check. The family of one of the ministers, Mrs. Willard discovered, was in hiding in her boarding-house. This and the knowledge that so much depended on her friend, Lafayette, made her feel very much a part of those critical days. When the sentence of life imprisonment was announced, the mob was infuriated. The soldiers threw down their arms in a rage, shouting, 'Vive la République! Vive La Fayette, notre Président!' But urged to return to their posts out of loyalty to Lafayette their Commander-in-Chief, they obeyed.

All that night and the next day the city was in an uproar. People thronged streets. The entire National Guard was called to arms. From her boarding-house window, Mrs. Willard anxiously watched the street, the men and women hurrying past, the soldiers marching by. In her journal, she wrote:

We apprehended something dreadful; we hardly knew what. Towards evening we saw pass near our window, a great number of young men marching in regular files; with here and there an officer in the uniform of the national guards. They shout, but for a moment we know not what. They wear a placard in their hats; of this also we know not the meaning.

They come nearer, and shout, 'Vive le Roi! Vive le Roi!' We
see that their motto is, 'Liberté et l'ordre, Public, Public.'
We breathe free, for we had feared that the multitude would
prevail against the government. Soon after we saw a numerous body of troops, their spears glittering by the light of the
lamps. They shouted, and again we were all anxiety. At
length we hear distinctly, 'Vive le Roi!' We waved our hand-
kerchiefs from the windows as they passed; and in the joy of
deliverance, hardly restrained ourselves from joining the
shout. Candles were carried to the windows of the houses
which they passed, to light the welcome band as they pa-
trolled the streets. This was also a demonstration of rejoicing;
and as such, the spirit was caught from house to house; and
thus without any directions from authority, or preconcerted
plan, Paris is illuminated.... All is becoming tranquil.
Every one we see praises the national guards, and declares
that La Fayette has saved France from another revolution.

Then events followed which filled Mrs. Willard with
indignation. Bit by bit the news reached her. The
King had deliberately snubbed Lafayette by omitting to
invite him to the review of the troops. The same day,
the King's party in the Chamber of Deputies introduced
a law abolishing Lafayette's office of Commander-in-
Chief of the National Guard. A great eulogy of Lafayette followed, and it was announced that the King
would confer upon him the honorary title of Commander-in-Chief. Thereupon Lafayette tendered the King
his resignation. All of this had happened because the
Royalists feared the popularity of Lafayette.

'I have done with French politics,' commented Mrs.
Willard with impatience, 'and I have learned a good deal
of French character; or rather of human nature. . . . The
ill-disguised satisfaction of the royalists, the hypocritical
pretences of those, who wish to stand well on all sides,
suit so ill with my feelings, that I now choose to keep

silent, or retire when these events are made the topic of general conversation.'

Soon after, Mrs. Willard called upon Madame George Lafayette, hoping to learn more about the unfortunate affair. She found her crushed by what had happened. 'Oh! my dear Madame,' she exclaimed as she greeted Mrs. Willard, 'what will the Americans say to this? America could remember the services of my father for fifty years. France can scarce remember them five months. Yet, it is not the people of France. They say republics are ungrateful, and monarchies are not — let this treatment of my father bear testimony.'

Lafayette's next soirée was attended by his many friends, Mrs. Willard included. They were eager to express their friendship and loyalty. 'He appeared calm and benevolent as usual,' chronicled Mrs. Willard, 'not the least touch of chagrin, or resentful feeling was visible in his appearance; but his countenance was to me, as though he was struggling to overcome an inward sorrow, and wished not to be disturbed in this work of self-government.'

Mrs. Willard had made many interesting acquaintances in Paris. She met William Cabell Rives, the American Minister, and his wife, James Fenimore Cooper and his family, and Amelia Opie frequently at the many soirées which she attended, and often exchanged calls with them. A conversation with Mrs. Opie was always a treat, for she received instruction as well as entertainment from it, and found in it 'a vein of pious and philanthropic sentiment.'

'Some of my best hours,' Mrs. Willard wrote, 'are spent with Mr. Cooper and his family. I find in him, what I do not in all who bear the name of Americans, a genuine American spirit. His conversation on various subjects, particularly his descriptions of scenery, are delightful. . . . Mr. Cooper is esteemed in France as a better writer than Sir Walter Scott, by the majority of those with whom I have conversed on the subject. In fact, they place him here quite at the head of the novel writers of the day.'

Mrs. Willard was invited by one of her friends to hear the 'Barbier de Seville,' but unfortunately was not pleased with the performance. 'Those singers,' she recorded, in her journal, 'seemed to me to consider it the perfection of singing, to shake, and trill, and quaver, and make an enormous squall, and take a breath longer than anyone else had ever taken before. It is certainly a physical exertion, at which I can be astonished as well as others; but it is not the soul of music; — it does not find its way to the heart.' She was also troubled by the effect the opera might have on the morals of the young, for old age was made contemptible, youth taught to condemn it, and the hero and heroine plotted and acted lies. 'I like to be amused,' she observed, 'but not at the expense of virtue. That, in fact, is not amusement to me, which I find serves the interests of vice.'

Paganini's music affected her differently. She wrote: 'We went one evening to the Grand Opera, to hear the astonishing Paganini. To me his music appeared so curious, so wonderful, so unearthly, that I was not certain whether I was pleased, or not. It had the effect to impress itself strongly on my imagination, and to give me a great desire to hear it again. I make this remark of his peculiar inventions. He gave some specimens of simple plaintive airs, in which the rich soul of music itself was expressed.'

As Mrs. Willard had been so lavishly entertained in Paris, she wished to reciprocate in some way, and ar-

ranged with the other members of her party to give a
soirée. The proprietress of her boarding-house prepared
everything. Seats covered with velvet cushions were
provided; chandeliers were hung, and 'elegant con-
fectionery' was ordered. About seventy people attended, among them General Lafayette and his family.
'To be presiding lady of a fête in Paris,' confided Mrs.
Willard to her sistér, 'gave me more the feeling, of
wondering at the wonders, and most of all "to see myself there" than anything else I have experienced.'

One Sunday afternoon, Mrs. Willard and her son presented a letter of introduction, which Professor Amos
Eaton had given them, to Alexandre Brongniart, a
celebrated French savant. Mrs. Willard was not accustomed to making Sunday afternoon calls, nor did she ap-
prove of them, but she had come to the conclusion that
she might as well make visits on that day as to sit in her
room endeavoring to be pious, while the sounds of music
and dancing drifted in from other rooms. This visit
was a very happy one, for both Monsieur and Madame Brongniart were interested in her educational
work. Monsieur Brongniart complimented her on her
'Republic of America' and told her that she had orig-
inated a new method of developing historical subjects.
He was astonished that her pupils were studying chemistry and making chemical experiments.

Always eager to improve her mind, Mrs. Willard went
to the College of France to hear Baron Cuvier deliver a
lecture which was introductory to a course on natural
history. It was just the subject she wished to hear,
and as his enunciation was perfect she understood his
French very well. She was much impressed by his appearance, called his large and strongly marked head
sublime, and compared him to Lafayette. 'They both

have noble countenances,' she reflected, 'but mental strength is Cuvier's leading characteristic — benevolence that of Lafayette.'

One of Mrs. Willard's plans in coming to Paris was to learn to speak French fluently. She found this more difficult than she had supposed, because most of the people whom she met spoke English, and because she did not wish to converse lamely in French at times when she ought to make a good impression. However, she did make noble attempts to speak French whenever possible and took French lessons daily. Talking with the shop-keepers gave her excellent practice, and she spent a great deal of time in the shops, collecting books, prints, and paintings for her school. She hired French women to sew for her and encouraged them to talk about their lives and customs, for she was eager to observe French character from all angles. She decided that French-women were improving in manners and chastity, and hoped that American women would maintain their characters. Frenchwomen, she felt, could teach Americans a great deal about dress, for they had a real *flair* for dress, and took such good care of their clothes. They never wore their nicest things in the morning or on the street. She was delighted with their morning costume, a plain dress of calico, or some cheap material, made close, with a kerchief of plain Jaconet muslin or tulle, beautifully plaited, and a cap of tulle. She profited by everything she saw, and although she did not relinquish her fixed principles in morals or taste, she bought a very up-to-date French wardrobe, not only to wear in Paris, but to take back to America with her. It gave her a great deal of pleasure one morning in church to discover that the Queen wore a cloak very much like one that she had just purchased, a blue-black gros des Indes with a broad velvet cape. At first, she was rather displeased to see gray-haired women at evening parties with their hair beautifully curled and put up without a cap, but as she thought it over, she saw no reason why ladies should conceal their gray hairs more than gentlemen. One French custom which she refused to adopt was to have her ears pierced for earrings, and this caused a great deal of comment. Many of the ladies considered her lack of earrings a deformity and even the men remarked upon it, but Mrs. Willard always had a ready answer for them. She told them she always fancied she had an uncommonly well-shaped ear and could not bear to spoil it. When a gentleman asked her whether it was unfashionable in America to wear earrings, she replied, 'Oh, no. Men as well as women wear them there; not only at the bottom of the ear, but throughout the whole rim, and in their noses besides.' Another gentleman said to her, 'Madam, if you were my wife, I should order you to change that turban for a cap, since you refuse to wear earrings.' 'When I am your wife,' she retorted, 'you will find me very obedient.'

The dangerous influence of French society upon young American girls was a subject which Mrs. Willard discussed thoroughly in a letter to one of her friends. In general, she found nothing but the most perfect decency on the face of society except the very low-necked gowns and such dances as the waltz and gallopade. The danger, she believed, lay in mingling with people of charming manners and great fascination whose lives transgressed God's commandments. She feared, too, that young girls would often hear shocking principles uttered by people whom they would otherwise have every reason to respect. For example, Madame Tallien, who was well received in Paris and was one of the most beautiful

women that Mrs. Willard met at Court, was, as Mrs.
Willard expressed it, that 'infamous woman, who was
drawn shamefully through the streets of Paris, during
the old revolution, to personate the goddess of reason.'
On the other hand, there were many virtuous women in
Paris, women of high ideals, like Lafayette's daughters
and granddaughters, and the Queen, who was considered by all a pattern of conjugal virtue. French character, she concluded, was much like the city of Paris,
'a series of contrasts where you are forever finding side
by side, the grand and the mean.'

The attitude of many of the French toward the common people was a continual surprise to her. They regarded them with contempt, as wretches who deserved
to plod along in any occupation they could find. When
in a conversation with a Royalist she championed the
people with her natural enthusiasm for democracy, he
retorted with sarcasm, 'The people are not the nation!'
'I dropped the conversation,' she wrote in her journal,
'thinking that one might as well discuss a mathematical
question with a person who denied that the whole was
greater than its parts.'

Mrs. Willard had an unusual opportunity for observing life in Paris, for in addition to her own indefatigable
tours of investigation and her very pleasant social life
with the friends that she had made, she had the honor of
being presented at Court. This was at the request of
General Lafayette. In preparation for the event she
consulted with Mrs. Rives, the American Minister's
wife, who told her that the more elegantly she was
clothed, the more honored the Queen would be. There
were some points which were not to be overlooked; her
shoes must be of white satin, jewels must be worn, and
her dress must be new.

One of Lafayette's friends, Madame Z——, accompanied Mrs. Willard to the presentation. Arriving at the entrance of the palace a little before half past eight, they gave their tippets to Madame Z——'s servant, and then passing between ranks of the King's liveried servants and the military guard, mounted a magnificent marble staircase at the top of which gentlemen at writing tables took their names and addresses and directed them to the main salon. The brilliant lights, the rich hues of the velvets, the bright sheen of satins, the turbans and toques of glittering materials, the beautiful plumes, the bandeaux of jewels and flowers, all made the scene a gorgeous one. Mrs. Willard and Madame Z—— were joined by Mrs. Rives, and the other American ladies who were to be presented.

Soon there was a movement in the upper end of the room [wrote Mrs. Willard], and the Queen! the Queen! passed from lip to lip. She came forth elegantly, but not gorgeously attired; in blue, with a berri of white, with four white plumes. Instead of taking her stand, as I expected, at the head of the room, and there receiving severally, the ladies presented, she suffered us to keep our places and came to us. When she had arrived at our party, Mrs. Rives named to her the ladies one by one. She addressed some conversation to each. Her manner was perfectly courteous and ladylike. If she erred, I thought it was rather seeming too much to court, than to command respect; but all on this occasion were pleased, and said after she passed, how affable! how gracious is the Queen!
When I was presented, she asked me how long since I left my country, and remarked that I might if I chose, address her in English. I said I was charmed to find that I might speak in my native tongue, and be understood by her majesty. She said she did not speak it well, though she understood it. The King spoke it well; he was much attached to the Americans. I made her a complimentary reply; — she smiled, courtesied, and passed to the next. We had not space for any great flour-

ish in our courtesies, but made them as respectfully as we might.

The Queen's two daughters, the King's sister, Mademoiselle d'Orléans, and the Duc d'Orléans next addressed a few words to the ladies who were being presented. Soon after the Queen retired from the room, Mrs. Willard and Madame Z—— took their leave. 'We promenaded the long halls of the Palais Royal with somewhat of a lighter step, republicans as we were, than that with which we had entered,' wrote Mrs. Willard. '... At ten o'clock I was at home, having been absent two hours.'

Not many days after Mrs. Willard had been presented at Court, she received an invitation to a ball at the Palace. She hired an Italian servant to accompany her, one whom she called 'the very Talleyrand of domestics.' Almost as soon as she entered the Palace, Mr. C—— (probably James Fenimore Cooper) greeted her and escorted her to the dancing salon, where Mrs. C—— was waiting for them. The ball was a very splendid one, and Mrs. Willard enjoyed to the full the beautiful gowns and elaborate headdress of the ladies. She never wearied of admiring the 'elegant and delicate artificial flowers of Paris,' and thought them very beautiful worn in the hair, especially the crowns of roses which had a fine effect in the dance. She was very much interested in the dancing, and found the dances very similar to those in her own country, only performed with more grace. 'How differently at different periods of our lives do similar events affect us,' she wrote, as she thought over the Royal Ball. 'At fifteen I was all in a flutter at the thought of entering a village ball-room, with plenty of company; how could I then have believed that a time would come, when I should enter the court of France

alone, pass through long rooms, guarded by files of
soldiers, officers, and other royal attendants — and all
this without any particular emotion whatever. My
general feelings were, that I should see a show which it
would perhaps, be a satisfaction to myself and my
friends hereafter that I had seen, and I hoped it would
be worth the trouble I had taken to see it.'

There were times when Mrs. Willard grew tired of the
social whirl. She still grieved for her husband and was
very anxious over the health of her adopted niece Mary.
There were days when she fought sadness and roused
herself with great effort to attend soirées and mingle in
the gay life of Paris. 'It is far easier,' she observed, 'to
quit the gay world than it is to live in it, and yet above
it. Yes; amidst all the gaiety which I describe, I often
bear an aching heart, though I endeavor as much as
possible to conceal it. — That is not the kind of life to
make me happy; rather give me back my toils and
cares, with the consciousness of living to a good and
useful purpose; give me back too a society, whose conversation shall lead my mind to better things, than the
toys of this world.'

When Mrs. Willard had been in Paris a little over
four months, a letter came bearing the news of the death
of her mother and of her adored niece Mary. She was
crushed with grief, but attempted to comfort herself
with continual assertions that it was God's will. Her
friends were very kind. Lafayette's daughter, Madame
Latour de Maubourg, sat by her, took her hand, and
wept long and silently. Lafayette called, spoke a few
words of condolence, and spent the evening with her and
her son. She was comforted to hear that he was planning to visit America again.

It was about this time, that Madame Belloc came into

Mrs. Willard's life. Aside from Lafayette, the person whom she had most wished to see in Paris was Madame Belloc. She had read her articles in the 'Revue Encyclopédique' and their 'elevated moral tone and elegant diction' had so attracted her that she determined to seek her acquaintance when she reached France. At one of Lafayette's soirées, she obtained her address from Monsieur Julien, the editor of the 'Revue Encyclopédique,' and later called upon her. Madame Belloc had heard of Mrs. Willard as a writer and was eager to read her 'Republic of America,' but as Mrs. Willard did not have a copy of this book with her, she presented Madame Belloc with her 'Plan for Improving Female Education' and her book of poems. The two soon became warm friends, drawn together by their enthusiasm for the advancement of women. They spent many happy hours together and with Madame Belloc's very close friend, Mademoiselle Mongolfier, discussing the education of women. Mrs. Willard was soon calling them Louise and Adelaide. This friendship meant everything to her, coming at a time when she was struggling with grief over the death of her mother and niece. It also meant a great deal to these two aristocratic, intelligent Frenchwomen to hear of the progress made by women in America. Besides, they were charmed with Mrs. Willard's personality. Madame Belloc said of her, 'Ah, oui, elle était bien belle.' As Madame Belloc was a friend of Maria Edgeworth as well as the translator of her books, she was glad to give Mrs. Willard a letter of introduction to her. Preserved in a notebook, yellow with age, is a copy of what would seem to be this letter. It reads: 'Madame Belloc to Miss Edgeworth. She seems to me to be one of the most sane and complete minds one ever meets; a person of resolution, wit, heart,

imagination — a union of beautiful and rare qualities.'
Underneath this and signed with the initials 'E. W.'
is the epigrammatic comment, 'Beautiful characters
serve to show us what one must be.'

Through the influence of Madame Belloc, General
Lafayette, and Mr. Cooper, Mrs. Willard was able to
visit many of the best schools of France. While they
were all of interest to her, she found nothing which
compared in any way with her Seminary in Troy. Her
analytical mind was ready with many criticisms. A well-
educated girl in France was able to speak several languages, play several instruments, draw, and perhaps had
some knowledge of mythology and history. What a
contrast to the keen-minded pupil of the Troy Female
Seminary taking her oral examination in geometry, natural philosophy, or chemistry! French schools, she felt,
kept their pupils in a state of perpetual infancy, and instead of learning much from them, as she had expected,
she found that she had many suggestions for them if
they would but receive them. She was convinced that
French character would continue to be unstable until
French women received a more solid and more suitable
education.

At an institution which she visited Mrs. Willard was
attracted to a bright, pretty, eleven-year-old orphan
with a remarkably sweet voice, and at once thought of
taking her to America and educating her at the Seminary. The necessary arrangements were made and Pauline Gertrude de Fonteview became a protégée of Mrs.
Willard. She also engaged a French teacher for the
Seminary, a very pleasing young lady of good family,
who, with little Pauline, was to meet her later in Havre
when she was ready to sail for America.

Pauline spent eight years at the Seminary, where she

became an accomplished musician. After teaching for two years at Washington, Pennsylvania, she married a young lawyer, William McKenna. When Mrs. Willard in her travels suffered a broken arm from the overturning of a stagecoach in the mountains of Pennsylvania, Pauline had the opportunity to repay her kindness in some measure by caring for her in her home in Washington until she was able to continue her journey.

About the middle of April, Mrs. Willard and John definitely decided to leave Paris and spend the remainder of their time in England and Scotland. They had planned to visit Italy, Switzerland, and Belgium as well, but friends had persuaded them that the times were too dangerous and unsettled. As Mrs. Willard wished to spend some time in England and be at home by the first of August to attend the examinations at the Seminary, she unfortunately could not accept the invitation given her by General Lafayette and his family to visit them at La Grange. It was hard to leave the dear friends she had made in Paris, but she was setting out on more adventures and there was much in England that she longed to see. They traveled by diligence from Paris to Calais, and there embarked on the steamboat Lord Melville. 'The morning was fine,' recorded Mrs. Willard, 'and the coast looked beautiful, as receding from it, I said, with a softened heart, though not with all the pathos with which Mary, Queen of Scots, once uttered the words, "Farewell France!"'

CHAPTER XVIII

IMPRESSIONS OF ENGLAND AND SCOTLAND

'IN going from French to English ground, I had a feeling
of getting home, among my own people, far beyond
what I had expected,' wrote Mrs. Willard in her journal.
'The English language, after having so long listened to
the French, was grateful to my ear.' She felt this even
on the steamboat, crossing the Channel, and when she
first glimpsed the white cliffs of England in the distance,
she was moved to poetry. Taking out her notebook, she
jotted down these lines:

> Hail, Britain! hail, thou island queen,
> That sits enthroned on yonder chalky cliffs,
> And stretchest far thy sceptre o'er the main!
> Land of my fathers, hail! The vital stream
> Within my veins, true to its ancient source,
> Warms through my heart, as I approach thy shores.

In London, Mrs. Willard took lodgings in a boarding-
house where there were twenty or more regular boarders,
and was pleased with the arrangement as it enabled
her to get acquainted with English people and English
customs. Arriving in England during a renewed agitation for the Reform Bill, she found this subject the main
topic in newspapers and in conversation. When King
William IV expressed his approval of the bill by dissolving Parliament, a big public demonstration followed.
London was illuminated and crowds thronged the
streets. Mrs. Willard and her party drove about the
city in a carriage, admiring the brilliant lights, amused
and yet frightened by the surging crowds, especially
when they saw the mob hurling pennies through the
unlighted windows of an anti-reformer's house.

Because the lower classes were impudent and the
streets were not patroled by military guards as in Paris,
Mrs. Willard felt it unwise to walk about alone. However, in her thoroughgoing way, she saw all there was
to see in London, and was even better pleased with the
city than she had expected to be. Regent's Park, Hyde
Park, Kensington Gardens, and the many fine squares
laid out in the English style of gardening, with trees
and shrubs growing in the rich green turf, and gravel
walks bordered with flowers, delighted her, as she had
not expected so much natural beauty in the city. She
gazed with admiration at the women riding horseback
in their close-fitting, graceful costumes. 'I know of no
more beautiful ornament to a sylvan scene,' she observed, 'than such a fair rider, with an elegant cavalier,
well-mounted by her side.'

Saint Paul's Cathedral, she found sublime; and West-
minster Abbey, although less magnificent than some of
the Gothic cathedrals on the Continent, she felt was
more interesting to an American than any other spot on
earth. 'When I found myself in the poet's corner, surrounded by the almost "animated busts," and breath-
ing statues of men, from whose spirits my own had
drawn many of its best energies, I felt delighted,' she
wrote, 'and I made it a point to pay my respects to the
company, by addressing to each of them some of their
own verses; and I was guided in my selection by the
face which each one seemed to wear, whether grave or
gay. For a handsome face among the men, I thought
Prior stood first; but there appeared to sit upon his
fine lip, a little conscious pride of his own personal attractions. Milton looked as though he might have been
composing the last part of his invocation to light.' In
another visit to the Abbey, she thoughtfully surveyed

the tombs of the kings, queens, lords, and ladies. 'There they lay,' she wrote, 'in marble semblance, stark and stiff . . . in all fantastic vanities of costume, which were fashionable in their different periods. No tombs interested me more than those of Elizabeth, and Mary, Queen of Scots. . . . Mary's monument is more elegant than Elizabeth's. Her sculptured face (which had just been washed by a man who was cleaning the tombs) is thinner, and not so beautiful as I had expected, but the countenance of Elizabeth is hideous; — not a line of a woman's face about it, but wholly the visage of a man.' What interested her most at the Tower was the armor, especially that belonging to Joan of Arc. 'It does seem to me,' she reflected, 'that our race must have degenerated in size and physical strength, since those days. I do not believe a modern lady could budge an inch with a weight equal to that of the armor of Joan of Arc.'

In London as well as in Paris, Mrs. Willard met many celebrities. Soon after her arrival, she sent Maria Edgeworth, who was then in London with her sister, the letter of introduction which Madame Belloc had given her, for there was no one in London whom she was more eager to see. Miss Edgeworth immediately invited her to spend the evening. In a letter to her sister Almira, she described minutely this first meeting:

The drawing room, as in all the houses I had visited, was on the second floor. There was little difference in their style of furniture and that of genteel families in America. Everything appeared tasteful and convenient, but nothing gaudy. At length Miss Edgeworth and her sister entered the room. Miss Edgeworth is small, but symmetrically formed, with not one single blue-stocking oddity about her. Her dress was ladylike — a delicate-colored satin, with a turban — reminding me of that in the pictures of Madame de Staël. In her manners, there is nothing that marks the slightest consciousness of her superior powers. Attentive to please, she seems liberal of her fine conversation, and observant of little attentions to her guests. She appears more proud of her sister than herself; and remarked that she had educated her, and that while she had been writing those books which I had read, she was climbing her chair or pulling her papers. . . . There was a degree of intensity in my feelings toward Miss Edgeworth, of which I myself was hardly aware, until I saw her. I had long communed with her through her writings, and often wished to see and converse with her. . . .

It was through Miss Edgeworth's influence that Mrs. Willard was able to visit some of the schools of England, but she received no more satisfaction from these schools than from those in France. Again, she was astounded at the superiority of female education in America.

An American friend in London took her to Hempstead to see Mr. Coleridge. 'He has all the poet in his large dark eye, and intellectual face,' she commented, 'and his manners seemed to me, such as suited his portly and dignified person. I was told that if he became fairly engaged in conversation, he would need but little response. He found in me a delighted auditor, and he was on subjects that interested him. . . . Yet though I was delighted at the time, I cannot now recall many of his expressions, or even his ideas. Who that should hear twenty pages of Coleridge's metaphysics, could tell afterwards what it was; and yet who, but would feel that it was passing strange, and very grand. You look intensely for his ideas, as you look through the dark rolling cloud for the outline of the distant mountain.'

Washington Irving who was in London in the spring of 1831 called on Mrs. Willard soon after he had received a letter of introduction. Referring to him as 'another of nature's nobles,' she described their meeting to her sister:

As I had known and appreciated different members of his excellent family, our conversation took a turn which brought out his warm attachment to his friends and country. . . . He spoke too of his return to America. I had told him that I presumed he was not ignorant, that we Americans were a little jealous of his long stay in Europe — regarding his literary fame as a national property, which we were unwilling should be alienated. He said nothing was farther from his intention than to remain abroad.

In another part of Mr. Irving's conversation, I thought I could perceive the foundation of the prejudice that he was not American in his feelings. . . . He took occasion to remark concerning some of the faults that his countrymen were apt to fall into, in visiting England. They were too much in the way of considering themselves in a state militant, and were sometimes too prompt for battle, if any question, however innocent or trivial, was made touching the superior excellence of anything, and everything American. This was, in some companies, and on some occasions extremely ill-judged. Mr. Irving had probably said the same to other Americans . . . because he did care for us, and wished we should make ourselves, and our nation respectable and respected, and because he knew himself to be better acquainted with the views and feelings of the English, than his countrymen, newly arrived, could possibly be. It was not saying that the cause of the Americans was bad, but that it might be injudiciously maintained. . . . It is Mr. Irving who has done, and is doing more to make his country honored in the eyes of the British nation, than any other American of the present day.

Mrs. Opie had given Mrs. Willard a letter of introduction to Mrs. Elizabeth Fry, whose reform work in the English prisons was being discussed by all progressive women. 'I went to Newgate with it on Friday, this being the day when she ordinarily reads in the Bible, and lectures to the prisoners,' wrote Mrs. Willard to her sister Almira. 'This day, however, her lecture was omitted. I then proceeded to her residence, enquired for her, and was shown to the parlor by a female servant.

After the usual salutations, I gave her Mrs. Opie's letter.
... I felt a great interest in her favorite object, the reformation of prison discipline; — and she in mine — that
of female education; and we talked an hour in the full
flow and mingling of soul. She modestly said the public
had given her more credit than was her due — she but
acted with, and was the organ of a society of ladies. She
was going that afternoon to visit a prison-ship in which
women were confined.'

Mrs. Willard called on Mrs. Fry again some weeks
later, but as Mrs. Fry was not at home, she was cordially received by her son. 'I had heard (and indignantly
combated the accusation) that Mrs. Fry's own children
had charged her with being a negligent mother,' wrote
Mrs. Willard to her sister, 'and for the purpose of drawing out her son on this subject I remarked, that when
women were in any way distinguished before the public,
there were always those who were ready to attribute to
them some failure in domestic virtues. He said that
as to his mother, so far was this from being the case,
that she was distinguished for uncommon attention and
kindness to her household, and private friends.'

Mrs. Willard also had a letter of introduction to a
lady whom she designated in her letters as Mrs. R——,
and it was Mrs. R—— who introduced her to Robert
Owen. She was shocked by her first conversation with
Mrs. R——, who was a hater of men, called them a race
of brutal, selfish, unfeeling tyrants, talked against marriage, and doubted the wisdom and benevolence of God.
'Yet, from my soul, I pitied her,' wrote Mrs. Willard.
'What can be more horrible than for a woman of an
intelligent and sensitive mind, loving justice herself, and
desiring good, really to believe that there is no benevolence in the government of the universe; — and that

men who have the power to govern us, and whom our
nature obliges us to love, are our tyrants and enemies?'
Yet, as she thought over all that Mrs. R—— had said,
she realized that there was a great deal of truth in her
indignation at the treatment which women received in
England. She felt she would be a traitor to her cause if
she did not acknowledge it. From all that she had seen,
she knew that the attitude of the men of England toward women was such as to drive them to deceit or
desperation.

In spite of her dislike for Mrs. R——'s views, she
accepted an invitation to spend an evening with her,
possibly because she thought she might be able to work
some little reform. It was then that she met Robert
Owen and several of his friends. 'Never did I meet a
man with a smoother face, or a smoother tongue,' she
wrote afterwards, describing that very trying evening.
She decided at once to avoid all controversial discussion,
but that proved impossible, as Robert Owen insisted
upon talking about his theories, and Mrs. Willard could
not let his remarks pass uncorrected. Robert Owen's
assertions that man was a creature of circumstance and
that all children should be educated by the community
at large brought forth vigorous objections from Mrs.
Willard, which she ended with this decisive statement,
'But it is useless for you to wish me to agree to your
views. There is an insurmountable barrier — I am a
Christian.' Then one of the party argued that Christianity could be disproved in two minutes, and Mr.
Owen suggested that, although Mrs. Willard was a
Christian now, she might later change her belief. But
Mrs. Willard stood firm for Christianity. 'No, sir,' she
retorted, 'I never shall change — I never will change —
a Christian I will live, and a Christian I will die.'

When Robert Owen remarked that of course she considered it right to keep an open mind, she replied with firmness: 'There is, sir, a time to be investigating, and a time to be decided. When a mathematician has brought the best and maturest energies of his mind to bear upon a subject — when he has carefully attended to what others could say on both sides of the question — when he has thus perfectly satisfied his own mind where the truth lies; and when he finds that everything agrees to his solution of the problem — his operations on the supposition having never failed, his expectations never been deceived — is he to go back, and labor through the whole process of his investigation, because he may find others who think differently from himself? No, sir, I will not reinvestigate the evidences of Christianity — I shall never change my belief.'

This silenced the discussion for a time, and Mrs. Willard had the opportunity of observing that Mr. Owen was well-informed and very intelligent about the details of education. He urged her to visit his school in Lanark when she went to Scotland.

The disparaging attitude of Englishmen toward America and Americans was a constant source of distress to her, for she was so completely convinced that her beloved country offered the world so much more than other nations. She was continually galled by the condescending way in which Englishmen talked down to women. 'Englishmen,' she said, 'are afraid women will know too much, and consider that the perfection of our nature is to amuse them, or to do menial services for their convenience; — but for us to claim to be something in, and of ourselves — to think we have higher moral obligations than those we owe to their sex — to assert our equal right to intellectual cultivation; —

this is all very shocking to an Englishman. There is a
certain something in his manner when he addresses you,
which makes you feel that you are a lady accosted by a
gentleman — a woman, spoken to by a man — one of
nature's lords.' For these reasons, she knew she would
never be content to live in England. 'My lot,' she said,
'is cast with my sex and country.'

From London, Mrs. Willard and her son traveled by
stagecoach and post-chaise through Windsor, Oxford,
Stratford, and Birmingham to Manchester. Between
Manchester and Liverpool they had a thrilling experience, their first ride on that new invention, the railway.
'At the appointed hour,' recorded Mrs. Willard, 'the
cars set off, and the motion soon became fearfully rapid.
The fields, the houses, and the trees seemed to fly to the
east, as we sped on our westward course, scarcely giving
us time to view them as they hurried on. The novelty
of the scene would have delighted us, but for the feeling
of danger which came strongly over us, as thus we were
shot, by the power of steam, along these high embank-
ments. Suddenly there was a terrific whiz, like that of a
rocket when first let off; but louder. The first impression
was, that something about the engine had gone wrong.
We looked for an instant in each other's pale faces, and
then at the strange appearance of an object, passing by
our side, which seemed to present long horizontal lines
of colors, while the whizzing noise grew yet louder. This
was the train of cars from Liverpool passing with the
apparent velocity of the two, which was about fifty
miles an hour.'

In Liverpool, Mrs. Willard was very happy to find
a girls' school which more nearly met her standards.
American textbooks were used, among them her own.
The ladies in charge urged her to write an article about

her Seminary in Troy for an educational periodical published in London, and it was gratifying to her to find another acknowledgment of her international reputation.

A boat trip from Liverpool brought Mrs. Willard to Scotland, where she was able to satisfy her love of nature to the full. Memories of Scottish history were revived and scenes from 'The Lay of the Last Minstrel' and 'The Lady of the Lake' passed through her mind. She was continually quoting lines from her beloved Scott.

She was pleased with what she saw of Robert Owen's experiment at Lanark — the factories, the comfort and neatness of the workers' houses, the school which the factory children attended where they studied botany, music, and dancing, as well as the rudimental branches. 'There certainly appears to be much to admire in the regulations here, which combine profitable industry, with physical and mental improvement,' she recorded.

Edinburgh fascinated her with its 'wild and wonderful scenery,' and the intelligence, wit, and warm affection of its people. She had never been so moved anywhere except at the tomb of Washington, for here were the graves of many of the fathers of her mind, as she expressed it. Although public schools for women had been sadly neglected here and throughout Scotland as well as in England and France, she found the general attitude toward women more satisfying. 'In Scotland,' she said, 'when men converse with you, you are permitted to feel that you are a human being, in communion with those of your own kind.'

Leaving Scotland was doubly hard because it meant saying good-bye to Mr. and Miss D——, who had been their traveling companions for so long; but the time had come for Mrs. Willard and John to prepare for their homeward voyage. After returning to London for a few days, they set out for Havre, accompanied by a young Englishwoman whom Mrs. Willard had engaged as music teacher. Here they met the French teacher and Pauline, the little orphan girl, who was to become Mrs. Willard's ward, and together they sailed for America about the middle of June on the packet Sully. It was a long voyage of forty-seven days, but a very pleasant one. Sailing along day after day in mid-ocean, looking out over the vast expanse of water, Mrs. Willard felt her own utter helplessness, and turned constantly to God for protection. With such thoughts in her mind, she wrote the poem which she called 'Ocean Hymn,' but which is better known as 'Rocked in the Cradle of the Deep,' the one poem which has lived and brought her fame. A fellow passenger, Count de Choiseul, set it to music, and during the rest of the voyage, it was sung as the evening hymn. The melody to which it is now sung was arranged by an Englishman, Joseph P. Knight. Every evening as she joined in the singing of the words that had come to her so spontaneously, she felt assured of their truth and they brought her renewed comfort:

> Rocked in the cradle of the deep,
> I lay me down in peace to sleep;
> Secure I rest upon the wave,
> For thou, O Lord, hast power to save;
> I know Thou wilt not slight my call,
> For Thou dost mark the sparrow's fall;
> And calm and peaceful is my sleep,
> Rocked in the cradle of the deep.
>
> And such the trust that still were mine,
> Though stormy winds swept o'er the brine:
> And, though the tempest's fiery breath
> Roused me from sleep to wreck and death,

In ocean-cave, still safe with Thee,
The germ of immortality;
And calm and peaceful is my sleep,
Rocked in the cradle of the deep.

Early in August, Mrs. Willard was back in Troy,
attending the examinations of her Seminary. She was
welcomed like a queen.

CHAPTER XIX

DAYS OF PROSPERITY AND THE SEMINARY IN GREECE

THE warm words of welcome and admiring glances of teachers and pupils, the unpacking and displaying of treasures from the Old World, the ceremony and bustle of the August examinations, accounts of all that had passed at the Troy Female Seminary during those long months when she was in Europe, all these things filled the first days of Mrs. Willard's homecoming with excitement and gratification.

'I well remember her arrival, and the joy with which she was greeted by the teachers and pupils who had known her before,' recalled Elizabeth Cady Stanton, who was then a pupil at the Seminary. 'She was a splendid-looking woman, then in her prime, and fully realized my idea of a queen. I doubt whether any royal personage in the Old World could have received her worshipers with more grace and dignity than did this far-famed daughter of the Republic.'

Mrs. Willard was highly pleased with the progress of the Seminary during her absence. Her sister, Mrs. Lincoln, had filled the office of principal as well as she herself could have done, and had been ably assisted by her cousin, Miss Nancy Hinsdale, who had previously conducted a female seminary in Pittsfield in the days when Almira Hart was a school girl, and had come to Troy to help govern the Seminary while Mrs. Willard was in Europe. It was not long, however, before Mrs. Willard found that she was to lose the services of her sister. That same year Almira Lincoln married Judge John Phelps, of Guilford, Vermont. Their marriage proved to be very happy, for she was most acceptable to his large

family of sons and daughters, and he was proud of her
love of study and literary ambition. Through her influence, his five daughters attended the Seminary during the next few years, and she devoted herself to writing, publishing in close succession, 'Geology for Beginners,' 'Botany for Beginners,' and 'Lectures to Young
Ladies.' This last book was a collection of her Saturday-
morning talks given to the pupils of the Troy Female
Seminary. By 1835, she had become so well known as
a writer that J. & J. Harper published her 'Caroline
Westerley' as Volume XVI of their 'Boys' and Girls'
Library of Useful and Entertaining Knowledge,' a series of books which, in the language of the prospectus,
had enlisted many able pens in the service of the young.
'Caroline Westerley, or The Young Traveller from
Ohio, containing the Letters of a Young Lady of Seventeen, Written to Her Sister,' was a very proper book for
young ladies, instructing them in geography, religion,
and manners, through the medium of letters, and undoubtedly was entertaining to young ladies of 1833.
Caroline Westerley, contemplating a trip to Connecticut, was awed at the thought of visiting the haunts of
the famous daughters of the State, Mrs. Sigourney,
Miss Beecher, Mrs. Willard, and Mrs. Phelps. She
wrote:

> I shall visit the hills and groves, and moss-covered rocks,
> where long before she was of my age, Mrs. Willard meditated
> those plans of improving the mental condition of her sex,
> which she has since so successfully carried into operation. I
> shall pluck the wild flowers from the same turf where her
> sister, whose work on botany we have loved to read, sat in her
> girlish days, and mused upon glimpses of future usefulness
> and mental illumination. . . .

Meanwhile, Mrs. Willard returned to her work with

renewed vigor. Her Seminary had attained an unrivaled reputation, and was looked upon as the fashionable school of the country. More than one hundred boarders and two hundred day scholars were enrolled, while the number of teachers was correspondingly increased. As its income now greatly exceeded expenditures, financial problems no longer menaced its existence. The revised editions of 'Republic of America,' which Mrs. Willard called 'History of the United States,' had a tremendous sale, making her a rich woman. As a contemporary expressed it, she lived in unusual style for a teacher, with beautiful pictures and treasures from the Old World in her parlors, with horses and carriages at her disposal, with many servants to look after her wants, with adoring teachers at her beck and call. Troy, then, was in its heyday, a little New York, bustling, making money, awed and impressed by wealth and position. Mrs. Willard met its standards. Troy was proud of her and of the Troy Female Seminary.

Since her return from Europe, Mrs. Willard had followed French styles in dress. 'She was always robed — one must use the word "robed," so majestic was her bearing — in rich black silk or satin, and her head was crowned with a large white mull turban,' said Elizabeth Cady Stanton. She thought her a beautiful woman. 'She had a finely developed figure, well-shaped head, classic features, most genial manners and a profound self-respect (a rare quality in woman) that gave her a dignity truly regal in every position.'

Admiration, fame, prosperity, all these were very dear to Mrs. Willard, and yet they were as nothing compared with her love for and devotion to the cause of woman's education. If she had her triumphs, such as repeated requests from Europe for accounts of her work and lists of the textbooks used at the Seminary, she had her disappointments and slights, as when George Barrell Cheever published 'The American Common-Place Book of Poetry with Occasional Notes' and omitted any mention of her work. Mrs. Phelps expressed her feelings regarding this in a letter to Madame Belloc, '. . . this is not a solitary instance in which some of the other sex have shown a disposition to set aside the claims of Mrs. Willard to literary distinction from what appears to be a jealousy for her bold and decided stand in favor of her own sex.'

Superintending such a large institution as the Troy Female Seminary was no easy matter, and there were days when Mrs. Willard was weighed down by the strain of the work and felt 'dragged from one thing to another from morning till night.' But it had its compensations. The letters which kept pouring in from all parts of the United States asking for teachers made her realize what a real service she was rendering her country, for the training of teachers was still her pet project, and many were sent out from the Seminary every year. The reports which came from Catherine Beecher in Cincinnati showed how acute the need was. A million and a half children were growing up in ignorance. Men opening up the wilderness were too busy to think about schools. Thirty thousand teachers were needed at once, and ten thousand more each year to take care of the increasing population. This was woman's first great opportunity and woman was able to meet it, because Emma Willard, Catherine Beecher, Mary Lyon, and other far-seeing pioneers had prepared the way. Mrs. Willard, through her teachers, was now playing an important part in that great westward movement of the empire.

It was in the summer of 1833, that Mary Lyon, traveling to Philadelphia and Detroit, stopped in Troy to call on Mrs. Willard. Unfortunately no record of their conversation has been found. This was before Mary Lyon had made any definite plans for establishing her endowed seminary at Mount Holyoke.

Like Mary Lyon, Mrs. Willard saw the need of establishing permanent educational institutions for women and the need of giving women of moderate means the educational opportunities which now only daughters of the rich enjoyed. With this in view, she sent an appeal to influential citizens of Vermont, hoping that the matter might be brought before the Legislature. The unsettled state of affairs at the University in Burlington led her to hope that it might become a female university supported by the state. In a letter to her brother-in-law, Mr. Phelps, she ventured to say that men's colleges, which she had looked up to as models fourteen years before, might now make improvements in their system by studying hers. Her system produced a creditable moral effect upon pupils, while many young men left college demoralized. 'The facilities for intellectual improvement are far greater in the college than we can want,' she wrote, still feeling that women did not require the same sort of education as men. 'Yet,' she added, 'because our system, by appealing to the affections, guiding the will, and guarding the pupil from temptation, does give us a moral control, which, ordinarily, the faculties neither seek nor obtain, therefore the intellectual improvement of our pupils has, proportionally to the time spent with us, been greater than theirs.'

About this time she sent a copy of her 'Plan for Improving Female Education,' which she had published in 1819, to Edward Everett of Boston, and fastened with

white ribbon in the back of the booklet were several
pages closely written in her clear, legible handwriting,
explaining the progress made in her Seminary since she
first offered her plan of education to the public. Among
other things, she observed that it was unwise to give
too much power to boards of trustees. Ways should be
devised 'of so dividing the power of ultimate decision'
that 'evil resulting from their injudicious interferences
be obviated.' Her board of trustees, she said, had no
control over her in the management of the school. She
was delighted with the success of her committee of
ladies, which met twice a year to hear reports of the
progress of the school and of the conduct of the pupils,
and always attended the examinations. When she
established that committee, she had in view 'the improvement of her sex, both as regards the rising and the
risen generation.' These ladies, she said, were a guarantee to the public that nothing went on inconsistent
with female propriety. On the other hand, they received a great deal of benefit from attending the examinations and were in this way able to keep up with
advancing female education. 'The consideration of
improvements which may be made in the education of
their own sex, is calculated to prevent that contraction
of mind which sometimes follows a woman's confining
herself to domestic cares and the observances of visiting
etiquette,' she wrote. 'It gives also to those minds
whose native energies will not be thus confined, a field
where they may expatiate without intruding upon the
province of the other sex, which some, of the many
Ladies' societies of the present day, have perhaps done.'

With her usual interest in world affairs, Mrs. Willard
had watched the struggle of the Greeks for independence from the tyranny of the Turks. Like all those in

Europe and America who appreciated the glories of ancient Greece, her sympathy went out to the oppressed people of that country. Like all ardent Christians, she rejoiced in their triumph over a race of infidels. When in 1832, Greece became an independent state with Prince Otto of Bavaria as its King, she began to plan for the women of Greece, hoping to bring them some of the improvements in education which she had given American women. Her plan was to establish a school in Athens which would train native teachers, and finding the Episcopal Board of Missions ready to coöperate to the extent of allowing their missionaries, Mr. and Mrs. Hill, to take charge of the school, she set to work to raise the money for the undertaking. Her first step was to interest the women of Troy, and the response to the first meeting, in which the clergymen of Troy and Mr. Hill, the missionary, took part, far exceeded her expectations. She wrote her sister that the week in which she had prepared for this meeting was the happiest she had ever spent in Troy. People's expressions of delight in the stand which she had taken caused her to observe, 'They probably thought me too cold a Christian.'

She wrote a series of addresses on the 'Advancement of Female Education,' the first of which was read in Saint John's Church by the Reverend Mr. Peck at a meeting of the Troy Society for the Advancement of Female Education in Greece. In this address, she pleaded eloquently for the Greeks and described her plans for helping them, saying in her characteristic way, 'In ancient story we are told that one of our sex remaining in Troy wrought harm to the Greeks. In modern recital may it be said, that women of American Troy have done them lasting good.' This address and two others were published by the Troy Society and were widely circulated to arouse interest in the female seminary for Greek women. Not only did these addresses emphasize the deplorable conditions in Greece, but they were filled with vital information for those who were interested in the advancement of women. They told of the progress of female education in this country and the benefits derived therefrom; they compared with this the status of women in other countries; and all in all stated more forcibly than ever before Mrs. Willard's opinions regarding the rights of women.

Mrs. Willard would not listen to the suggestion that the seminary be named for her, because she knew that she and her pupils could not raise the necessary funds and would have to appeal to others for help. Through the efforts of Mrs. Sigourney, who wrote a poem to aid the cause, the ladies of Hartford were so aroused that they threatened to outdo Troy. In Boston, Greek women found an advocate in Mrs. Sarah J. Hale, editor of the 'American Ladies' Magazine,' who not only contributed an original hymn for the Troy meeting, but offered to print Mrs. Willard's plea in her magazine, which was circulated in every State in the Union. Scarcely an issue of the magazine appeared in 1833 without some mention of this plan for furthering female education in Greece.

Mrs. Phelps did much to aid the cause, and pupils of the Seminary aroused interest in New York, Portland, Maine, and elsewhere. The sum of three thousand dollars was the goal in view, and Mrs. Willard, always ready with a practical method, offered to publish her 'Journal and Letters from France and Great Britain' and sell it at a dollar a volume for the benefit of the fund. The book was eagerly bought by her pupils and friends who had been urging her to publish the story of her trav-

els. The 'American Ladies' Magazine' recommended it
highly to its readers and assured them that they would
find it of deep and abiding interest and usefulness. 'The
letters are characterized by the playfulness and enthusiasm of a mind delighted with new impressions,' read
its review, 'and a naïveté which seems like the fresh
glow of youthful feelings; but when she draws her
deductions and enforces her principles, it is with the
penetration of a philosopher, and the dignity of a
Christian.'

The 'American Quarterly Review,' published in
Philadelphia, felt differently about Mrs. Willard's
'Journal and Letters from France and Great Britain.'
In a long, sarcastic article, evidently written by some
one who was amused at woman's assumption that her
ideas were worth printing, it ridiculed the book from
beginning to end, criticizing Mrs. Willard especially for
giving more lavish information about herself than about
Europe. Its only kindly comment was the acknowledgment that her aspirations, views, and pursuits were of
an elevated character.

Readers, however, delighted in the personal touch
which the 'American Quarterly Review' so bitterly
condemned. It was a new note in the formal, stilted
style of the thirties. The sale of this book alone provided a large portion of the fund for the seminary in
Greece.

Although Mrs. Willard received a great deal of praise
for her work in behalf of female education in Greece,
she was also harshly censured. There were those who
thought it a foolish infatuation and saw no reason for
such interest in distant lands when there was plenty to
be done at home. Others accused her of wishing to gain
notoriety. She wrote Mrs. Sigourney that her influence

in the cause had been injured by the slanderous assertions that she was seeking fame. These accusations
always hurt Mrs. Willard, for she threw herself into a
cause so whole-heartedly and with such sincerity that
she could not understand how any one could possibly
misjudge her motives.

Finally, the training school for teachers was established in Athens, and the Greek Government not only
publicly expressed approval of the undertaking, but
announced its intention of paying the expenses of twelve
pupils. A Greek statesman, pointing to the Parthenon,
said to Mrs. Hill, who was in charge of the school, 'Lady,
you are erecting in Athens a memorial more enduring
and more noble than yonder temple.' Dr. Samuel G.
Howe, the American whose services in Greece earned for
him the title 'Lafayette of the Greek Revolution,' wrote
Mrs. Willard a letter of praise in which he said, 'The
members of your society, are, indeed, the friends of
Greece, and deserve more of her gratitude than many
who joined her in her struggle for independence.'

Through the efforts of Mrs. Willard and her co-
workers, five hundred dollars a year was sent to the
seminary in Greece until the Episcopal Board of Missions intimated that they preferred to have entire control of their agents and would therefore, if possible, provide for the support of the school's normal department.

It was Mrs. Willard's interest in world affairs and
causes such as this one that made her such an inspiration
to her pupils. She did not keep them close within four
walls, buried in their books, but gave them an international outlook and the urge to work for the good of
humanity.

CHAPTER XX

WORK AND PLAY AT THE TROY FEMALE
SEMINARY

INTEREST in Greece did not keep Mrs. Willard from intensive work in her own school. Although she no longer taught regular classes, she was an indefatigable supervisor, training her teachers, introducing improved methods, and adding new subjects to the curriculum. It was physiology which now caused the greatest consternation among her critics. For women to study physiology was the height of indiscretion. It would rob them of all delicacy. Mothers visiting a class at the Seminary in the early thirties were so shocked at the sight of a pupil drawing a heart, arteries, and veins on a blackboard to explain the circulation of the blood that they left the room in shame and dismay. To preserve the modesty of the girls and spare them too frequent agitation, heavy paper was pasted over the pages in their textbooks which depicted the human body. Mrs. Willard was ready to make concessions such as these, but she would not allow criticism to interfere with what she felt ought to be taught. Besides, she was especially interested in physiology herself. Therefore, it remained a part of the curriculum in spite of the wails and protests of the decorous and the slurs of the indignant male.

Mrs. Willard still considered the study of mathematics of prime importance. She believed that woman's daily duties tended to make her look at everything from a personal angle and led her to depend upon the authority of others for ultimate decisions. Mathematics would train her to think for herself in an orderly way, would help her impersonalize her problems and solve them on the basis of abstract truth. Woman, a creature of impulse and feeling, must learn to reason and face a subject squarely. Mathematics, alone, would give her this training.

As she believed correct English to be the mark of a good education, she required a great deal of writing in every subject. Each week the girls wrote an original composition and copied it carefully in their neatest handwriting. Frequently, they were obliged to write out their translations to make them more polished and perfect than oral translations could ever hope to be. They studied subjects in groups, their history being supplemented by geography and literature of the same period. For example, ancient history, ancient geography, and the Iliad were studied together. They, of course, learned their history lessons by means of chronological charts which grouped historical matter in epochs, as this was Mrs. Willard's favorite method of teaching. They came to geography class with their blackboards under their arms, and painstakingly drew maps from memory to illustrate the salient points of the lesson. Shakespeare's dramas served as textbooks for oral reading. A teacher selected a play for her class to read and study, assigned a character to each pupil, and when the reading had been practiced in class until it was perfectly done, the play was read before the whole school to the delight of readers and audience. The youthful Portias, Shylocks, and Bassanios lived in an enchanting make-believe world for weeks, a wonderful bit of romance in the clock-like routine of the school. Nor was there ever anything more impressive than a rosy-cheeked Portia, dressed in her best, her skirt billowing and her curls neatly arranged, reading with feeling and perfect intonation:

THE EXAMINATION ROOM

'The quality of mercy is not strained.
It droppeth as the gentle rain from heaven
Upon the place beneath . . .

A few subjects were required throughout the course:
Bible, composition, elocution, drawing, singing, gymnas-
tics, and dancing. The modern languages, now taught,
included Spanish and Italian as well as French and
German. Among the higher studies were Latin, algebra,
geometry, trigonometry, moral and natural philosophy,
logic, botany, chemistry, geology, astronomy, zoölogy,
natural theology, rhetoric, literature, and history. It
was an imposing curriculum, not equaled by any girls'
school in the country in those years. Mrs. Willard's experience led her to observe, 'The very pupils who excel
most in those studies, which men have been apt to
think would unsex us, such as mathematics and mental
philosophy, are the most apt to possess the elegant
simplicity of truly fine manners, without mannerisms.
Even personal beauty is advanced; for as a woman
improves in taste, and as her will gains efficiency in
every species of self-control, she rarely fails to improve
herself in symmetry of form: and while not a rose or a
lily falls from the cheek or the neck; men see that the
beautiful statue is animated by a living soul of intelligence. In fine, genuine learning has ever been said to
give polish to man; why then should it not bestow added
charms on woman?'

It was at examination time that Mrs. Willard showed
off her girls and their accomplishments to her complete
satisfaction. There were two public examinations during the year, one in February at the close of the first
term and the annual examination which began the latter
part of July and lasted for eight days. The annual examination drew crowds of spectators — parents, friends,

and prominent educators, legislators, and clergymen, who were invited by Mrs. Willard. It was one of the great social events of the year for Troy and Albany. In the large examination room with its rows of ascending seats on two sides, the spectators gathered. They were seated on one side, while the excited, expectant girls, in white dresses with bright sashes, filed into the seats on the opposite side. In the center of the room at a long low table, sat Mrs. Willard, the examiners, and the various teachers whose classes were being questioned. Prominent educators were invited to be examiners, and often they were men who had never before seen young women prove problems in geometry nor heard them give analyses of Stewart's philosophy. Every class was examined thoroughly. The girls were questioned one by one, standing at the table as they recited, and usually two stood there together as this made it less embarrassing. Some of the best compositions were read, but never by the authors themselves, as this would have been too great a strain on the modesty of young ladies. As a blushing young girl rose to read the composition of a friend, she was supported throughout the ordeal by another girl, close beside her. Everything was done to preserve modesty and to keep girls from becoming too forward or bold.

The girls always brought their blackboards and colored chalk with them into the examination room. The blackboards were two feet square and were easily carried under their arms. When they were examined in history or geography, they sat at the table in the center of the room, resting their blackboards against it, and drew map after map to illustrate what they had learned throughout the year. For example, the pupils who had studied Mrs. Willard's 'History of the United States' were expected to draw from memory all the maps in the Atlas and a map for each year of the Revolutionary War; they were to recite the events of history and explain them with the help of their maps, and were to give an analysis of the Introduction of the textbook, of the Constitution of the United States, the Declaration of Independence, and Washington's Farewell Address.

The walls of the examination room were covered with pictures painted by the young ladies, and comprised an art exhibit very pleasing to the audience. Their eyes might wander to a bright bit of color and find diversion if the examination grew monotonous. Occasionally between recitations, a few young ladies entertained the spectators by singing or playing on the harp or piano, and frequently the whole school joined in a song. Every day at the close of the session the pupils sang an appropriate hymn to emphasize the fact that it was the Creator who gave them minds capable of improvement. The favorite hymn for the end of the examinations was one written by Mrs. Willard, which the bright-eyed, white-robed maidens sang with fervor:

> O Thou, the First, the Last, the Best!
> To Thee the grateful song we raise,
> Convinced that all our works should be
> Begun and ended with Thy praise.
>
> It is from Thee the thought arose
> When chants the nun or vestal train,
> That praise is sweeter to thine ear,
> When virgin voices hymn the strain.
>
> Lord, bless to us this parting scene;
> Sister to sister bids farewell;
> They wait to bear us to our homes,
> With tender parents there to dwell.

Oh, may we ever live to Thee!
Then, as we leave earth's care-worn road,
Angels shall wait to take our souls,
And bear them to our Father God.

No marks, no medals, and no rewards were given at
the examinations. To have recited admirably before
such a distinguished assemblage was as great an honor as
one could achieve. Contemporaries who attended the
examinations were amazed at the ability of the girls,
gratified to see them rosy-cheeked and healthy in spite
of their arduous mental labors, and pleased with their
quiet, unassuming manners.

Although the girls acquitted themselves nobly
throughout the long examinations, they spent weeks
agonizing over them and cramming for them, and wrote
many verses describing their horrors. The following
verses written by the precocious poetess Lucretia
Davidson were favorites:

One frets and scolds, one laughs and cries,
Another hopes, despairs, and sighs;
Ask but the cause, and each replies,
    Next week's Examination.

One bangs her books, then grasps them tight,
And studies morning, noon, and night,
As though she took some strange delight
    In these Examinations.

The books are marked, defaced, and thumbed,
Their brains with midnight tasks benumbed;
Still all in one account is summed,
    Next week's Examination.

Thus speed ye all, and may the smile
Of approbation crown your toil,
And Hope the anxious hours beguile
    Before Examination.

The girls were studious and serious, and yet they were full of fun, always ready for a frolic, a bit of tomfoolery, or a chance to break the rules. According to one student, they might be classed in three groups — the dulls, the romps, and the flirts. The dulls were always good and very studious; the romps played pranks and always planned some mischief; the flirts' chief interest was young men and the mark of membership in that group was waving a handkerchief from a Seminary window at some passing man. The sight of a Rensselaer-School boy caused many a heart to flutter. That was one of the compensations of the required walk when the long line of girls, two by two, headed by a watchful teacher, tripped along the streets of Troy for their daily exercise.

In the recreation plot in the rear of the school buildings, the girls vied with each other in the swings, climbed onto the seesaws in spite of their impeding long full skirts, and shrieked with delight and fear as they teetered high above the ground. Some flitted gleefully here and there in a game of tag, others tossed bean bags, while the more sedate walked slowly arm in arm around the yard, exchanging confidences.

What a rush and a stampede there was for peanuts, molasses squares, and chocolate balls on Wednesday and Saturday afternoons when women with big baskets of goodies for sale gathered in the lower hall of the Seminary. After the plain meals, the ever-present bread pudding, and the lunches of plain bread which Mrs. Willard allowed between meals, baking day was a treat, and the four girls who served their turn in Cooking Class often lunched on applesauce and shortcake and took little cakes or pies to their rooms, much to the envy of their friends. The great achievement of Cooking Class was baking pies for Sunday's dinner.

From the music rooms where the girls were sent to practice, there often came strains of the 'Russian March,' 'Napoleon Crossing the Rhine' or popular airs of the day, and it required a watchful music teacher to keep them at their lessons. There was great consternation among the guardians of the younger generation over the popular songs of the thirties. That young ladies should express in singing, sentiments which they would blush to utter in conversation caused their elders to sigh for the beautiful chaste songs of Mrs. Hemans.

After the examinations, when most of the girls left the Seminary, the Southern and Western girls who were far from home often remained and continued their studies throughout the summer. The work then was not so difficult, usually study and reading under the guidance of a teacher. They lived together much like one big family, and evenings when they gathered with their sewing, Mrs. Willard often read to them. 'The Lay of the Last Minstrel' was her most frequent choice, and she read it with the greatest pleasure, for Scott was always her favorite. To a remark that Scott was not a great poet, she replied with vehemence, 'Scott not a great poet? As well might you say that a gun fired on the Alleghanies, that was heard upon the shores of the Atlantic and Pacific, was not a great gun, as to say that Scott, whose poems are read wherever the English language is spoken, and are translated into the languages of Europe, is not a great poet.'

During these years when Mrs. Willard was so busy with her girls at the Seminary, she was at the same time keeping a watchful eye on all the young teachers whom she had sent out into the world. In 1837, she organized the Willard Association for the Mutual Improvement of Female Teachers. She was its president, and Madame Necker de Saussure, Madame Belloc, Mrs. Phelps, Mrs. Hale, and Mrs. Sigourney were among the honorary members. Not only did the Association aim to encourage teachers and help them improve their work, but it also hoped by correspondence with them to gauge the actual state of female education and to learn what was promoting or retarding its progress in various parts of the country.

By means of circular letters and addresses, Mrs. Willard was able to disseminate her views and her good counsel. She had many sound, practical suggestions to make. She reminded the young teachers that they could do more for their children in eight hours of healthful, active labor than in twelve of languid, sickly exertion. She warned them against overexertion, advising them to take time for exercise, mental recreation, regular meals, and sufficient sleep. She told them that in order to succeed they must always strive for self-improvement, and suggested her method of teaching a new subject and studying it at the same time. This, she felt, would develop independent methods of teaching and so interest the teachers that they could not fail to interest their pupils. They were to see that their pupils really understood their lessons and did not merely memorize. 'Remember,' she said, 'that there is no special reverence for human opinions, because they are printed in a book.' Upon religious instruction, she, of course, laid special emphasis. 'Bring God into all subjects,' she advised, for in so doing they would show His sway over all human affairs.

Mrs. Willard was not only interested in her young teachers. She was just as solicitous about her girls who were married and established in homes of their own. In fact, she was very much concerned with their problems, especially those that dealt with the bringing up of children, and because of the many questions asked by young mothers on this subject, she was delighted to find, when she was in France, a book which was especially suited to meet the needs of young mothers and infant-school teachers. This book, 'Progressive Education, Commencing with the Infant,' had been written by a scholarly woman, Madame Necker de Saussure, the sister-in-law and biographer of Madame de Staël. Mrs. Willard and Mrs. Phelps set to work to translate it, and in 1835, William D. Ticknor, of Boston, published their translation.

In the Preface and in Notes scattered throughout the book, Mrs. Willard and Mrs. Phelps freely expressed their own opinions. 'Nothing can be more pleasing to the true friend of woman,' wrote Mrs. Willard in the Preface, 'than the sight of a well-educated female bringing all her faculties into exercise in the performance of the appropriate duties of her sex, as mistress of a household, as a wife and mother. To prepare the rising generation of women for these important duties, and to bring forward teachers to aid me in this, has been the grand object of my life.' The views expressed by Madame Necker de Saussure coincided with those held by Mrs. Willard and were extremely helpful to any one wishing to bring up children intelligently and scientifically. Many of their theories sound surprisingly like twentieth-century child psychology and mental hygiene. For instance, Mrs. Willard stated emphatically in a footnote that she believed it wrong to break the will of a child, as will was the very stamina of the mind. While she, of course, felt that a child should be taught obedience and should know that his own wishes could not always be gratified, yet she maintained that this could be done in an affectionate manner which would not break the child's spirit. 'Insult and ignominy,' she wrote, 'are heaped upon the defenseless being, as ungovernable passion or mistaken views of discipline may prompt, and either a sullen obstinacy, a morbid melancholy, or a servile abjectness of spirit, takes the place of that ingenuous frankness, that playfulness of disposition and noble independence which are so lovely and interesting in the young. ...

Her clear, penetrating philosophical thinking is shown in another footnote: 'It is certainly questionable how far we have a right to sacrifice ourselves. God has given to each of his great family the care of one being, that is, of himself — and if he neglect this one, or inflict upon him unnecessary pain, or deny him reasonable gratifications, is he not unfaithful to his trust? To *have right*, as well as to *do right*, seems to be the duty of each individual.'

Another book was published by Mrs. Willard in 1837, entitled, 'A System of Universal History in Perspective, Accompanied by an Atlas, Exhibiting Chronology in a Picture of Nations and Progressive Geography in a series of Maps.' It was a textbook developed in an original way and afforded new facilities for teachers and pupils.

In writing her 'Universal History,' Mrs. Willard was again inspired with the desire to be of service to her country. She wished to acquaint people with 'the virtues which exalt nations and the vices which destroy them.' She felt that the study of universal history was at this time peculiarly important to Americans, because the world was looking to them for the answer to this question, 'Can the people govern themselves?' The next ten years would probably decide it for coming generations. 'Shall monarchy in its palaces,' she asked, 'and aristocracy in its lordly halls, then exult, as it is told that America is passing through anarchy to despotism — while mankind at large mourn, and reproach us that we have sealed their doom as well as our own, and that of our posterity? Or shall we continue to be that people which of all others heretofore, or now existing, possess the most equitable government; and to whom national calamity is as but a phrase ill understood?'

While never so popular as her 'History of the United States,' the new textbook was nevertheless well received and highly endorsed by prominent educators. The Ward School Teachers' Association of New York considered it 'essentially adapted to higher classes of schools because of its vivacity, lucidness, and intelligent mode of arrangement.'

Both of these books, 'Progressive Education' and 'Universal History,' drew considerable attention to the Seminary. It received further publicity through articles printed in the 'American Ladies' Magazine,' published in Boston. The September number, 1833, contained a short article on the Seminary by the editor and an article by Mrs. Willard, entitled 'Places of Education,' which pointed out that education is gained not only in the schoolroom, but in every experience in life if the mind is alert and receptive. These articles were followed by pupils' contributions which, according to the editor, were printed to show their attainments in prose and poetry and their habits of thought and reflection. There were a variety of titles: 'Mind,' 'Stilling the Tempest,' and 'Examinations' in poetry; in prose, 'De Vere — The Suicide,' 'Time, Truth, and Falsehood,' and 'Philosophy of the Mind.' The frontispiece of the magazine for December, 1835, was a full-page picture of the Seminary, and a long article in the same number described the workings of that celebrated institution.

The 'American Ladies' Magazine' also called the attention of its readers to the fact that already seventy-nine incorporated colleges and universities for men existed in the United States and not one single Protestant incorporated and endowed female seminary. 'Men of America,' it asked, 'shall this neglect of your daughters be perpetual?' Then followed the recommendation that the Troy Female Seminary which had proved its usefulness, be incorporated and endowed so that it might be preserved for future generations.

The importance of the Troy Female Seminary was also emphasized in a letter to Mrs. Willard written in 1837 by George Combe, the renowned phrenologist whom she had met while she was on her European tour and who had been interested in her work ever since the publication of her 'Plan for Improving Female Education.' The letter read:

Your school is so extensive, and the influence of women on the state of society is, in my opinion, so important that I regard you as the most powerful individual at present acting on the condition of the American people of the next generation. ... You may never live to see the good you are doing, but you may see it by faith.

Realizing her influence in the educational field and the responsibility which such influence conferred upon her, Mrs. Willard endeavored to work for the establishment of another institution for the education of young ladies — a school for teachers. This, she hoped the New York Legislature would establish and endow, and she wrote out her plans for Governor Marcy in a most remarkable letter:

SCHENECTADY, *Dec.* 20, 1836

His Excellency Wm. L. Marcy,

SIR: Pardon my intrusion if I again bring to your recollection the subject of female education. In the large share of the surplus revenue, of which the interest will accrue to the State of N. York, there now seems to be the means of doing something for this object, which from the explanation you were so kind as to give me last winter, I then plainly perceived there was not.

I do think it would be for the permanent honor of the empire state, and for those who should lead her destinies for the time, to come forward the first in giving durable form to improvements which are already on their course with mind and tide favourable. There would be some difficulties to encounter respecting location — So there is in locating any public building, be it even a state's prison. Perhaps this might be obviated by giving the institution to that place which would make the largest private donation. The difficulty of this would be that it might in this case be carried into the heart of a large city or to some other unfavourable location. Should it become a contested point which place had already done the most for female education, Albany and Troy would probably both claim to stand first — What if the difference should be divided and an institution be placed somewhere along that beautiful ridge between Albany and Troy next of the road? I do not think the state presents a finer location. Both cities need their present schools for the education of their females who board with their parents. To make a female school on the best model there should be none but boarders, others cannot attend to their duties with regularity but the institution should have within its own precincts ample grounds for exercise. This suggestion concerning location I would thank your Excellency not to mention as from me.

You are aware, Sir, that my views for the advancement of female education are connected with those I entertain of the improvement of common [schools]. I had partly completed a letter to your Excellency on this subject last spring but before I had time to complete it the season was past for making it of any use. Allow me here briefly to state my views. Common schools will never be well managed while there is a change of teachers every spring and fall — There should be settled teachers as in Academies. In a country presenting so many objects for enterprize as ours these cannot be men. — Neither would men do so well (generally) as women properly qualified. Men are not happy as women are to spend their lives in communing with children nor can they teach the girls such handy works as they ought to learn in common schools, whereas women of talents may be prepared by education to teach boys all they need to learn even to the languages and the higher mathematics. It is a mistake to suppose that a woman of talents cannot govern lads of fifteen or sixteen years of age. The civil law I believe gives them the authority — In Vermont a female teacher sued the parents of two boys who refused obedience to her regulations and she (having taken all previous measures correctly) obtained of the fathers damages to the amount of thirty dollars each. But these women must in order to be properly qualified to teach and to govern first be educated themselves and then they must be paid not one dollar a week but about $250 per annum. They can get more than that sum to go to the south and west. Another object connected with the improvements in female education is the amelioration of the condition of those hundreds of young women who are labouring like mill-horse drudges in factories though many of them are the daughters of those who achieved our revolution, and those who are to be the mothers of the next generation. Schools organized on a peculiar plan and allowing such of those young women who are disposed to learn, to spend half or one third of their time in learning should I think be made for their benefit in the vicinity of the great factories. This would elicit the talent there is among them and the first rate scholars might be taken and educated as teachers of common schools — and this brings us back to the starting point that there must be a right place to teach these teachers.

I hope to have the honour of paying my respects to Mrs. Marcy and yourself before long. The illness of Miss Knonen was the cause of much anxiety at the Seminary and her recovery of rejoicing.

With profound respect
Your obedient servt.
EMMA WILLARD

While Mrs. Willard was evolving these plans for the
education of women and was trying once more to interest
a Governor and a Legislature, Mary Lyon was putting
her heart and soul into plans for an endowed permanent
seminary for women. Addressing public meetings, collecting contributions in her little green bag, going from
door to door and from town to town urging men and
women to make an investment for the education of their
daughters, Mary Lyon aroused severe criticism because
she was defying the conventions, but she pressed steadily
on, and was able to raise more than twenty-seven thousand dollars. She explained her project by referring to
the Troy Female Seminary, Miss Beecher's Seminary
at Hartford, and her own work at Ipswich. She did not
have to argue for woman's mental capacity as did Emma
Willard. Her plea was for a permanent institution with
lower tuition. It had become fashionable to attend a
celebrated seminary. Mary Lyon's seminary was to
bring education to poorer girls. On November 8, 1837,
before the new school building was completely finished
or furnished, Mount Holyoke Female Seminary at
South Hadley, Massachusetts, received its first pupils.
At first its course of study was quite similar to that of
the Troy Female Seminary except that it included none
of the ornamental branches. Mount Holyoke, however,
had entrance requirements and a regular three-year
course, while the Troy Female Seminary with no entrance requirements, admitted pupils at any time on
the condition that they attend the examinations at the
end of the term, and awarded diplomas to pupils who
had creditably passed examinations in the full course of
English studies with Latin or one modern language.

Meanwhile, another educational institution had
opened its doors to women. The Oberlin Collegiate

Institute, founded in 1833 in Ohio, admitted men and women, black and white. The female department, which was regarded as separate, gave instruction, according to the catalogue, 'in the useful branches taught in the best female seminaries.' It also promised that higher classes of the female department might have the privilege of some of the higher departments of the Institute. Wheaton Seminary, founded in 1835 in Norton, Massachusetts, by Judge Wheaton in memory of his daughter, was patterned after Mary Lyon's Ipswich Seminary. Endowed with twenty thousand dollars to be used for the cause of education and guided by the progressive advice of Mary Lyon, it became an important institution for women.

Emma Willard was seeing woman's education accepted and supported in the East and in the West, in the North and in the South. She was seeing it take strides toward college education and she knew that she perhaps more than any one else had blazed the trail.

CHAPTER XXI

DISILLUSIONMENT

IT was a great satisfaction to Mrs. Willard to look back over her life and think over all that she had accomplished. She had built up a successful school without State aid. She had proved that women were capable of comprehending collegiate studies and were unspoiled by them. She had sent hundreds of teachers out from the Seminary and they were bringing education to an ever-increasing number of American girls. Her textbooks were being read throughout the country.

Now that the constructive pioneering work was done, Mrs. Willard felt more and more like turning over to others all her work at the Seminary. She was eager for new fields which would widen her sphere of usefulness and put into play her independent methods of investigation and organization. The training of teachers and the writing of textbooks had become her chief interests, for through them she could reach the common schools and the minds of hundreds of readers.

In a sense, the Seminary had come to a standstill. Mrs. Willard was bound up with the City of Troy, from whom she still leased most of the school property, and occasionally there were differences of opinion which made her wish heartily that she had entire control. The city, however, turned over enough property to the trustees in 1837 to make the Seminary eligible for a portion of the State literature fund. This allotment from the State was the first money contribution that Mrs. Willard ever received for her school. She had built it up entirely by her own hard, unremitting work. Every attempt for an endowment which would insure permanency for the Seminary had proved futile, and a real college for women still seemed out of reach.

All that was necessary now was an alert, intelligent manager who would uphold present standards. This manager, Mrs. Willard had at hand in her daughter-in-law, for John had married a few years before, and had chosen one of her own girls, Sarah Lucretia Hudson.

When Sarah was eleven years old, her mother sent her to Mrs. Willard's Academy in Waterford. Although her father had died, leaving the family in straitened circumstances, her mother made every effort to give her daughters an education. They moved to Troy, and when Mrs. Willard opened her Seminary there, Sarah and her younger sister, Theodosia, were enrolled. Both girls were promising students, and Mrs. Willard, hearing of their financial struggles, offered to give them an education. She eventually adopted Sarah as her daughter. At sixteen, Sarah began teaching at the Seminary, and at twenty-one, was made second vice-principal.

When John returned from Europe with his mother, he found his old playmate very much grown up and more attractive than ever. They were separated again for a time while he studied medicine with Dr. Morris in Bennington, Vermont, but in 1834 they were married. Then John took over the business management of the Seminary and Sarah continued as vice-principal.

It was during these years when the Seminary ceased to be an all-absorbing interest, that Mrs. Willard made the acquaintance of Dr. Christopher Yates, a physician of Albany and New York. They were at once very much attracted to each other. Mrs. Willard had always been partial to physicians, while Dr. Yates could hardly fail to appreciate Mrs. Willard's charm and graciousness, or to be impressed by her ability and fame. A contemporary, writing of her at this time, called her a beautiful woman. Her weaknesses, he said, were egotism, vanity, and love of admiration, but these were soon lost sight of in her gracious smile, her kindness, and her lofty ideals.

There is no doubt that Mrs. Willard was often lonely in spite of her success and the adulation which she received as Principal of the Troy Female Seminary. She missed the loving, steadying companionship of Dr. Willard. She saw John happily married and well established, no longer needing her care. She often thought of Almira's fortunate marriage with Judge Phelps, of her leisure for writing, of the joy of having a strong man by her side. She had always sentimentalized over married life and idealized it. Nothing seemed more beautiful to her than a noble, protecting husband and an adoring wife. A poem of hers called 'The Bouquet,' published in the 'American Ladies' Magazine' in 1835 reveals her thoughts. It is addressed to Mrs. C., who sent her a beautiful bouquet:

> Lady, I take thy fragrant gift,
> Of many a sweet and lovely flower,
> And bear it from the public gaze,
> To place it in my secret bower.
>
> Its varied fragrance scents the air,
> Its modest beauties charm my sight.
> Thus female virtues, when combined,
> The dear domestic scene delight.
>
> Thus thy fond husband turns to bless
> The flower that blooms for him alone;
> And dearer than the garden's pride,
> The cherished treasure all his own.

MRS. JOHN H. WILLARD

JOHN H. WILLARD

Perhaps it was only natural under these circumstances that when Dr. Yates proposed marriage, Mrs. Willard accepted. He was an agreeable man, highly respected in the community. She was looking forward to the happy companionship which her sister Almira had found in her second marriage and there were times when she longed to leave Troy. She wrote Sarah in April, 1838:

I felt clear in my own mind in making the engagement. . . . We have had time for acquaintance, and we have not yet found a stone that jars. His daughter Catharine is one that I do think you will love and be loved by. She and I love each other sincerely, and I feel that she will be most essential to our arrangements, which are, to go to house-keeping in some central part of the city, such as is best for his business . . . Dr. Yates wishes me to arrange every thing in reference to my own time to please myself, and Catharine is an excellent house-keeper, and fond of it, and pleased to be useful, and I intend to give strict attention to my school books. This is an honorable and sacred act, which I am about to perform solemnly and deliberately, and I do not hold my dignity any the less on account of it.

When Mrs. Phelps heard that her sister had decided to marry Dr. Yates, she wrote her at once, giving her excellent advice:

I conclude that, having decided, you will not wish to delay the consummation of this event for any length of time, as your position, at the best, is a very trying one, though you will, no doubt carry it through with dignity. But the case of a widow at your time of life, being engaged, is somehow so regarded by the world, and is so awkward, that the sooner you change your position the better. I trust you will remember the good advice you gave me in respect to keeping the command of your own property; and I pray that all your counsels may be aided by Divine wisdom. You have not mentioned whether Dr. Yates is a pious man. I trust you would not engage yourself to one who did not, at least, respect religion; and real piety would be truly desirable. I hope, also, he is of your own denomination; for, though these things do not enter into the romance of life, they are of great importance in realities. You have said nothing about the pecuniary affairs of your intended, by which omission I infer there is not much to be said. If he is a good man and will make you a good husband, this is no great matter, perhaps, as you will yet have to exercise your faculties, which may be better for you than to have nothing to do but enjoy a fortune, and certainly will be for the advantage of the world.

Meanwhile, various disturbing rumors about Dr. Yates reached Mrs. Willard. She was told that he gambled, and there were insinuations about a suit in which he had been involved. But although she investigated all these things thoroughly through friends, nothing could be proved against him. When her old friend, Professor Amos Eaton, came to the defense of Dr. Yates, she poured out her gratitude to him in an impulsive letter:

TROY, *May 15th*, 1838

MY DEAR FRIEND:

Certainly whatever you wish in regard to Laura Anne and Kate shall be done — and it can be in this case without any inconvenience.

As to that third page I shall keep it with your leave, and shall send two or three copies of it abroad — one to Dr. Yates. I could kiss your hand (if that would please you) for having written it. I had heard yesterday that amidst the general din which has been raised against my friend by those who know nothing of him that you had raised a friendly voice, but I was not aware that you possessed the knowledge of that abominable prosecution. The people seem to have become possessed with an idea that I had lost my wits, and made the most important leap of my life, wholly in the dark, whereas it has been many months since I have been secretly making enquiries concerning his character he having been twice to Troy and written me numbers of letters. When I first heard of that prosecution I at once determined to reject him, but in order to be quite sure I was right about the facts I sent to Hermanus Bleeker of Albany by Col. Stone who subsequently made enquiries also of Chancellor Kent and others. The result was entire conviction of the deep injustice done to Yates' character; and a more tender feeling towards him than otherwise I might have had. It has seemed to be my fate with the knights of old, though I am a woman, to right wrongs; and this injustice which common fame has done to a noble man, is one of those wrongs which my esteem and affection may help to set right. Unless something had happened to call this question up anew, he might have gone down to his grave without any one coming forward as you have now found occasion to do and setting the matter in its right light. Nothing you could have said or done for me personally could have raised such grateful emotions as that you have undertaken the defence of one of whose preference and affection I am proud and with whom I am happy to find another congeniality in being.

Your sincere and affectionate friend

EMMA WILLARD

Disquieting rumors, however, continued to come to Mrs. Willard, and when she heard that Dr. Yates lacked respect for religion, she was deeply concerned, for noble religious principles were to her the essential qualifications of character. His attitude on the subject, when she discussed it with him, was not satisfying, and, hard as it was for her, she broke the engagement. She sent John to New York at once to return Dr. Yates's gifts through a mutual friend, Colonel Stone.

Unfortunately, Colonel Stone did his best to bring about a reconciliation. He wrote Mrs. Willard of the suffering she had brought upon Dr. Yates, of his consternation and inability to understand her decision. He told her that Dr. Yates felt he had been cruelly and unjustly treated and feared his reputation would be ruined when the break became known, as the public would

surely think it was due to some disgraceful act on his
part which she could not overlook. He assured her that
Dr. Yates was a Christian and a church member, and
closed his pleading with this decisive counsel, 'My own
opinion is, that the separation, after matters had proceeded so far, must be in a greater or less degree,
disastrous to you both.'

Mrs. Willard had great respect for Colonel Stone's
judgment and allowed herself to be persuaded to recon-
sider. When Mrs. Phelps heard of her sister's indecision,
she would have done anything to prevent the marriage,
but Mrs. Willard felt herself in duty bound to marry
Dr. Yates, since she had promised and nothing had been
proved against him. She wrote later of these trying
days, 'I think I have never been more unhappy than
at this period. My health could not stand against my
mental struggles, and I determined to marry him.'

She did, however, draw up a marriage agreement by
which she turned over to trustees a large portion of her
property. She was to receive the income from the trust
fund and use it as she saw fit. This was the only means
by which a woman, in those days, could retain a hold
on her property, for in the eyes of the law, all of it au-
tomatically became her husband's after the marriage
ceremony. The Seminary was left in charge of John and
Sarah, who now received the title of Principal.

The 'Troy Budget' of September 18, 1838, printed the
following notice:

Married

In this city at 11 o'clock yesterday morning by the Rev.
Mr. Cox, Doct. C. C. Yates of New York to Mrs. Emma
Willard, Principal of the Troy Female Seminary.

Only two hours after the wedding ceremony, Dr.
Yates called upon his wife to pay for their wedding din-

ner in Albany. From that time on, it became more and more evident that he intended to have her pay all of his expenses. They moved to Boston in January and took a house on Louisburg Square. Determined to live in luxury and idleness, Dr. Yates demanded money continually, and when his wife remonstrated, accused her of being penurious, selfish, and mean. He demanded ten thousand dollars from her separate funds to purchase a pretentious home for himself and his daughter, Catharine. He took possession of all her books, silver, paintings, and jewels, many of which she had collected in Europe. He claimed everything, even her separate trust fund. Catharine, with whom Mrs. Willard had expected such happy companionship, joined with her father in exasperating her and wearing down her resistance.

The man who had appeared so congenial and agreeable that she could write of him to Sarah during their engagement, 'We have not yet found a stone that jars,' had become a veritable fiend. He saw what disillusionment and sordid family quarrels were doing to her refined nature, and he set to work with persistent mental cruelty to break her spirit and bring her completely under his domination. Scoffing at religion, making their family worship ridiculous with jests, telling her cruel falsehoods about her family, neglecting her shamefully when she was ill, he made her existence unbearable. In the presence of outsiders, he treated her with the utmost courtesy, trying to give the impression that she was to blame for the dissension between them.

He did his best to break up the friendship between Sarah Hale and his wife, a friendship which had continued through years of common interest in the cause of woman. He gave Mrs. Hale to understand that his wife insisted upon teaching against his will, and so winning

were his ways and his confidences about his married life
that Mrs. Hale censured her old friend severely. Not
content to be malicious in his own circle, he went to New
York and published disparaging articles about his wife
in the 'Sunday News.'

Humiliation and bitter disillusionment were heaped
upon the head of a woman who had in her previous experiences known devoted love, admiration, and success.
It is useless to speculate how a woman of her caliber and
keen discernment could have been so completely deceived as to the character of Dr. Yates. Perhaps she
was blinded by prosperity and popularity. Perhaps a
craving for affection, an undue confidence in the perfection and generosity of men, clouded her thinking and
led her into a step which brought her untold suffering
and irreparably wounded her pride, but which at the
same time gave her an understanding of life that she
previously lacked.

All her views of married life were turned topsy-turvy.
She began to learn, as the scorned Mary Wollstonecraft
had learned, how cruelly women could suffer under the
domination of brutal men. For a woman of Mrs. Willard's principles even to consider separation meant a
struggle with pride and conventional virtue, but she
was convinced that if she did not leave Dr. Yates, she
would collapse and that he, in some way or other, would
finally get possession of her separate funds which were
now maintaining her school and which she intended to
hold for her son John. So she took the step. She drew
up an agreement of separation, giving as reasons 'difference of opinion and uncongenialities of mind.' When it
was signed, Dr. Yates told her he would force her to live
with him. He published the agreement in the paper,
casting aspersions on his wife. But she left him in June

of that year after nine months of torture, going at once to Berlin, Connecticut, to the home of her sister Mary Lee, and there in the peace of the country-side, among those hills that she had so loved in childhood, she hoped to find strength and courage to pick up the broken threads of her life.

CHAPTER XXII

WORK WITH HENRY BARNARD IN THE COMMON
SCHOOLS OF CONNECTICUT

THE Lee home was in that part of Berlin known as Kensington, a substantial red frame house on a country road. Here, there was peace under the big elms and in the views of the rugged, clear-cut hills. Here, with her older sister Mary, who had mothered her as a child, Mrs. Willard found refuge and seclusion. She found kindness, sympathy, and understanding which brought healing to her wounded spirit.

Nothing had ever been harder for her to bear than criticism and censure. She had a horror of misrepresentation. Now, it seemed as if all three were heaped upon her. When a friend like Sarah Hale could misunderstand, what would others think? Every one discussed the affairs of a woman who left her husband, and a woman was always blamed when she stood out against a man, no matter what his faults might be. To think of divorce took unlimited courage in those days when a divorced woman was looked upon as a social outcast. It was doubly hard for Mrs. Willard, who so highly respected certain conventions and prided herself on her reputation.

The days were a struggle with indignation and despair. She turned more and more to God for comfort and strength, trying hard to quell the bitterness which crowded into her thoughts. She wrote to a friend, '... my final dream of earthly happiness is passed; and I am more ready, I think, in mind, than I have ever been to be devoted to His service who will, if we love Him, make all things, even our afflictions, work for our good.'

She was among friends, and every kindly greeting and warm handclasp filled her with overwhelming gratitude. Very near the Lee house, so near that she could see its chimney over the treetops, was the home of her brother Samuel Hart. Samuel had died a few years before, but his wife, Mary, still lived in the home with her son Samuel and his family. All through the neighborhood were relatives and friends. 'I am now like a mariner who has escaped shipwreck,' she wrote, 'thankful for what is saved — for life, for reason, friends, and a thousand comforts with which a kind Providence has surrounded me.'

Gradually, she began to take an interest in the affairs about her. She took long drives in the country. She visited in Hartford, and in Troy, but always came back to Mary's as to a haven of refuge. A visit to Troy was now an ordeal, as there the shame of her position weighed heavily upon her. Even her beloved Seminary seemed better off without her since she had defied the conventions. It was thriving under the efficient management of Sarah and John. Her future course was undecided. She often thought of going back to her old home in Middlebury. To occupy her mind, she once more took up her scientific and physiological studies and began to write out a treatise on 'Respiration and Motive Power,' a surprisingly unconventional subject for a lady of 1839.

The country was rich in beauty that autumn, the first autumn in many years that Mrs. Willard had driven leisurely through lanes of brilliant foliage, or seen such clusters of wild purple asters and cornfields bright with pumpkins. The dry leaves rustled as she walked through the grass to pick ripe grapes from the vine or a rosy apple from a limb weighed down with fruit. She felt the tang of frost in the air. She breathed deeply to catch the pungent odor of autumn woods. There was much to remind her of happy October days in Middlebury long ago. The bustle of the busy harvest season soon cast its spell over her, and her old eagerness for work returned. She spent many hours at her writing. Then came the opportunity to help Henry Barnard build up the common schools of Connecticut.

Mrs. Willard and Henry Barnard had become acquainted through their mutual friend Dr. Eli Todd, of Hartford, a man who had inspired them both with his fund of knowledge, his interest in education, his enthusiasm for Pestalozzi, and his work for the more humane treatment of the insane. Henry Barnard was making Connecticut think about education. He was a well-educated, brilliant young man who, after graduating from Yale and preparing for the practice of law, had spent several years in Europe studying social, educational, and political conditions. Returning to this country, he was elected to the Legislature, where he engineered the passage of a bill which would enable him to improve the schools of his native state. Investigations had revealed that from six to eight thousand children did not attend school, that only three hundred of the twelve hundred schoolhouses were fit to be used, that there were no fixed standards for teachers, no examinations to test their ability to teach, that two hundred varieties of textbooks were in use. People of wealth and influence sent their children to private schools, and as a result the common schools had been outrageously neglected.

In order to remedy this, it was necessary to rouse the mass of the people out of their apathy, and as Secretary of the State Board of Commissioners for the Common

Schools, Mr. Barnard traveled throughout Connecticut holding meetings to explain actual conditions and urge a reform.

For one of these meetings to be held in the Kensington church, Mrs. Willard was asked by Mr. Barnard to write an address. She of course gladly complied with his request, but as it would have been too great a strain on the proprieties for a woman to read her own address in a church and before such an assemblage, Elihu Burritt read it for her, and according to reports, it was listened to 'with deep and thrilling interest.'

In fact, so telling was Mrs. Willard's plea for education that a committee of leading citizens asked her to take charge of the four schools of the district, and shortly after, the voters of Kensington elected her Superintendent of the Common Schools, 'to take oversight of them for the ensuing season.' A woman had been elected by men to fill an important office, a woman who thought she did not believe in political rights for her sex. It was a great honor and she accepted on the condition that the women of Kensington as well as the men support her in her work. To show the people that she was willing to contribute her share in money toward improving the schools, she offered to pay a school tax equal to that paid by the wealthiest member of the community.

She took up the work with her old enthusiasm and at Mr. Barnard's request wrote out her plans. As the schools were convening in May for their summer session, a female teacher had been placed in charge of each one, and older pupils chosen to assist in the work with the younger children. While Mrs. Willard preferred to employ a regular corps of well-trained teachers, she knew this was impossible on account of the expense.

Pupil-teachers could help out very well as they had for so many years at the Troy Female Seminary. Three rooms seemed necessary for each school, a main room for assembly and two smaller rooms, one for the youngest pupils, the other for the most advanced, who could be trusted to govern themselves.

'Each schoolhouse,' she wrote Mr. Barnard, 'should we think be provided with a clock; no matter how plain, if it do but perform its office correctly. Whatever is to be done regularly requires a set time as well as a fixed place; and teachers on low wages cannot afford to buy watches; nor would they serve the purpose of a perpetual memento of the coming duty of the scholar, like a clock.'

Grieved at the amount of fiction that had been put in the hands of the children, she selected new textbooks. 'Fiction,' she explained to Mr. Barnard, 'may mislead, even when it intends to do good — truth never. The mind that feeds on fiction becomes bloated and unsound, and, already inebriated, still thirsts for more. And has not so much of the mental ailment of our times been fiction, that this delirium of the mind has become an evil so pervading that we ought resolutely to shun its source, and turn now to the simple element of pure truth. . . . In general, sacred objects are the best for schools. There is even among children, an awe and quietness diffused by ideas pertaining to God and religion, which tend to good order; and shed around the true atmosphere of the soul.'

She drilled the children in reading, in geography, and arithmetic, paid special attention to their penmanship and spelling, dictated model business and social letters, and encouraged the writing of compositions. Finding that many children under ten had not learned to write, she set to work to remedy this and kept them busy with their slates and at the blackboard.

'When the little children found that they themselves could produce the written language,' she wrote Mr. Barnard, 'it seemed to give them the most vivid delight; and instead of manifesting the reluctance to composition which older scholars almost invariably have, they were troublesome with bringing me their little compositions. This experiment has convinced me of what I before expected, that the unconquerable distaste for composition which is found in schools of older pupils, arises from our passing by the proper period of early childhood, before we begin to teach the communication of ideas by writing.'

Another fault which Mrs. Willard corrected was toning, that monotonous, unintelligent manner of reading which was so common in the schools of that day. She would not let the children memorize the answers to questions, but tried to have them gain a general knowledge of every subject they studied. 'What we wish to effect,' she wrote Mr. Barnard, 'is not so much to give our schools a few facts from books, as to give them the power of using books to profit.'

She taught the children Bible history, supervised their music, wrote a song for them, 'Good Old Kensington,' which they loved to sing, and a simple prayer which they recited at the close of each session. She offered a prize to the girl who could make the best shirt, for in her opinion the making of a shirt had from time immemorial been the test of good common sewing. She introduced a 'normal class' for those who were planning to become teachers and for those who assisted in teaching the younger pupils, and in this work she found an able helper in her niece Harriet Hart, who had been

trained at the Troy Female Seminary. She also spent a
great deal of time training the teachers whom she found
sadly in need of attention. She held classes for them on
alternate Saturdays, instructing them in history, reading, algebra, geometry, and in methods of teaching. So
interested was Mrs. Willard in her work that she talked
to every one about it and aroused a surprising amount
of interest among the townspeople. She organized a
'Female Common School Association' among the
women of Kensington. Her address to them, 'The Relation of Females and Mothers Especially to the Cause of
Common School Improvement' was printed in the 'Connecticut Common School Journal,' as were many of her
addresses and suggestions regarding the schools, but
this address in particular received notice outside of
Connecticut and was read before the annual meeting of
the Western College of Teachers at Cincinnati, Ohio.
In fact, Mrs. Willard's work in the common schools of
Kensington was looked upon as a model in improving
other schools throughout the country. Many educational and literary societies asked her to meet with them
to tell them of her work, those at a distance requesting
her to write addresses for them.

The public examination, which she had found so useful in the Troy Female Seminary, she forthwith introduced into the Kensington schools. The first one
held at the church in September, 1840, was a gala occasion, attended by parents and prominent educators
from all parts of Connecticut and even from other
States. Although the exercises commenced soon after
nine in the morning and continued with but an hour's
intermission until six-thirty at night, contemporaries reported that there was 'no abatement of interest in the
audience or weariness in the children.'

Meanwhile, Henry Barnard had become a national figure as regards education. Through his 'Connecticut Common School Journal,' he was disseminating his ideas and describing Connecticut's constructive educational work. As his fame as an orator had traveled far and wide, he was in constant demand for lectures. Horace Mann called upon him again and again to speak for the cause in Massachusetts and his work, as well as Horace Mann's, helped to make possible the founding of the first State normal school in Massachusetts in 1838. Mr. Barnard's Teachers' Institute held in Hartford in 1839 for six weeks with daily class instruction did much to arouse interest in a normal school for Connecticut, but it took more than ten years to crystallize that interest into action.

Nevertheless many efforts for a normal school were made, and Mrs. Willard with her wide experience as a teacher was looked upon as the logical head of such an institution. The people of Kensington urged her to head a normal school there and Hartford too offered opportunities. While she felt she would be happier in Kensington where there was no aristocracy to look down upon the enterprise 'with withering and blighting influence,' yet the Hartford proposition seemed better and was the one which she eventually attempted to carry out.

'There is a desire manifested by Mr. Barnard, and others,' she wrote at this time to her cousin Nancy Hinsdale, 'that I should go to the head of a school for teaching teachers for the common schools, and the proposition has been, this last week, taking some form and shape. . . .' She told of a large brick building in Hartford which was being considered for the normal school. It was occupied in part as an orphanage, but as she

wished a model school for her teachers, she was delighted
at the prospect of conducting the orphanage and normal school simultaneously. The orphans, she felt, would
make exceptional pupils for a model school as there
would be no unreasonable parents at hand to interfere.
Her idea was to have a series of teachers' institutes
rather than a permanent normal school, with two sessions of four weeks each, held when teachers could
attend without giving up their positions. Students were
to enroll for four successive sessions and complete the
prescribed course of study. This type of normal school,
she felt, would reach more of the men and women then
actively engaged in teaching and would therefore bring
more immediate good to the schools of the State.

But none of the plans materialized, and as political
changes in the State terminated Mr. Barnard's work
there, normal-school activities ceased temporarily.

Meanwhile, Mrs. Willard had been honored by a request for a poem for the bicentennial celebration of the
settlement of Farmington. She lost herself in a maze of
ancient records and then spun out her verses with
exuberance. The result was her poem, 'Our Fathers.'
Writing about it to her son, she said, 'I had to read and
make investigations concerning facts which it was not
easy to find out; and my poetical mill will not work
without full headway. . . . It is to be read by a gentleman whom my friends here recommended as an elegant
reader, the Rev. Mr. Andrews, of West Hartford. He
spent part of the afternoon here, and I read it to him.
He says he likes the poem; that there are passages in it of
thrilling interest; and he intends to become so familiar
with the whole as to deliver it without the manuscript.
I wish you could come. . . .'

She wrote still another poem for the occasion, which

was read in the evening at a historical party where the guests in old-fashioned costumes revived the customs of their forefathers. This poem, 'Bride-Stealing, A Tale of New England's Middle Age' told the story that she had heard so often as a child as she sat on her father's knee before the blazing logs in the kitchen fireplace. It told of the wooing of her great-aunt, Tabitha Norton, of Tabitha's marriage to the famous Isaac Lee, and of the unsuccessful attempt to steal the bride, a prank quite common in the early days of the colony, when a party of young men and women would carry off the bride soon after the ceremony, take her from tavern to tavern, and finally bring her home the following day. It was a spirited poem picturing well the customs of her ancestors, and with great satisfaction, she saw it printed a few years later with a short biographical sketch in Everest's 'The Poets of Connecticut.'

A great deal of Mrs. Willard's time was now spent with friends in Hartford as she had decided to appeal to the Connecticut Legislature for a divorce from Dr. Yates. In this connection, a relative, Mr. Norris Wilcox, was of great assistance. The divorce petition was presented to the Legislature in May, 1843, its pitiful story written by hand on both sides of seven large sheets of paper, securely fastened together with a green ribbon. This publicity was agonizing for Mrs. Willard, and yet it comforted her to have her case clearly and fairly stated. Her plea was favorably considered by the Legislature, the marriage dissolved, and 'Emma Willard released and discharged from all obligations arising out of same.' She was declared sole, single, and unmarried and was given the right thereafter to 'be known and called by her former name, Emma Willard.'

This was a blessed relief. She had not seen Dr. Yates

since she left him four years before in June, and she
never saw him again. Now that she was free, a great
burden was lifted, and although she was still often filled
with indignation over her treatment during this unfortunate experience, she was, according to Dr. Lord who
saw her at this time 'far from becoming bitter or radical
or revolutionary, as many women become under similar
provocation.' From now on, he said, her character was
tinged with sadness and she never recovered her old
joyousness. Yet through it all she did not lose her good
humor, wit, and vivacity.

Soon after this, Mrs. Willard spent some time in
Philadelphia. She grew very fond of the city, spent
many hours in the libraries working on her books, and
revising her histories, and often conferred with her publisher, Mr. Barnes. She thought seriously of making
her home here and editing an educational journal which
she proposed to call the 'School-Mistress.' Her sister,
Mrs. Phelps, was not far from Philadelphia, at Ellicott's
Mills, Maryland, where she and Judge Phelps at the
request of the Bishop of Maryland had taken charge of
the Patapsco Institute, an Episcopal school for young
ladies. Mrs. Phelps was prosperous and happy in her
educational work and had developed a practical business
judgment which now often steadied her more impulsive
sister. She was not much in favor of Emma's editing
an educational periodical because she feared it would not
pay.

'You know how the "Journal of Education" failed,'
she wrote Emma in 1844, 'and the "Annals" died a
lingering death. You must not count on making money;
but you might benefit the school at Troy, and aid in
the business of sending out teachers. The idea of the
periodical I should like very well on my own account,

and might sometimes give you aid. I would send you some of our best compositions — and we have some very good — and, perhaps something original once in a great while. But I would not like the "School-Mistress"; such a title would suit better some country-school journal. The "Educator," or the "Educational Intelligencer," would sound much better to me than your title. "Woman's Mission" would not be bad, but, since the thing is in the dim distance, and may never come, there is no use in taking that name. If Mrs. Hale and Miss Leslie and yourself could write, you might do something popular and useful at the same time; yet, again, there are so many jealousies among literary ladies that you might not get on well, even if you could be agreed enough to begin.'

This plan was put aside, and in the summer of 1844, Mrs. Willard returned to Troy to make her home in a little red-brick house in the shadow of the Seminary.

CHAPTER XXIII
EDUCATIONAL TRAVELS

IN the little red-brick house on the corner of the Seminary grounds, Mrs. Willard now spent many happy years. She could look out from her windows, across her well-kept garden to the Seminary buildings and lovingly watch the institution which was the pride of her heart. Her vigorous personality still dominated its policies. She loved all of its ever-changing family and shared their interests, affectionately calling the girls her 'granddaughters.' In a trailing black satin or velvet gown with soft creamy lace neck-ruff and hand ruffles and a lacy headdress which set off her gray curls, she was the commanding figure at all their entertainments and at the annual examination. Her presence in the dining-room for Sunday dinner roused a flutter of excitement. To the girls, she was an oracle and a queen. They listened with awe to the occasional talks which she so gladly delivered, impressing them with the importance of education and the duties of their sex.

The school catalogue now read, 'The Founder of the Institution, Mrs. Emma Willard, has her residence on the Seminary grounds, and is at all times ready to extend to its members the results of her successful experience as an educator.' She was again a vital part of the Seminary, happy to be there among those who loved and respected her, stimulated by the adulation of the Seminary girls, and proud and pleased, like all grandmothers, over John and Sarah's own family of five children.

Her favorite niece, Jane Lincoln, lived with her as companion and secretary, and often other nieces and

EMMA WILLARD

relatives temporarily made their home with her. In
fact, she was always surrounded by a bevy of young relatives who were being educated at the Seminary, including the daughters of her stepsons, Gustavus and William
Tell Willard. Gustavus's daughter, Lucretia, came all
the way from Ohio for an education.

The Seminary girls were always welcome at the little
red-brick house. Mrs. Willard was at home to them on
special days and when two or three of them shared a
simple meal with her, as they frequently did, she entertained them as if they were distinguished visitors,
always eager to interest them and to encourage them
to express themselves on serious subjects. She stayed
young with them, and they loved her and knew she was
their friend, though they remained in awe of her. How
eager she was to keep them improving their minds when
they left the Seminary! She urged a teacher's career as
the height of useful service, and quoting Dr. Gallaudet,
she advocated one or two years of teaching in the common schools for every woman who was a friend of her
country.

'But if you do not teach yourself,' she often told them,
as in a commencement address she told the girls of
Washington Seminary, 'pass not by unnoticed the
teacher who does. . . . Seek her out and help to give her
a standing in society that may make her respected by
herself and her pupils. Visit her in her school, and then,
between yourself and her, give her any hints that you
see she needs; and why not take an hour a day, if this
too is needed, in helping her to teach.'

Again and again, she repeated to the girls the remarks
of foreign statesmen who feared for the stability of the
country's democratic institutions and who said, 'If
America is saved, it is her women that must save her.'

She did her best to prepare her girls for this task and urged them to be studious, steady, and intelligent, avoiding vain amusements and the snares and follies of luxury.

Always, she urged self-improvement, and sensing the temptation that befell young mothers to give up everything for the routine work of caring for home and children, she wrote these characteristic lines to her niece, Emma Lincoln O'Brien. 'I hope you will not drop your pen, and shut up your piano, and make your education of no avail, because you have a child. A little extra resolution is needed to find or make time, but that is all that is necessary. Mrs. John Willard, with five children, performs well the duties of principal of this school.'

Mrs. Willard, herself, had in no sense retired from active work. She now found herself in constant demand as an advisor, teacher, and speaker in the educational revival taking place in New York State. Her first invitation came from the County Superintendents of Common Schools, who were holding a convention in Syracuse in the spring of 1845. She was made an honorary member of their association and was asked to take part in their public debates. She went to Syracuse, but instead of speaking at the convention, she followed the more lady-like way of allowing sixty of the gentlemen to call upon her and then reading them an address which she had prepared for the occasion. In this address, she mapped out the place that women should hold in the common schools, recommending especially the formation in every town of a society of women to coöperate with men in improving the schools. It was published in the newspapers and in the common-school journals, and as a result, she was asked to make a tour of several counties in southern New York to attend teachers' institutes.

She set out in September in her own carriage with a companion, Carry Richards, one of her former pupils, whom she called a little, though not a spoiled, beauty. They spent a week in Monticello, where Mrs. Willard taught a hundred teachers, men and women, and persuaded the men of the town to invite the women to form an educational society. She was gratified to hear later that the men had given the women fifty dollars to spend and that with it they had clothed the poor children and sent them to school. Driving on to Binghamton, Owego, Cairo, and Rome, she conducted similar teachers' institutes, traveling in all seven hundred miles and instructing as many as five hundred teachers. In all her educational work, she stressed the importance of employing teachers who were more or less permanent in the profession, as children could not be expected to progress rapidly when they were given new teachers every few months. She felt, too, that women were especially suited to the profession, and unlike men, were willing to spend the greater part of their lives with children, training and guiding them. Most men made teaching a temporary profession until they could find something more satisfying and lucrative. She also brought the question of salaries before the people continually, trying to make them see the need of more adequate compensation.

These educational travels suggested to her the possibility of writing a book called 'Home-Travels of a Schoolmistress,' of writing it in the form of letters addressed to Mrs. Sigourney, who was still her staunch, highly respected friend. She wrote Mrs. Sigourney about it, asking her opinion. 'I could in this way,' she said, 'bring this remarkable movement which is going on in this state before others to stir them up — I could

give some of the results of my long experience in sketches
of instructions given to the teachers — and in accounts
of my discourses with the people. I could bring forward
the doctrine which I wish to promulgate. But the time
is passing and passing away in which it should be done
if ever and I have nothing done as yet.'

This book was never written, as other literary work
filled her days, and an unexpected opportunity for a
trip through the West presented itself. She wrote Mrs.
Sigourney how it all came about:

When I wrote you last I had no thought of making this long
journey but one day soon after, my son having been looking
over our demands against many persons in different parts of
the Union said to me, 'We must send out an agent and such a
person will go if I wish it.' 'Why,' said I, 'if we must be at
this expense should I not go myself. I have long had the intention to make a tour of the U.S.' 'Most assuredly' said
John, 'if you will go — but talking of going won't answer.'
'Well, give me twenty-four hours to consider.' Then I called
Jenny Lincoln and on my asking her how she would like such a
tour, her face lightened and her eyes sparkled with pleasure.
This decided me.

In March, 1846, on the day after her granddaughter,
Catharine, was born, Mrs. Willard and her niece, Jane
Lincoln, started out on their journey, stopping first in
New York and Philadelphia. While Mrs. Willard was
in Philadelphia, she again saw her old friend, Sarah
Hale, from whom she had been estranged since her
separation from Dr. Yates. Mrs. Hale, after leaving
Boston, had become editress of 'Godey's Lady's Book'
in Philadelphia. One evening at dusk as Mrs. Willard
was returning to her hotel, she saw Mrs. Hale sitting at
the window of her boarding house, and on a sudden
impulse, went in to see her. She wrote Mrs. Sigourney
about this visit:

I reflected how lately I had been on the brink of eternity, and our Saviour's precepts of love to all — no matter how they had treated us came to my mind — and she was sitting as if she might be pensive and sorrowful. I alighted — enquired for her — and she came forward — 'Who is this?' said she for it was almost dusk — Emma Willard said I — she sprang forward and embraced me with real feeling. She knew I doubt not that she had not deserved this attention at my hands. She and Josepha came the same evening with her youngest son to the hotel to see Jane and Emma (Mrs. O'Brien, Jane's sister) and I never saw Mrs. Hale when she appeared better. But though I do not wish to quarrel and feel the Scripture injunctions to live in peace — yet there is little pleasure in intercourse where confidence is lost. . . . But yet I have long been acquainted with Mrs. Hale and have loved her, and I wish her well, and had rather be at peace with every human being and even with brute creation than to live in quarrels.

Mrs. Willard's journey of eight thousand miles through the South and West was made by stagecoach, packet, and canal boat, and often by private carriage, as no railroad yet connected this vast empire with the East. She visited all the principal cities in every State west and south of New York with the exception of Florida and Texas. It was, in a way, a triumphal tour, as her former pupils, now settled in every part of the country, welcomed her with joy, entertained her, and honored her. Her reception in the South was especially gratifying, for here the majority of her pupils lived, many of them the belles of society, many of them teachers in Southern seminaries. Traveling through the States that formed the western boundary of the country, Arkansas, Missouri, Iowa, and Wisconsin, she found even here close to the frontier her 'daughters' and her teachers. At all the seminaries which she visited, she was looked up to as a pioneer educator, as the woman of all women to whom they owed their existence. Everywhere, she answered questions and gave advice. Everywhere, she urged women to take an interest in the common schools. She was taking the principles and ideals of her Female Seminary out of Troy into the world. She was stepping out from her work there into the wider sphere of national education. Like Henry Barnard on his nation-wide lecture tours for the cause of education, she left behind her a zeal for more and better schools. She brought to women a consciousness of their responsibility in educational matters.

It was an experience very dear to the heart of a woman who cherished praise, very comforting after the years she had spent struggling for the recognition of women's educational rights. So much had happened since those days in Middlebury when she was secretly planning her address to the Legislature. So much had happened since, heart-broken and discouraged, she had learned she could expect no financial aid from the State. Now, she was reaping her reward. She was filled with joy and gratitude as she realized the progress women had made in the last thirty years, and knew that she had been largely responsible for that progress.

When Mrs. Willard returned from her long tour of the United States, she found an invitation awaiting her from the County Superintendents of New York to attend a meeting at Glens Falls. As she had been injured by the overturning of a stagecoach in Ohio, she was unable to make the trip and instead wrote a long letter to Mr. A. W. Holden which was read at the meeting and was filled with excellent suggestions for the improvement of methods in the common schools. In fact, it was so filled with practical advice that the son of Mr. Holden republished it in 1916 in the 'Educational

Review' with an article in which he said the letter was interesting in the light of modern pedagogy.

Again in this letter, Mrs. Willard called women to the common schools, and again in urging this innovation she used her old tactics of flattering the men into acquiescence. She wrote:

If the men amidst their many occupations have not more time to command, there are educated women who have; and who would be honored and their minds made more active and comprehensive, by serving under the superintendents on various committees connected with the welfare of the schools. I do not wish women to act out of their sphere; but it is time that modern improvement should reach their case and enlarge their sphere, from the walls of their own houses to the limits of the school district. In the use of the pen, women have entered the arena, and if we take all the books which are now published, I believe those which well affect the morals of society are, the one-half of them, the works of women; but, in the use of the living voice, women are generally considered as being properly restricted to conversation. St. Paul has said they must not speak in churches, but he has nowhere said they must not speak in school-houses. To men is given the duty of providing for children, to women that of applying to their use this provision; and why should not the men and women in school-districts meet together for discussion? . . . These suggestions may now sound strange, as they foreshadow a new shade of things. But I see it in the future, and rejoice in it as the harbinger of a brighter moral day than the world has yet seen. And when the time of the women shall be occupied under the auspices of the men, and made by their means efficient, then will the whole frame of society be regenerated. Men will be relieved of a burden which, however their conscience may feel, they cannot fully discharge. Women will be honored and elevated, and children will have the full benefit of their mutual and united cares and labors. . . .

Mrs. Willard had meanwhile published several text-books. Her 'Temple of Time, or Chronographer of

Universal History,' appeared in 1844, and this was followed during the next years by a 'Chronographer of
English History,' a 'Chronographer of Ancient History,'
and an 'Historic Guide to the Temple of Time.' The
'Temple of Time' was a unique invention, a chart on
which the world's history 'from Creation to the Present
Time' was set forth. The chart pictured a temple with
pillars in groups of ten, each pillar representing a century
and inscribed with the name of the outstanding sovereign. On the floor of the Temple, the principal nations
of the world were grouped, with important battles listed
on the right-hand margin, and on the left, the epochs
from Willard's 'Universal History.' The roof was
emblazoned with the names of heroes.

There was considerable demand for the 'Temple of
Time' and at the World's Fair in London in 1851, Mrs.
Willard was awarded a gold medal for this original plan
of teaching history. She, herself, was extremely enthusiastic about it, feeling that she had revolutionized
the teaching of history. With every history that she
completed came the feeling that she had rendered her
country a real service. Her 'Temple of Time' she
knew would save time for both teacher and pupil. 'We
have great need,' she said, 'to quicken the process of
education to meet the demands of a new age of steam
and electricity. We must learn to value the time of
children.'

She was indefatigable in giving demonstrations of
teaching history with the 'Temple of Time.' She taught
every class in history at the Seminary to illustrate the
advantages of the new method, and spent four weeks in
Philadelphia introducing it into the school conducted by
her niece, Helen Phelps. This kept her very busy, but
as she wrote in a letter to a friend, she preferred the
name of teacher to that of lady-loafer.

She was made very unhappy and indignant about this time by attacks on her histories by Marcius Willson, who also was the author of textbooks on history. He claimed that his books should be used by the schools, as previous histories, including Mrs. Willard's, were filled with errors. Her friends, on the other hand, claimed that he had been plagiarizing her books. The result was a succession of controversial pamphlets with such titles as 'An Appeal against Wrong and Injury, Written by Emma Willard in Answer to a Pamphlet Issued by Marcius Willson and Widely Circulated Injuring Her Books' and 'An Appeal to the Public Especially Those Concerned in Education.' In these pamphlets, Mrs. Willard forcibly defended her reputation as a historian and showed that Mr. Willson's accusations were groundless. She reprinted on a prominent page this most favorable review of her 'History of the United States,' entitled, 'More from the Boston Traveler':

Bancroft has written us a noble history. It will live as long as the story which it so well records. But Bancroft's work is a grand and vast one, like our own Niagara, and interminable forests, and boundless prairies. But around that waterfall, beneath those lofty pines and sycamores, and on those vast plains, there smile beautiful flowers, sweet blossoms of the heart which only woman's delicate hand could pluck. It was fitting too, that the intelligent young ladies of our land should have a history in which they could delight. But Mrs. Willard's work has not alone the grace of woman's pen. It has other useful qualities. In perfect arrangement, comprehensiveness, and well digested detail, it is the best book for reference of any published.

Through the ever-increasing prestige of its founder, the Troy Female Seminary continued to prosper. In spite of the many sister institutions that had sprung up throughout the country, including Mary Lyon's endowed Seminary at Mount Holyoke, the growth of the Troy Female Seminary was such that an additional building was erected in 1846 — a large building, five stories high and fifty feet square, heated by steam and lighted by gas. According to the six prominent men who acted as Examination Committee in 1845, this Seminary had 'the same superiority over other female seminaries which Harvard and Yale have over colleges of more recent date.'

CHAPTER XXIV

WOMAN'S SPHERE AND WOMAN'S RIGHTS

In the year 1848, the country was startled, indignant, and amused by what the newspapers termed an 'Insurrection among Women.' The first Woman's Rights Convention, to which they referred, had been held in Seneca Falls, New York, in July of that year, and there a group of women had issued a Declaration of Sentiments, patterned after the Declaration of Independence, and a set of eleven resolutions outlining their aims and demands.

Tired of being denied the right to take part in Anti-Slavery and Temperance Conventions, of having their sphere mapped out for them by pious clergymen claiming undue familiarity with God's will, feeling keenly the injustice of their legal disabilities, these courageous women bravely came before the public to demand their rights, and in spite of almost unbelievable persecution, continued their fight for what they believed to be the cause of woman. Foremost among them was one of Mrs. Willard's former pupils, Elizabeth Cady Stanton, who proposed the most bitterly debated resolution of the eleven, which read, 'Resolved, That it is the duty of the women of this country to secure to themselves their sacred right to the elective franchise.'

Mrs. Willard was not a party to this convention. Nor is there any record of what she may have thought of this unprecedented action on the part of women. Yet, we can feel quite certain that however much she may have sympathized with their demands, she would have considered this convention most unwise and even harmful to the advancement of her sex. In her mind first and foremost always was the cause of woman's education, and anything which might in any way react against it was out of the question. As she had been before the public for so many years as one of the leading advocates of woman's education, she felt that she must keep herself an example above reproach, nurturing all the womanly virtues and never exposing herself to slurring attacks from the press. She still hoped that when women were adequately educated all the other things would naturally come to them. In spite of all her difficulties with legislators in securing their support and financial aid for woman's education, she still seemed to have sublime faith that noble men would honor virtuous women by conferring upon them in God's good time the rights and privileges of which they were worthy. She had made this very clear in a poem entitled 'Prophetic Strains,' published in 1830:

. . . .

Listen. The deep prophetic voice doth speak
Of woman. There shall be a council held
Of matrons, having powers to legislate
In woman's province, and to recommend
To man's prime rule, acknowledged first and best,
As wife to husband, whatsoe'er, to her
Maternal eye, seems for the general good.

Such council yet shall be: but distant far the day.
And let no woman's rash, ambitious hand,
Attempt to urge it. Let it come, as it will,
By God's own providence. Seek we to do
What duty bids, and leave the rest to him.

. . . .

And much must woman learn, and much reflect,
Ere she such council could with profit hold.
And let my warning voice again be heard.

Let not the day be urg'd: wait God's full time.
No hot-house plants have health, nor bear the winds;
And human institutions, forced in growth
Are sickly, and soon wither and decay.
Let woman wait, till men shall seek her aid.
A day will come, when legislative men,
Pressed by stupendous dangers to the state,
Will see how woman's power, wealth, influence,
And mind of quick invention, might be turn'd
By right machinery to great account.
Then woman, prompt to aid distress, and proud
To be found worthy, will the means invent,
Concentrating her power, her aid to give;
Then form such council as the vision shows.

Almost twenty years had now passed since she had
written that poem, and apparently the time had come
for women to give men at least a slight suggestion, to
prod them just a little, so that they would begin to
confer some of the honors and privileges upon them.
So in the year 1848 when younger women were demanding their rights, Mrs. Willard, who could not be quite
satisfied with the passiveness of her generation, nor
quite won over to self-assertion of the younger women,
published a very tactful letter in the 'American Literary
Magazine' of Albany, 'A Letter to Dupont de l'Eure on
the Political Position of Women.'

In a short letter 'To the American Public,' which pre-
ceded this letter, she explained that the drafting of a
new constitution in France gave her the opportunity to
present her views to the public, that she had held these
same views three years before when New York called
a constitutional convention, but she did not advance
them then because men would have said, 'Here is an
ambitious woman who wants a new order of things to
make a high place for herself.'

Her suggestions to the French were that they should invite the women of their country to meet and choose delegates to assemble in Paris as a female body invested with powers to act for their sex and that the Convention should give them 'those advisory powers which in the family properly belong to the mother.' These advisory powers, of course, she assured them, would find no place in men's deliberations on commerce, war, and foreign relations, and would be considered only when the rights, duties and liabilities of women were concerned. '... there you may find it wise,' she wrote, 'as well as just to defer to them, so far as to give them a negative upon any law which you may propose: and also to permit them on these subjects the right of introducing into your convention any bill which they may judge expedient, with the reasons by which they sustain it, leaving it for the supreme power to decide. This would be in fact but a modification of the right of petition. ... On subjects where each sex is alike concerned, as in the laws of marriage, each party could introduce bills which the other might negative.'

She went so far as to say that there were certain public duties, which she eventually hoped to see turned over to women — the care of the schools for young children, especially as regards religious, moral, and intellectual training, the care of female education beyond the primary schools, the care of the poor and of public morals. She reasoned this way: 'As a human being walks in safety using both his limbs, while with one only he hobbles, and is in constant danger of falling; so has human government forgetting that God has made two sexes, depended for its movements hitherto on one alone. The march of human improvement is scarce a proper term to express its past progress, since in order to march both limbs are required.'

She made several startling assertions — that in the framing of new constitutions, slaves were kindly remembered but the women forgotten, that women were persons and as such their rights were sacred, that since women had not been barred from succession to sovereignty and Isabella, Elizabeth, Maria Theresa, and Catherine II had proved that women were not unequal to questions of law and policy, why should women any longer be regarded as incapable of judging their own rights and responsibilities. Such sentiments might have been uttered by the scorned women at Seneca Falls, and Emma Willard when writing them forgot tact and voiced her own real feelings.

Even as early as 1833, when Mrs. Willard wrote her second address on the 'Advancement of Female Education,' she enumerated some of the laws which discriminated unjustly against women, the laws which gave a husband absolute right over his wife's property, even that accumulated by her own labor, that gave him the right to will to his children her property including the copyrights of her own books, thus making her utterly dependent on the children. She acknowledged the wrongness and injustice of these laws but said, 'I leave this matter to the reflection of those who regulate the law, and to the many educated women who are rising up, and who will hereafter be capable of investigating our rights, and explaining our claims.' Her work was to educate women and through education to free them.

There were times, however, when Mrs. Willard became so interested in a subject that she forgot her caution, her tact, and her resolution to be the perfect example of an educated woman. This was the case in her medical researches. In 1846, one year before any woman had been admitted as a student in a medical school in this country, she published 'A Treatise on the Motive Powers Which Produce the Circulation of the Blood.' It was a bold thing to do in an age when no perfect lady could make a scientific study of the human body. In fact, so bitter was the feeling about such study that when Elizabeth Blackwell in 1847 finally gained permission to attend the Geneva Medical College, women at her boarding house refused to speak to her and drew away their skirts to avoid contamination when they met her on the street. But Mrs. Willard, engrossed in her subject, gave no serious thoughts to critical comments. She had worked over her theory for years, had observed post-mortem examinations of the heart and lungs with her family physician, Dr. Robbins, and with Professor Smith of Troy, both believers in her theory, and now she felt it was her mission to present it to the world. In fact, she was so obsessed with the theory of circulation by respiration, worked so much over it during the remainder of her life, and made such courageous efforts to have it accepted by medical men that her family and friends often referred to her 'unfortunate mania' on the subject. Her first treatise was followed three years later by 'Respiration and Its Effects, Particularly as respects Asiatic Cholera.'

Because the theory of circulation by respiration was advanced by a woman, it was looked upon with skepticism by most medical men. Gradually, however, it won advocates, was defended and discussed in medical journals, and then finally was called the American theory rather than the Willardian. Mrs. Willard often remarked that when the theory was accepted, she would not be given credit for its discovery, and when later she found it taught in books and lectures without reference to her as its discoverer, she showed no bitterness but was glad her message had reached the world. She wrote in a New York medical journal: 'The time I had spent in devotion to this theory, the many rebuffs I had met in seeking to promulgate it — sometimes, unhappily, affecting my social life — had made painful the duty of publishing it. My historical works had been received with favor; but I believed that in publishing this, it would be charged against me that I chose a subject unsuited to my sex. I therefore said in my preface, "This is not so much a subject which I chose, as one which chooses me; and if the Father of Lights has been pleased to reveal to me from the book of his physical truth, a sentence before unread, is it for me to suppose that it is for my individual benefit."'

A few months after Mrs. Willard's death in 1870, her sister, Mrs. Phelps, wrote an address for a meeting of the American Association for the Advancement of Science on the 'History and Defense of Emma Willard's Theory of Circulation by Respiration.' Both Mrs. Willard and Mrs. Phelps had been honored by membership in the Association, and Mrs. Willard during the four years of her membership had wished to submit her theory but had been unable to do so. Mrs. Phelps assumed the task, although she had always been a little impatient with her sister for keeping her theory so persistently before the public. In the address, she felt called upon to make the following statement: 'Before concluding this imperfect sketch, I deem it proper to say, that, though Emma Willard might have seemed to step out of the province of woman in her physiological researches, she had no sympathy with the declaimers upon *women's rights;* those who advocate the mingling of women in political strife, or who would change the order of God's providence in fixing her condition in social and domestic life.'

To be sure, Mrs. Willard did not give her support to the work of Lucretia Mott, Susan B. Anthony, or Elizabeth Cady Stanton. She had had no sympathy with earlier feminists, such as Frances Wright. Yet, she herself was continually stepping out of the so-called sphere of woman, and had struggled all her life to widen that sphere for other women. It is difficult to see just where she drew the line, except that she felt that education rather than agitation would solve woman's problem. One cannot imagine Emma Willard with her interest in history and politics, refusing the ballot if it were offered her. Still the ballot seemed unimportant to her in comparison with the value of education to women.

During the past thirty years, she had seen a vast change in the attitude toward the education of women. Consternation at their study of geometry, history, the sciences, and even physiology, was gradually melting away. Anything new, of course, still aroused opposition, as for example the examinations in philosophy at the Troy Female Seminary which critics said were a fraud perpetrated upon the public, for women could not comprehend the meaning of philosophical statements and could only memorize them as they did Greek or Sanskrit. Such accusations, however, were now more easily silenced, and in this case the examining committee of six prominent men assured the public that there was no conspiracy between teachers and pupils, that in a searching examination they had found the young ladies intelligent students of philosophy.

Another innovation at the Troy Female Seminary, very pleasing to Mrs. Willard, was the placing of Mary A. Hastings at the head of the science department when it no longer seemed possible to secure the services of a professor of the Rensselaer Polytechnic Institute.

Miss Hastings was one of the first, if not the first woman, to give laboratory lectures with experiments, and her courses in mechanics and chemistry were said to equal those at Yale.

Yet, in spite of Mrs. Willard's years of work to improve and widen the curriculum for young women, we find her again and again making such statements as this—'We plead against giving to boys and girls precisely the same education, and claim that each sex should be taught its peculiar duties.' Although her mind traveled far along the road of woman's emancipation, it was halted periodically by the warnings of orthodox religion, which in that age so punctiliously marked out woman's sphere; and as year by year she became a more ardent religionist, the doctrines of Saint Paul regarding women never lost their hold over her.

Still, ultra-modern theories would persist in mingling with the orthodox. Even in the early days of the Troy Female Seminary, she courageously advocated the financial independence of women, urging them to give up the idea that they must be supported in order to be respectable or that they must marry in order to be supported. In 'Morals for the Young, or Good Principles Instilling Wisdom,' a book written in 1857 especially for the edification of the children of the common schools, she said, 'In making her calculations for the future, therefore, every young woman is wise to prepare herself to become independent, useful, and happy, without marriage; although her education should always fit her for those high and holy duties, which result from marriage and maternity.'

As the years went by, Mrs. Willard realized more and more the need of an endowment for the Troy Female Seminary if it were to continue in the future as a per-

manent institution. In spite of all her disappointments
in dealing with the Legislature, she again petitioned
them in 1852, asking them at least to put the trustees in
full possession of the Seminary property. She declared
it was the duty of the Legislature to encourage female
education by an endowment, thus putting it more
nearly in a class with education for boys and reminded
them that the pupils of the Troy Female Seminary had
always been taught quietly to perform the duties of
their sphere. She, however, believed, and she spoke for
herself alone, that the sphere of their usefulness would
in time be enlarged to the great benefit of society.
Nevertheless, in her characteristic manner so irritating
to the women who considered women's rights a natural
inheritance, she added, 'But they will await, as becomes
them, the time when men their natural protectors,
guardians, and rulers, shall invite them to these new
responsibilities, induct them into their places, and
watch over, and sustain them there.'

The publication by a woman of a textbook on astronomy was unheard of in those days, and yet Mrs. Willard, in 1853, published 'Astronography' or 'Astronomical Geography.' Educators considered this one of her
most valuable contributions. It was a textbook of
elementary astronomy simply and clearly written.
Professor Avery of Hamilton College said, 'She has
achieved a remarkable success in making the elements
of a difficult science, easy of comprehension.'

Meanwhile, another unusual book had been published,
a book which chronicled the achievements of women.
It was edited by Sarah Josepha Hale, published by
Harper and Brothers, and called 'Woman's Record: or
Sketches of All Distinguished Women from "The Begin-
ning" till A.D. 1850, Arranged in Four Eras with Selec-

tions from Female Writers of Every Age.' This pretentious volume was very pleasing to the ladies, because
it showed them all they had accomplished through the
ages. Mrs. Willard was proud of the record of her sex
and very happy over the tribute paid her. A long sketch
of her life and work, her picture, her 'Ocean Hymn,'
and three selections from her prose works gave her an
imposing share of space. It was very gratifying to be
ranked among the distinguished women of the world.

In the summer of 1854, the World's Educational Convention was held in London, and Mrs. Willard, then
sixty-seven years of age, made up her mind to attend,
not only because she was so vitally interested in the
cause of education, but because she felt women educators should be represented there. As her son John could
not accompany her because of his duties at the Seminary, she chose her niece, Jane Lincoln, who had been
her companion on previous journeys in this country.
It took a great deal of persuasion to win the consent of
Jane's mother to a voyage across the Atlantic, but it
was finally given and on June twenty-fourth, Mrs. Willard and Jane sailed for Liverpool on the steamship
Pacific. It was a voyage of thirteen days, very short as
compared with the twenty-four days that Mrs. Willard
had spent on the sailing vessel Charlemagne, in 1830.

On landing, they went at once to London, where Mr.
Barnard warmly welcomed Mrs. Willard and introduced
her to prominent educators of every country. She attended the Convention meetings with him and distributed many of her own educational writings which she
had brought with her. She was very well received not
only by educators, but by men and women of rank and
by Mr. Buchanan, who was then minister to London.

She spent many happy days sight-seeing with Jane in

London and throughout England, noting the changes
that had taken place in the twenty-four years since her
first visit. In August, Jane's mother joined them, bringing her son Charles and daughter Myra with her, and
after spending a month longer in England, they toured
the Continent, visiting Germany, Switzerland, Italy,
and France. In Paris, Mrs. Willard again met her good
friends, Madame Belloc and Mademoiselle Montgolfier,
with whom she had corresponded during the intervening
years. Paris was filled with memories — memories of
Lafayette and the happy inspiring days of her first visit.
Traveling now was almost commonplace in comparison,
and this trip, while it was filled with interest, new experiences, and honor for her, lacked the glamour and
adventure of that first voyage of discovery. They returned to America in November.

Mrs. Willard went back to Troy, while Jane accompanied her mother to Ellicott's Mills, Maryland,
and assisted her at the Patapsco Institute. Since the
death of Mr. Phelps in 1848, the full responsibility of the
school had fallen on the shoulders of Mrs. Phelps, and now
Jane's intelligent, conscientious help was a great comfort.

In the summer of 1855, the tragic news reached Mrs.
Willard that Jane had been killed in a railroad accident.
This was one of the most heart-rending experiences of
Mrs. Willard's life, for she loved Jane as a daughter.
For many years, both she and Mrs. Phelps struggled
with grief. Turning over to others her school at Ellicott's Mills, Mrs. Phelps moved to Baltimore and devoted herself to writing, while Mrs. Willard found comfort in revising her textbooks and in efforts to save the
Union. Mrs. Willard wrote her sister at this time, 'For
myself, I conclude, that since God has spared me, He
has something yet for me to do, and my wish is and my
mind is to do it.'

CHAPTER XXV
SAVING THE UNION

ANTI-SLAVERY agitation and increased bitterness between the industrial North and the agricultural South
over the extension of slavery, the tariff, and banking
measures had now racked the country for a long time,
and Mrs. Willard watching the trend of affairs grew
more and more apprehensive. Her ears rang with the
prophecies of foreign statesmen that America was
doomed to destruction, and she resolved to do everything in her power to work for peace and to preserve
the Union.

Although she believed slavery to be fundamentally
wrong, she was not an abolitionist. As the friend of
many Southerners, she felt she understood their point of
view and could do much to bring the North and the
South together. She identified herself with the American
Colonization Society, whose object was to solve the
slavery problem by establishing a negro republic in
Africa and aiding the emigration of free negroes.

In this, she again separated herself from Lucretia
Mott, Elizabeth Cady Stanton, and the more progressive feminists who worked actively with the abolition-
ists. The National Female Anti-Slavery Society had
been formed in 1833 and was the first organized woman's society and the first attempt made by women to
assert themselves on a political question. The continued
interest of women in the anti-slavery movement brought
forth in 1837 a pastoral letter from the General Association of Congregational Churches of Massachusetts,
condemning public work for women and saying: 'We

appreciate the unostentatious prayers and efforts of
women in advancing the cause of religion at home and
abroad and in leading religious inquirers to the pastor
for instructions; but when she assumes the place and
tone of man as a public reformer, our care and protection of her seem unnecessary, we put ourselves in self-
defense against her. She yields the power which God
has given her for protection, and her character becomes
unnatural. We say these things not to discourage
proper influence against sin, but to secure such reformation as we believe is Scriptural.'

It was at the World's Anti-Slavery Convention in
London in 1840 that the unjust treatment of women
delegates aroused the indignation of Lucretia Mott and
Elizabeth Cady Stanton and gave them their first idea
of calling a Woman's Rights Convention in the United
States.

So it was that the slavery issue, along with that of
education and temperance, gave women their first opportunity to work for their country and incidentally to
develop their own powers.

Mrs. Willard's work for her country had heretofore
been wholly along educational lines. Now, it was being
turned into new channels as she saw the Union threatened. Perhaps no other woman in America was so
familiar with the details of her country's history. In
1849, she added to her earlier works on American history, another volume entitled 'Last Leaves of American
History,' which recorded the Mexican War and the
history of California. This was followed in 1856 by a
revised edition which she called, 'Late American History: Containing a Full Account of the Courage, Conduct, and Success of John C. Frémont; by which
through Many Hardships and Sufferings, He Became

the Hero of California.' As Frémont was then being considered as a presidential candidate, this book was advertised as giving an impartial, copious account of his career.

Mrs. Willard had become very much interested in the exploration of the far West, in the opening up of Oregon and California, in the Mormons, in the gold rush of '49, and in the ever-increasing number of immigrants who were flooding the country. While on her tour of the United States in 1846, she had heard in St. Louis many unfavorable reports about the Mormons. She was in Nauvoo, Illinois, when the Mormons, in their white-topped prairie schooners, were setting out over a practically unbroken trail for the Western wilderness, and she wrote concerning this, 'Bad as their principles are, and as their lives, conformably to them, have doubtless been — from my soul, I pitied them.'

She was alarmed by the steady influx of foreigners encouraged by Northern industry, and felt that these immigrants, unused to our customs and standards, were largely responsible for the too frequent riots, robberies, and assassinations in New York, Philadelphia, and Baltimore. 'We are,' she wrote, 'in danger of anarchy.'

The writing of 'Late American History' kept her in touch with the happenings at Washington, and her correspondence and interviews with prominent men gave her a great deal of first-hand information. She received valuable information for her 'Late American History' from Senator Thomas H. Benton, and wrote him fully and frankly in January, 1850:

Hon. Thomas H. Benton   Troy, *January 7*, 1850

DEAR SIR: Accept my grateful acknowledgments for your generous favor of four bound volumes, with accompanying maps, charts, etc., and for the still greater favor of your interesting and gratifying letter. Frémont's journal and his trial I read attentively, making a synopsis of their contents while I was collecting materials for my history. The journal of Captain Johnson I shall read in the same manner, when I engage in a revision of the history; then your letter will also be useful to me, as would any further remarks you might find time to make.

You do me the honor to believe (and I will say the justice) that, having formed independent opinions from the facts within my knowledge, I have written them intelligibly, *and have fearlessly published them.* That you, sir, whom all know to possess these characters of mind have thus understood me, gives me a gratification that one, who *is* understood by the world he lives in, knows not how to appreciate. All that I have done in the department of history has been done in the same spirit. May I be allowed to add that, what I have done in other departments, has also been done in the same spirit? I am desirous that you should find a little time to bring down your powerful, clear, and far-seeing mental optics on that theory of the motive powers of the blood's circulation, which is set forth in my pamphlet on 'Respiration,' which I had the honor to forward to you, and which gives hopes of greater security against Asiatic cholera than has been heretofore enjoyed. I drew in patriotism from my mother's breast and on my father's knee; and I recollect being kept awake nights, while I was yet so small a child as to sleep in a little bed beside my parents, by anxious fears lest some great predicted calamity was just about to befall my country; and I never knew the time when the croakers lacked one to predict. . . .

These remarks, though egotistic, are intended to introduce something which I wish to call your attention to; and, for mentioning which, I want you, sir, to give me credit for patriotism, and nothing else. I feel uneasy about the Mormons getting possession of such a central and important part of the country. There is, it seems to me, a spirit of false liberality out, which fails to see the real danger that may accrue from allowing that people to organize a State with their *peculiar institutions;* which from what I have been able to learn concerning them, are far more dangerous than slavery; and I feel

the more on this subject as the progress of the sect involves, as
I have reason to believe, the degradation of my own sex; and,
if of my sex, certainly the deterioration of the whole of society.
Are they to be allowed to set aside, by their laws, the sanctity
of marriage? Are they to have a secret system of religious observances, which shall give their rulers the power to make a
right and wrong, different from the common law of the land,
and that given by God in divine revelation? The time to consider these questions, it seems to me, is now; and I hope the
national legislature will have wisdom given them to act right-
eously and fearlessly. For one thing, I hope they will not allow the poor, mean word *Deseret* to become the name of a
State. . . . The aboriginal name, reckoning by the name given
to the natives, might have been Utah — a far better word. . . .
It appears to me that the men of this nation were at one time
ultra in their notions of liberality in regard to religion, but
have now become sensible of their own error. A nation cannot exist without religion. France tried that, and failed. We
were born a *Protestant Christian* nation, and, *as such*, baptised
in blood. Our position ought to be considered as defined as
that. If we tolerate others, that is enough. We should not
allow them to form governments or exercise political powers
on any other basis. If they want to do this, let them go elsewhere. . . .

Your views concerning the great central railroad I regard
not only as just, but of the utmost importance. But for this
connecting link, which now, in imagination, holds them to
their native land, I think there is great reason to apprehend
that California and Oregon would soon unite and form a
separate nation, which would be unfortunate for us all. . . .
Pardon me, sir, if I grow tedious, and permit me, in closing, to
offer you my best wishes for the coming and future years, and
may the Lord perfect that which concerns you, especially
wherein connected with the destinies of our country!

With great respect, sir, your obedient servant,

EMMA WILLARD

Mrs. Willard was in the galleries of the Senate in 1850
when Henry Clay delivered his famous compromise
speech which temporarily settled the bitter debate over

the extension of slavery in territory newly acquired
from Mexico and over the abolition of slavery in the
District of Columbia. In fact, so intense had been the
feeling in the South, that there had been threats of secession, and in view of this, Mrs. Willard called Clay's
speech 'the crowning action of his useful life.' She summarized the speech for her history, and sending it to Mr.
Clay to learn if he were satisfied with it, received his
reply, 'Perfectly.'

While in Washington at that time, she prepared an
address for the Columbian Association of Teachers,
which was delivered at the Smithsonian Institution and
in which, after discoursing on 'How to Teach' and
'What to Teach,' she voiced her fears of a divided nation. She declared, however, that before the mothers of
the land would allow this to happen they would assemble and plead that the Republic be spared, and
teachers would send their pupils to the Capitol, 'to
stretch forth their little hands and cry, "Oh, leave not
unto us, you, who received from your fathers a rich inheritance, leave not to us only the miserable legacy of
national disgrace, of danger, poverty and death."'

Mrs. Willard had great confidence in the conservatives
in Congress — Clay, Webster, and Crittenden — and
hoped they would be able to hold the country together.
She attended the meeting of the Colonization Society in
Washington, in 1852, when Daniel Webster was asked
to preside in place of Henry Clay, who was critically ill.
She treasured every word of Webster's eulogy of Clay,
and the next morning, when she called on Mr. Clay, she
told him of the praise he had received and of the prayer
for his health. 'Never will the deep expression of Mr.
Clay's countenance be forgotten,' she wrote, 'as he
listened, sitting in his chair, and raising his wasted hand

to hide the rising tears, which soon trickled between his fingers.'

The Compromise of 1850 from which Mrs. Willard had expected so much, was only temporary. Clay and Webster passed away and with them the welding power of the conservatives. With the deepest concern, she watched the progress of her beloved country. She saw her countrymen stirred by the publication of 'Uncle Tom's Cabin,' as nothing else before had stirred them. She read with anxiety reports of the tempestuous debates on the Kansas-Nebraska Bill, of the speeches of Sumner, Seward, and Chase, attacking slavery and accusing the South of a breach of faith. Brooks's assault upon Sumner, the Dred Scott Decision, the ruling of the Supreme Court upholding the Fugitive Slave Law, and John Brown's raid followed, one close upon another. She watched the rise of that uncouth, impelling man from the West, Abraham Lincoln. Like the rest of her countrymen, she eagerly followed his debates with Douglas, sensing the greatness, clearness, and justice of the man. She stood aghast at Seward's prophecy of 'irrepressible conflict,' and read in dismay those dynamic words repeated by Lincoln, 'A house divided against itself cannot stand.'

It seemed to Mrs. Willard as if a vast tidal wave were engulfing her beloved country and that she must stop it. She wrote many letters to prominent statesmen, pleading for peace and for the preservation of the Union. She was sure that the breach could be healed by more wisdom, by more efforts at conciliation. In the presidential campaign of 1860, her sympathies naturally were with the Constitutional Unionists, headed by John Bell and Edward Everett, for, like the men of this party who shrank from conflict, she felt that high-

sounding phrases and good resolutions would still save
the Union. But she was satisfied with the election of
Lincoln. She had confidence in him and confidence that
the Republican Party would not favor abolition and
would uphold the Constitution. Yet, several Southern
States had threatened secession, if Lincoln were elected,
and to avert this, she sent many appeals to the newspapers. Her 'Appeal to South Carolina' was published
in the 'New York Express,' December 19, 1860. In it,
she strayed far from her old-time clarity of reasoning and
made some pitifully weak concessions to slavery. It was
a desperate cry of peace at any price, for she was convinced that her country was falling into the snare that
the reactionaries of Europe had laid for her. She called
attention to the fact that the condition of the negro in
Africa was far below that of American servitude and
explained that it was *servitude* not *slavery*, for as she
expressed it, 'The master owns not the man, but his
time. He has a perpetual servant, not a slave.' As the
negroes were here and incapable of taking care of themselves, the Southerners would be obliged to care for
them, and must then necessarily have the benefit of their
labor. She urged South Carolina not to secede, warning
her that peaceful secession was impossible, as the Union
must be preserved. But on December twentieth, South
Carolina determined to secede.

Next, Mrs. Willard undertook the work of presenting
to Congress a memorial from American women. This
received the approval of many distinguished men, but
Mr. Seward, with whom she had an interview at the
Astor House in New York, January 15, 1861, looked
upon her as an advocate of slavery, and, as she expressed
it in her diary, gave her a severe, insulting rebuke.
Nevertheless, she persevered, indomitable as ever at

seventy-four. She went to Washington in February, hoping she could influence some of the political leaders then holding a peace convention.

She wrote Sarah Willard, her daughter-in-law:

I felt that I *must* come; and I feel that the voice of the women in this crisis will not be unheeded, but will tend to peace. . . . My sister and her sweet daughter are here with me; and my sister has exerted herself to get signatures to my memorial. I have modified it since it was first sent out, as the ultras on both sides objected to it, while some (judicious people, as I think) believe it will do much good by calling attention from mere political considerations to those of right and duty. This change of memorials and other causes made such a delay in the affair of getting signatures at New York that I shall not have as many as I expected from there. But Troy has done and is doing very well, and Philadelphia has already sent me a goodly number, and I am to receive more. The memorials are now circulating in Washington, Baltimore, and other places. . . . In undertaking to do something, though a little, for our beloved country, in this her hour of peril, I find I am but doing what many expected of me.

Finally, the Memorial with its signatures of four thousand ladies was presented to the Senate by Senator Crittenden, of Kentucky, and to the House of Representatives by John A. Gilmer, of North Carolina. 'Our humble petition is,' read the Memorial in part, 'that those to whom, in our feebleness, we look for help, will not allow party or sectional prejudices to prevail over a spirit of mutual conciliation.' In order to have this Women's Memorial presented with perfect propriety, it was accompanied by two paragraphs of commendation by men of all parties, signed by nine men, giving the assurance that they saw nothing unbecoming in such a memorial from American women.

Many friendly, pathetic letters passed between Mr.

and Mrs. Gilmer and Mrs. Willard during the next trying months, and after the fall of Fort Sumter continued for a time, showing how overwhelmed they were by the course of events. 'If I thought that the Northern armies were going to make aggressive war on the South,' wrote Mrs. Willard to Mrs. Gilmer, 'I should feel as unhappy about it as you would. So would the greater part of the Northern people ... and, should any rising of the slaves occur within reach of our troops, confident I am that they would join you to put it down. Did I believe that any opposite course was thought of and would be tolerated at the North, especially against the faithful and respected State of North Carolina, I would not live here. My bones should not be laid to moulder into this soil, but I would make it obligatory on my executor to carry them to North Carolina, and, if you permit, lay them near where you expect to be laid.'

Nevertheless, Mrs. Willard heartily endorsed the North's determination to put down the rebellion. In 1855, when Judge Miller, of Mississippi, had voiced to her the possibility of secession, adding that the South, of course, would take the government and government buildings, she had retorted with vehemence, 'not till you have killed every man, woman, and child north of Mason and Dixon's line; for, when you have finished with the men, you will then have to fight the women and children.' She recalled those words in a letter to her sister Almira, who was in Baltimore when it was forcibly occupied by Northern troops, and when anxiety for the safety of Washington was intense throughout the country. She added that in her opinion the North should firmly hold the sword in one hand and proffer the olive branch with the other. 'Let them show plainly that they have no thought to *conquer* the South by force of

arms,' she wrote, 'but that their *ultimatum* is this — the
Government shall not be illegally broken up.' A few
weeks later, she wrote again to her sister: 'I sympathize
in your divided feelings and in your love for your Maryland friends: but I do rejoice that you are enabled to see
the truth as it is, in our national affairs. . . . My heart is
lifted up as our country rises from the mire of degradation which she was placed in when our Congress was
daily insulted by the traitor-servants who had sworn
to support her, and who were receiving her pay. . . . The
South have some views concerning the North that I
think will be corrected by this war.'

Mrs. Willard was now busy with plans for making
underclothing for the army and aiding the families of
volunteers. After publishing her plans in a Troy paper,
she received a letter from Professor Davies of West
Point saying that her article contained more valuable
suggestions and showed more knowledge of the wants
and claims of the army than anything he had read since
the beginning of the war. She was made president of
the Associate Relief Society of Troy Women which was
organized at the Troy Female Seminary for the purpose of furnishing hospital supplies and assisting 'poor
females' by giving them employment.

She could not refrain at this time from writing President Lincoln, whom she felt needed support and encouragement during these trying days. She sent this
letter:

TROY, October 5, 1861

To Abraham Lincoln
  President of the United States of America

DEAR SIR: Presuming that I am known to you as a writer of
my country's history, and having just heard that the great
cares which weigh upon you begin to tell upon your physical

health, I determined to write to you my high approval of your general course and leading measures, and the judgment I entertain that, if your soundness of mind and body continue, so that you can weigh these great matters as you have done, and, with the same calmness and steadiness, pursue and cause to be carried out the great measures you have decreed, success will, by the aid of Him in whom you have trusted, finally crown the efforts headed by you, and that your name will go down to posterity near to that of Washington. If, as I believe, your acts have been characterized by that boldness and moderation combined which the circumstances of the times demanded and warranted — they being more trying than any President of the republic has heretofore encountered — this will certainly be the case.

When a great man's heart is encouraged, he is strengthened; and, in the view here taken of your position, your health is shown to be of great importance to your country.

With profound respect,

EMMA WILLARD

Mrs. Ellet, who had become famous for her books, 'Women of the Revolution' and 'Pioneer Women of the West,' came to Troy to see Mrs. Willard with a message from the ladies of New York asking what they could do for peace. Peace was still foremost in Mrs. Willard's mind, and while she was busy with her work for the soldiers, she was at the same time evolving a plan. She had written Mrs. Gilmer in the spring of 1861, 'Who knows but the women may yet contrive some way of peace, for we love one another South and North, and Christian women will watch for opportunities to make peace, and pray that peace and righteousness may prevail.'

In May, 1862, Mrs. Willard published her 'Via Media,' which she hoped would be the means of bringing the North and the South together. It was her solution for the problem of slavery which had so far baffled

all the statesmen of the country. Its full title read, 'The
African in America: To Find His True Position and
Place Him in It, the *Via Media* on Which the North
and the South Might Meet in a Permanent and Happy
Settlement.'

She began her treatise by stating definitely that political equality for the negro race would be a menace to the
country, that only educated white men should be given
political power. Assuming that God had intended to
rank the negroes as servants and had marked them for
this province by their color, she suggested 'regulated
servitude.' As God had sanctioned the servants' place
in the family by the Ten Commandments, she believed
He might possibly have had it in mind to create a race
to serve the white women, and add strength to their
physical weakness. Experience had shown that Liberia
had not proved to be the solution for the slavery problem, that neither free negroes nor slaves were willing to
migrate, and four million negroes were in America and
must be dealt with intelligently and justly. Since the
negroes who had been freed had not been able to get
along in this country and most of them had ended in the
gutter, she felt that they needed the supervision of a
master and that for this supervision the master was
entitled to their services. However, the rights of the
black man must be respected, the slave market must be
abolished, and families must not be cruelly separated.
If a master found an unusually talented negro in his
service, he should encourage his aspirations for freedom
and help him get to Liberia where the best negroes were
needed. That this change could be brought about by a
tribunal of the best American statesmen, Mrs. Willard
was confident.

Since the war had placed a large number of Southern

slaves in the hands of the government, she felt that the North should look upon them as their responsibility. She suggested that the President and Congress appoint commissioners to deal with them and recommended that Northern families take one or two of them into their homes. Then after ten or fifteen years of service when they would be fitted to go to Liberia, their employers would be bound to send them. Or, if they did not wish to go to Liberia and preferred to stay in service during their lifetime, laws should be made to regulate this servitude. Such a solution of the negro problem would also solve the servant problem for the Northern housewife and in many cases would avert death and invalidism for the conscientious, over-worked woman.

In spite of all the hopes that Mrs. Willard entertained for the conciliatory powers of 'Via Media,' it could not stay the onrush of events. In some quarters, it received the highest praise, in others the severest condemnation. 'My pamphlet has already procured for me,' wrote Mrs. Willard to a friend, 'some of the highest compliments I have ever received (you must not mention if I tell you that Colonel Gardner says it will give me the credit of "profound statesmanship"; and, what is better, he gives as his opinion that I had laid down principles on which the difficulties between the North and the South will ultimately be settled, though not yet).'

A long, appreciative letter from General McClellan assured her that the views set forth in 'Via Media' were identical with his own, and that had the power been placed in his hands, he would have tried to establish such a system as she advocated.

Her nephew, John Willard, however, in a letter acknowledging the receipt of 'Via Media' told her plainly but kindly that the time for the adoption of such a plan

was long past and that the only thing left was to continue the war to the bitter end. To press 'Via Media' on
the country at this time, he felt, would do more harm
than good. John Willard's opinion was one to be respected, for he had progressed far since those days when
as a young student he had lived with Aunt Willard in
Middlebury. As Judge of the Supreme Court of New
York, member of the Court of Appeals, and State
Senator, he had gained a national reputation for ability,
integrity, and justice.

After giving 'Via Media' to the country, Mrs. Willard
published nothing relating to the war except her 'National Hymn,' which was included in a book edited by
Mrs. Phelps for the benefit of the United States Christian and Sanitary Commission. In this book entitled
'Our Country — In Its Relation to the Past, Present,
and Future, A National Book Consisting in Original
Articles in Prose and Verse Contributed by American
Writers,' Mrs. Willard poured forth her patriotic sentiments in the following verses:

> God save America!
> God grant our standard may
>   Where e'er it wave;
> Follow the just and right
> Foremost be in the fight,
> And glorious still in might
>   Our own to save.
>
> CHORUS — Father Almighty!
>   Humbly, we crave,
>   Save thou America,
>   Our country save.
>
> God keep America!
> Of Nations great and free
>   Man's noblest friend:

Still with the ocean bound
Our continent around,
Each State in place be found,
    Till time shall end.
CHORUS —

God bless America!
As in our Father's day,
    So evermore.
God grant all discords cease,
Kind brotherhood's increase,
And truth and love breathe peace
    From shore to shore.
CHORUS —

CHAPTER XXVI

IN THE SHADOW OF THE SEMINARY

'GOD save America' was Mrs. Willard's continual prayer throughout the war. This frightful carnage in her beloved country was almost more than she could bear. She watched the steady progress of General Grant's troops in the West, grateful that the cause of the Union was being upheld; yet at the same time, she grieved over the plight of her Southern friends. Warfare seemed very near in July, 1864, when the train on which she was traveling homeward from Baltimore was seized by Confederate soldiers. The 'Troy Daily Times,' July 13, 1864, described her capture as follows:

Mrs. Emma Willard taken prisoner by the rebels. — A dispatch received this morning from Mrs. Phelps, at Baltimore, states that Mrs. E. Willard, of this city, was among the passengers on the train from Baltimore to Philadelphia, which was captured by the rebels when Major-General Franklin was taken prisoner. Nothing since then has been heard of Mrs. Willard, but no fears are entertained by her friends here of personal harm — although it may be possible that she has suffered in loss of property. Mrs. Willard's authorship of several valuable standard works, and her association with the Troy Female Seminary, have given her a wide-spread reputation. Her numerous friends here and elsewhere, will await further tidings with great interest. Mrs. Willard left the city a few days ago for Baltimore and Washington and was on her return when this unfortunate incident occurred. Her capture by the rebels was hardly one of the calculations of the journey.

On July 19, 1864, the paper commented further:

The adventures of our townswoman, Mrs. Willard, on the Gunpowder bridge railroad train captured by the 'rebs' were quite romantic. — Mrs. Willard took the precaution to place all her valuables in her pocket, as soon as she realized the situation, but she does not think the raiders would have robbed the lady passengers. Before Mrs. Willard could leave the car, the forward part of the train was on fire. As she was stepping to the ground, Major Harry Gilmor approached the high platform and asked the privilege of assisting Mrs. Willard to the ground.

Although Mrs. Willard's captors treated her with consideration and she was not robbed nor harmed, it was all very frightening and exhausting as well, as she was obliged to walk some distance in the hot sun to find a boat to take her North.

With the horrors of war all about her, Mrs. Willard pondered more and more on the subject of peace, resolving to dedicate the remainder of her life to that cause. Peace, however, was no new interest, for even in 1820, when hard at work establishing her female seminary, she had published a peace plan under the title, 'Universal Peace to Be Introduced by a Confederacy of Nations, meeting at Jerusalem.' During these past years, her attention had been attracted by Elihu Burritt's work for peace, by his League of Universal Brotherhood, and by the yearly Peace Congress held in Europe. Now, she craved a talk with him, and while on a visit in Farmington, determined to meet him. They had met years before, and in fact, were related through her mother's side of the family. Since the outbreak of the war, Elihu Burritt had devoted himself to farming, and lived near the home of Mrs. Willard's niece, Harriet Hart Dickinson. So one spring day Mrs. Willard drove from Farmington to West Hartford to pay Harriet a visit, and almost immediately asked if it would be possible for her to see Mr. Burritt. As Harriet had happened to see him pass earlier in the day on the way to his hayfield, she watched for his return and stopped him

MADAME EMMA WILLARD

to tell him that Mrs. Willard wished to talk with him. Elihu Burritt, embarrassed by his appearance, protested that he could not come in to see her in his working clothes. In a short time, however, he returned very much dressed up, with gray gloves and all the accessories essential for a proper call. Then he and Mrs. Willard became engrossed in a discussion of peace plans, and Mrs. Willard resolved to go to Europe again, this time to work for the cause of peace. •

And while this was going on, Harriet's small daughter, Emma, watched proceedings from afar, very much awed as usual by the presence of Aunt Willard. For although Aunt Willard was always kind and smiling, her young namesake dreaded her visits, fearing that she could never satisfy such a model of perfection. She much preferred to gaze at the handsome photograph of Aunt Willard, which always stood on the mantel.

Although Mrs. Willard was not able to go to Europe to promote peace because of the objections of her family, she continued to ponder on the subject and published another peace plan similar to the one she evolved in 1820. This, she called 'Universal Peace,' and it was included in 'Our Country,' the book edited by her sister, Mrs. Phelps, in 1864. Again, she suggested that the nations of the world form a permanent judicial tribunal to which by mutual consent, their disputes be referred, and again she chose Jerusalem as the seat of this tribunal. Such an organization, she explained, was much more possible now than in 1820 when she had previously proposed it because of the wonderful inventions, ocean steamers, and the telegraph. Delegates to the Permanent Peace Council could reside in Jerusalem for a term of years and might easily be accompanied by their families. She had chosen Jerusalem because of Bible

prophecies and because the choice of any other city
would arouse national jealousies. Although the Holy
Land was now in the possession of the Turks, England
and France, who had influence with Turkey, might
arrange to buy it. The Rothschilds, she felt sure, would
gladly furnish the money for the cause of universal
peace and could build a railroad to the coast and do
whatever was necessary to prepare for a meeting of the
Council. France, England, Russia, and America should
inaugurate this Council of Peace and then when delegates from all the nations assembled, they should prepare a code of international laws which would bind all
nations. The Gentiles of the world should then aid the
Jews to return to Jerusalem and thus fulfill Bible prophecy. Had this council been in existence before the Civil
War, contended Mrs. Willard, the South could have laid
her complaints before it and bloodshed might have been
averted. Even in 1820 and 1864 a woman was looking
forward to a league of nations.

Not only was Mrs. Willard at the age of seventy-
seven, planning for peace; she was also preparing to
write a history of the Civil War. Mrs. Phelps discouraged both of these projects, but although Mrs. Willard
gave up the trip to Europe which she hoped to take in
the interest of peace, she was determined to continue her
writing. She wrote Mrs. Phelps:

Now as I have ceded to your wishes so far as to delay, if not
wholly to abandon, my project of going to England, I hope
you will think I am good, and behave *yourself* accordingly.
But, since it would be a pity, after the steam is up, and the
engine all ready to move forward for grand objects, to let it
puff off, and no use be made of it, I am thinking this morning
that I will try whether it will not be available to move my
mind to write here, in this heavy atmosphere of unfaith, a
work to be published in New York, and perhaps simultane-

ously in London, made such a one as I would write in undisturbed retirement in England, where if I had had nothing to encourage me, I should at least have had no disheartening unbelief to contend with. One form of this unbelief is the impression, so clearly conveyed in this letter of yours, that, through age, I have lost my power. In England the prime minister, Lord Palmerston, is several years older than I. My health is better than it was last year, when I wrote, at your house, my 'Via Media.' I have this past winter been reading the London Times. These things I say to encourage you to feel that, if I do write, I shall not write ignorantly. For the last ten years I have been devoted to American history. I believe that, when the part I have taken to make peace is known, I should find more favor in England than even Mr. Seward or Mrs. Beecher Stowe. You may think my views are visionary. Perhaps they are, and perhaps they are not. But one thing is certain — I have had experience and observation of national affairs through a long course of years, and I am warranted in saying, not a mere sandy soil, where the miners, when its contents were thrown out found nothing but dirt, but occasionally a lump, larger or smaller, of some precious metal. One of these hammered out, became the Troy Female Seminary, another the *theory of circulation.* Now, some of these lumps I still have by me, and I think the most important duty which remains to me is to work them out, and forge them so that they may not be allowed to perish.'

When the war was over and the work of reconstruction had begun, Mrs. Willard was hard at work bringing her American History for schools up to date. Her publisher had many calls for school histories, especially from the South, as most of the textbooks offended Southern educators, and her books were in demand.

As she was writing, she was watching the work of reconstruction and as usual was drawing her own conclusions. These she confided to her nephew, General John Wolcott Phelps, whose military career she had followed with great interest. She was proud of his Civil War record in the lower Mississippi Valley and respected his independent opinions even if she did not always agree with them. She often thought of his differences with the authorities at Washington when, after the occupation of New Orleans, he organized negro troops, the training of which aroused such animosity throughout the South, that he received orders from Washington to disband them, and in consequence resigned, taking no further part in the war. One of her letters to him read:

... In her last letter to me Stella speaks of my being so hopeful about the country. I was once — but am sorry to say I cannot find it in my heart to be so now. I pretty much agreed with you in all you said in your letter. When Andrew Johnson first began his administration I had hopes he would improve matters. I never thought of undertaking to make things equal, which the Lord made unequal, and I wrote a letter to Mr. J—— suggesting to him the satisfaction it might give, if he would build up Negrodom by sending to Liberia an Embassador and Minister Plenipotentiary, who should also be an American agent for that country and we obtain the right to send members to a congress there, our negroes choosing they who would then be persuaded to go. Now if Mr. J—— would have heard to this — I had other plans ahead. You, whom I think the Lord has made for some extraordinary thing — I designed should have been this Envoy and Agent — and the likeliest negro in America, Fred Douglas, the Secretary of the Legation. Now see how well my plans tally with yours, as expressed in your letter to me. — If the Lord had seen fit in his Providence, to have us two to arrange the affairs of the nation just at this particular time — that would have been done which now there is no hope of. But as changes for the worse have been, we can but hope that hereafter there may be changes for the better. ...

During these years, Mrs. Willard received considerable notice in books and magazines. A long article, 'Educational Services of Mrs. Emma Willard' by Professor Henry Fowler of Rochester University appeared in the 'American Journal of Education' and later was included in a book entitled 'Memoirs of Teachers, Educators, and Promoters and Benefactors of Education, Literature, and Science.' Mrs. Willard was the only woman represented in this volume and took her place with Ezekiel Cheever, Caleb Bingham, William C. Woodbridge, Horace Mann, and Timothy Dwight of Yale. She furnished Professor Fowler with a great deal of the material for this article and spent many happy hours reliving her struggles and conquests. She also sent reminiscences of her life and work at Middlebury to Samuel Swift at his request for his 'History of the Town of Middlebury.'

When Hollister's 'History of Connecticut' was published, she was proud to find his comment, 'Mrs. Sigourney, Mrs. Ann S. Stephens, and Mrs. Emma Willard are among the most gifted and eminent writers of our country.' She presented a copy of this book to her sister Almira, inscribing on the fly-leaf this poem so filled with memories of her girlhood:

> Almira, youngest born, and sole to me
> Remaining of *my* father's house and thine,
> This history I give thee of that State
> Where the dear mansion of our infancy
> Reared its colonial front and simple form
> Near meeting roads, and in a pleasant vale.
> Orchards were near, nor far the murmuring brook.
> Fond recollection peoples all the scene!
> Father! I see thee! calm — with dignity
> That speaks of high communings, and of deep
> Affections overmastered — cheerful made
> By wit and warm benevolence. With thee
> Is she thine eye sought ever as thy foot
> Crossed the domestic threshold — Mother, dear!
> How many virtues light that blessed face!

Sister! we boast an honest ancestry
Of parents nobly virtuous, reared in thee,
Connecticut! whose earliest sires were ours.
Her annals read thou, then, with this poor verse;
For who but thee of all that loved abode
Is left, to feel and understand with me?
Soon will there be a sole surviving One!
By nature 'tis thy lot; nor be the doom
Reversed. *Christ* has prepared a better home.

Mrs. Elizabeth Ellet, who in her books was giving women a place in the historical records of the country, mentioned both Mrs. Phelps and Mrs. Willard in 'The Queens of American Society.' She described the 'splendid reception' given by Mrs. Phelps in 1858 at her home in Eutaw Place, Baltimore, to the members and guests of the American Association for the Advancement of Science. 'Mrs. Phelps,' she wrote, 'has for ten years contributed to the enjoyment of Baltimore society. Her literary and educational celebrity is as extensive as the country. She is the sister of Mrs. Willard, whose social influence in Troy was as much acknowledged as her fame as a teacher and author.'

In 'Eminent Women of the Age, Being Narratives of the Lives and Deeds of the Most Prominent Women of the Present Generation,' a compilation of biographical sketches by James Parton, Horace Greeley, Thomas Wentworth Higginson, Elizabeth Cady Stanton, and others, Mrs. Willard was given an important place under the section, 'Our Pioneer Educators.' The sketch of her life and work was written by the Reverend Mr. E. B. Huntington, and was supplemented by an excellent engraving.

To be acknowledged a famous, useful woman was the fulfillment of all of Mrs. Willard's dreams. As she let her mind travel back to her childhood days and then on through the years, she had much to be proud of. It was real joy now in these less active days, to live her life over again in memory. Emma and Almira, the two Hart sisters from the little town of Berlin, Connecticut, had won national prominence. They now returned to Berlin together, driving to the site of their old home. A new house had been built a little to the south, but the same well was there and they asked for water, wishing to drink once more from the well that had refreshed them in childhood. Realizing the interest which her birthplace would have for future generations, Mrs. Willard left a framed engraving with the owner of the house, asking that it always remain there, and it may be found there to-day.

Mrs. Willard still made her home in the little red brick house on the Seminary grounds. She had found a most congenial companion and secretary in Mrs. Celia Burr, and they lived happily together in spite of Mrs. Burr's decided leanings toward woman's rights and other liberal movements of the day. When Mrs. Burr left Mrs. Willard in 1865 to marry William H. Burleigh, well known in anti-slavery circles, Sarah Willard, a granddaughter, took charge of Mrs. Willard's household. Another young relative, a nephew, William Hart, also made his home with them. William Hart had come to prepare for Yale, as Aunt Willard insisted she could teach him as well as any one, but instead of going to Yale, William helped John Willard with the management of the Seminary, and later went into business in Troy. He lived with Aunt Willard for many years, even after his marriage, because she insisted, and two of his children were born in her home.

His little daughter, Helen, and Mrs. Willard were

great friends. Helen remembered her as 'an adorable, kindly, kissable, beautiful old lady.' She loved to run up to Aunt Willard's chair, stand on tiptoe, and kiss her behind the ear. At lunch time when Katie, the maid, appeared with Helen's tray, she would be hidden securely under Aunt Willard's big black silk apron, and Katie, hunting for her diligently high and low, would finally take off the sugar-bowl cover and look within. At this, Helen, with a burst of laughter, would run out from under the apron, to the great delight of all three.

Helen always thought of Aunt Willard in a black silk dress with a full skirt, a tight-fitting basque, and a fluffy tulle fichu, in a white cap which set off her six little gray curls. She was a very important, busy great-aunt, always writing or reading, or receiving callers, often starting off on a journey to Baltimore or New York, or driving off for an afternoon behind two prancing horses.

No soirée or dancing class at the Seminary was complete without Madame Willard. Enthroned in a big armchair, she sat at the foot of the stairs, and the girls coming down two by two curtsied as they passed her. She was revered and loved by the girls, and still attended their lectures and the annual examination. She grew more affectionate, gentle, and tolerant as the years went by, and was as cheerful, companionable, and witty now as she had been at forty. Her interest in public affairs never waned, and she read about them and discussed them as she had always done. There was always a new book on her table, and beside it the latest newspapers and magazines. Nothing gave her more pleasure than to gather her family about her on Sunday evenings and hear them repeat passages from the Bible, for the Bible to her was still the Book of books. She had studied

Greek and Hebrew after she was fifty in order to read it in the original.

When finally she moved from the little red brick house to the Seminary building where she could be nearer her son and his family, she occupied a study and bedroom on the first floor. She spent hours in the study in a big chair in front of a table desk. Here, in the heart of the thriving institution which she had founded, she wrote, planned, and thought over the past, conscious always of the orderly activities of her Seminary, hearing hourly the light footsteps of her beloved girls as they hurried to their classes. She was now in her eighty-third year, but with the years, she had lost none of her interest in life and looked forward to the future with peace and confidence. She still found great satisfaction in keeping her journal, recording punctiliously her estimate of Sunday sermons and every book that she read. In January, 1870, she began reading Liddon's 'Bampton Lectures.' The last entry in her journal was written April sixth. On April eighth, she received a call from General Sherman, who had come to Troy to attend the funeral of General Thomas. A week later, the newspapers reported her death.

If at times she had failed to receive full appreciation for her labors, it was not lacking now. Praise poured in from all parts of the world, from prominent men and women. Newspapers and magazines told of her work and of the great contribution she had made toward the education of women. The Legislature of New York, that body which had so persistently refused to endorse or carry out her recommendations for State-endowed seminaries for the higher education of women, now unanimously passed resolutions expressing appreciation of her life. She was called the pioneer in the cause of

woman's education, 'with a reputation in the world of
science as wide as the universe.'

During those last years, as Mrs. Willard had sat in
her big armchair reflecting on the past and future progress of her sex, she had seen with satisfaction and a glow
of happiness the unprecedented steps which were being
taken in woman's education. Vassar Female College
had been founded near by in Poughkeepsie in 1861 by
a far-seeing man who said, 'It occurred to me that
woman, having received from her Creator the same intellectual constitution as man, has the same right as
man to intellectual culture and development.' Four
years later, Vassar Female College, the first fully endowed institution in the world for the education of
women, had opened its doors, and in accordance with
the wishes of the founder, women had taken their place
with men on the faculty. It seems incredible that such
events could have transpired without letters of comment or encouragement from Mrs. Willard, but none
have been found, and as most of Matthew Vassar's correspondence was sold by a nephew to a ragman, it is
highly probable that Emma Willard's comments on
Vassar College were lost in that way.

But Vassar College was not the only institution for
the higher education of women which had sprung up.
Wesleyan Female College, Elmira College, Mary Sharp
College, and other colleges through the West and South
had been founded for women, and while their standards
were probably not as high as those of Vassar College,
they were assuredly bringing the higher education of
women to the fore. Antioch College in Ohio under the
guidance of Horace Mann, and in the Far West, Iowa
State University and the University of Utah had been
opened as coeducational institutions. These were all

possible because the Troy Female Seminary had proved that women were capable of pursuing higher studies and were unharmed by them.

This increased interest in woman's education was but one of the many signs of progress that had brightened Mrs. Willard's last days. Woman's sphere was very rapidly being enlarged. The war had made it necessary for women to take the place of men in teaching, in business, in industry, and on the farm. Even in the field hospitals women had made a place for themselves, and had brought with them order, cleanliness, and comfort. This had been Clara Barton's contribution, while Dr. Mary Walker, the first woman to be made assistant army surgeon, had been awarded a medal of honor by Congress for her bravery and services during the war.

Mrs. Willard had seen the fulfillment of her prophecy made in 1819 that educated women would render their country a great service, and as she thought of this, contrasting the past with the present, she knew that she had not lived in vain. She knew that because of her efforts the advancement of woman had been possible. She glimpsed only faintly what the future would bring, but she knew that women had seen the vision, and would now march courageously on.

THE END

BIBLIOGRAPHY

EMMA WILLARD'S WRITINGS

Abridged History of the United States; or Republic of America. Philadelphia, Barnes & Co., 1843.

Address to the Columbian Association of Teachers, in *Patapsco Young Ladies' Magazine*, 1850.

Advancement of Female Education, or a Series of Addresses in Favor of Establishing at Athens, in Greece, a Female Seminary, Especially Designed to Instruct Female Teachers. Troy, New York, N. Tuttle, 1833.

An Address to the Public; Particularly to the Members of the Legislature of New York, Proposing a Plan for Improving Female Education. Middlebury, Vermont, J. W. Copeland, 1819.

An Address to the Pupils of Washington Seminary. Pittsburgh, 1844.

An Appeal against Wrong and Injury. New York, A. S. Barnes & Co., 1847.

Ancient Geography, as Connected with Chronology and Preparatory to the Study of Ancient History; Accompanied with an Atlas. Hartford, Connecticut, O. D. Cooke, 1829.

Answer to Marcius Willson's Reply, or Second Appeal to the Public. New York, A. S. Barnes & Co., 1847.

Fulfillment of a Promise, by Which Poems by Emma Willard are Published, and Affectionately Inscribed to Her Past and Present Pupils. New York, White, Gallaher & White, 1831.

God Save America, in *Our Country*, edited by Mrs. Phelps. Baltimore, John D. Toy, 1864.

Guide to the Temple of Time and Universal History for Schools. New York, A. S. Barnes & Co., 1850.

History of the United States, or Republic of America. New York, White, Gallaher & White, 1829.

Same, Revised. Philadelphia, Barnes & Co., 1843.

Journal and Letters from France and Great Britain. Troy, New York, N. Tuttle, 1833.

Last Leaves of American History; Comprising Histories of the

Mexican War and California. New York, G. P. Putnam, 1849.

Last Periods of Universal History. New York, A. S. Barnes & Co., 1855.

Late American History; Containing a Full Account of the Courage, Conduct, and Success of John C. Frémont, by Which, through Many Hardships and Sufferings He Became the Explorer and Hero of California. New York, A. S. Barnes & Co., 1856.

Letter, Addressed as a Circular to the Members of the Willard Association of Female Teachers; Formed at the Troy Female Seminary, July, 1837. Troy, New York, Gates, 1838.

Letter to Dupont de l'Eure on the Political Position of Women. Albany, New York, Joel Munsell, 1848.

Memorial Relative to Female Education, in New York State Assembly Document 74, 1852.

Memorial to the Senate and House of Representatives of the United States of America in Congress Assembled. Washington, 1861.

Morals for the Young, or Good Principles Instilling Wisdom. New York, A. S. Barnes & Co., 1857.

Ocean Hymn. 1831.

Respiration, and Its Effects: Most Especially in Relation to Asiatic Cholera and Other Sinking Diseases. New York, Huntington & Savage, 1849.

A System of Universal History in Perspective. Hartford, Connecticut, Huntington, 1835.

Same, Revised. Philadelphia, Barnes & Co., 1844.

Treatise on the Motive Powers Which Produce the Circulation of the Blood. New York, Wiley & Putnam, 1844; London, Wiley & Putnam, 1846.

Universal History in Perspective. New York, Barnes & Burr, 1859.

Universal Peace, in *Our Country*, edited by Mrs. Phelps. Baltimore, John D. Toy, 1864.

Via Media: a Peaceful and Permanent Settlement of the Slavery Question. Washington, C. H. Anderson, 1862.

Willard's Historic Guide to the Temple of Time and Universal History for Schools. New York, A. S. Barnes & Co., and H. W. Derby & Co., 1849.

GENERAL

American Journal of Education. Edited by Henry Barnard, Hartford, Connecticut.

American Ladies' Magazine. Edited by Sarah J. Hale, Boston, 1828–36.

American Quarterly Review. Containing a review of 'Journal and Letters from France and Great Britain,' by Emma Willard, Philadelphia, March, 1834.

Andrews, Alfred: History of Deacon Stephen Hart and His Descendants. Hartford, Connecticut, Case, Lockwood & Brainerd Co., 1875.

Ballard, Harlan H.: Amos Eaton, in Berkshire Historical and Scientific Society Collections, Pittsfield, Massachusetts, 1897.

Barnard, Henry, editor: Memoirs of Teachers, Educators and Promoters and Benefactors of Education, Literature, and Science. New York, F. C. Brownell, 1859.

Beecher, Catherine: Suggestions Respecting Improvements in Education. Hartford, Connecticut, Packard, 1829.

Blandin, Mrs. J. M. E.: History of Higher Education of Women in the South Prior to 1860. New York, Neale Publishing Company, 1909.

Brainerd, Ezra: Life and Work in Middlebury, Vermont, of Emma Willard. New York, Evening Post Job Printing House, 1893.

Camp, David N.: History of New Britain, with Sketches of Farmington and Berlin, Connecticut, 1640–1889. New Britain, Connecticut, Wm. B. Thomas & Co., 1889.

Catt, Carrie Chapman, and Nettie Rogers Shuler: Woman Suffrage and Politics. New York, Chas. Scribner's Sons, 1923.

Coit, Rev. Thomas Winthrop: A Sermon in Reference to the Death of Mrs. Emma Willard. Troy, New York, W. H. Young & Blake, 1870.

Connecticut Common School Journal. Edited by Henry Barnard, New Britain, Connecticut.

Cubberley, Ellwood P.: Public Education in the United States. Boston, Houghton Mifflin Company, 1919.

Davis, Emerson: Historical Sketch of Westfield. Westfield, Massachusetts, J. Root, 1826.

Ellet, Mrs. Elizabeth F.: The Queens of American Society. New York, Scribner & Co., 1867.

Emma Willard Association Reports, 1892–93.

Everest, Charles W.: The Poets of Connecticut. Hartford, Connecticut, T. & B. Case, 1843.

Fairbanks, Mrs. A. W., editor: Emma Willard and Her Pupils, or Fifty Years of the Troy Female Seminary, 1822–72. New York, Mrs. Russell Sage, 1898.

Fitzpatrick, Edward A.: The Educational Views and Influence of De Witt Clinton. New York, Columbia University, Teachers College Contributions to Education, 1911.

Foster, John: A Sketch of the Tour of General La Fayette on His Late Visit to the United States, 1824. Portland, Maine, A. W. Thayer, 1824.

Fowler, Henry: Educational Services of Mrs. Emma Willard. Reprint from the *American Journal of Education*, 1859.

A Friend to Suffering Humanity. Mrs. Willard Reviewed, or a Short Examination of the Proceedings of 'The Society for the Advancement of Female Education in Greece.' Albany, New York, 1833.

Galpin, Ruth: Mrs. Almira Hart Lincoln Phelps, 1914.

Gibbs, Dorothy Day: Bibliography of Emma H. Willard. In Card Catalogue, New York State Library, Albany, New York, 1920.

Gilchrist, Beth B.: The Life of Mary Lyon. Boston, Houghton Mifflin Company, 1910.

Goddard, A. A., compiler: Trojan Sketch Book. Troy, New York, Young & Hartt, 1846.

Goodsell, Willystine: The Education of Women; Its Social Background and Its Problems. New York, The Macmillan Company, 1923.

Hale, Mrs. Sarah J.: Woman's Record; or Sketches of All Distinguished Women from the Beginning till 1850. New York, Harper & Bros., 1853.

Hart, James Morrison: Genealogical History of Samuel Hart. Concord, New Hampshire, Rumford Printing Company, 1903.

Hayner, Rutherford: Troy and Rensselaer County, New York. New York, Lewis Historical Publishing Company, 1925.

Hemenway, Abby M.: Vermont Historical Gazetteer. Burlington, Vermont, 1867.

Holden, James Austin: Emma Willard: A Sketch and a Letter. New York, Educational Review Publishing Company, 1916.

Hollister, G. H.: The History of Connecticut from the First Settlement of the Colony. Hartford, Connecticut, Case, Tiffany & Co., 1857.

Howard, Cecil H. C.: Life and Public Services of General John Wolcott Phelps. Brattleboro, Vermont, F. E. Housh & Co., 1887.

Hughes, James L.: Henry Barnard, the Nestor of American Education. Reprint from the *New England Magazine*, July, 1896.

Hunt, Gaillard: Life in America One Hundred Years Ago. New York, Harper & Bros., 1914.

Johnson, Clifton: The Country School. New York, Thomas Y. Crowell & Co., 1907.

Levasseur, A.: Lafayette in America in 1824 and 1825, or Journal of a Voyage to the United States. Translated by John D. Godman, Philadelphia, Carey & Lea, 1829.

Linford, Madeline: Mary Wollstonecraft. London, Leonard Parsons, Ltd., 1924.

Lockwood, J. H.: Westfield and Its Historic Influences. Springfield, Massachusetts, 1922.

Lord, John: The Life of Emma Willard. New York, D. Appleton & Co., 1873.

Lossing, B. J.: Vassar College and Its Founder. New York, C. A. Alvord, 1867.

Mayo, A. D.: Henry Barnard. Washington, United States Bureau of Education Report, 1898.

Merrill, Thomas Abbott: Semi-Centennial Sermon, Containing a History of Middlebury, Delivered December 3, 1840. Middlebury, Vermont, E. Maxham, 1841.

Necker de Saussure, Madame Albertine: Progressive Education Commencing with the Infant. Translated from the French, with Notes and an Appendix, by Mrs. Willard and Mrs. Phelps. Boston, W. D. Ticknor, 1835.

North, Catharine M.: History of Berlin, Connecticut. New Haven, Connecticut, The Tuttle, Morehouse, Taylor Company, 1916.

Northend, Charles: Elihu Burritt: A Memorial Volume Containing a Sketch of His Life and Labors. New York, D. Appleton & Co., 1879.

An Officer in the Late Army: A Complete History of the Marquis de La Fayette, Major General in the Army of the United States of America in the War of the Revolution, embracing an Account of his late Tour through the United States to the Time of his Departure, September, 1825. Hartford, Connecticut, S. Andrus & Son, 1848.

Parton, James, and others: Eminent Women of the Age. Hartford, Connecticut, S. M. Betts & Co., 1869.

Phelps, Mrs. A. H. L.: Caroline Westerly. New York, J. & J. Harper, 1833.

—— Familiar Lectures on Botany. Hartford, Connecticut, H. & F. J. Huntington, 1829.

—— The Female Student. New York, Leavitt, Lord & Co., 1836.

—— Genealogical Sketch of the Hart and Hooker Families, in the *New York Genealogical and Biographical Record*, Vol. XV, 1884.

—— Reviews, and Essays on Art, Literature, and Science. Philadelphia, Claxton, Remsen & Haffelfinger, 1873.

Phelps, Mrs. A. H. L., editor: Our Country in Its Relation to the Past, Present, and Future. Baltimore, John D. Toy, 1864.

—— Letter to a Son on Christian Belief, by Samuel Hart, Baltimore, 1875.

Ricketts, P. C.: History of the Rensselaer Polytechnic Institute, 1824–94. New York, Wiley & Sons, 1895.

St. James Magazine, containing 'Recollections of School Days in an American Seminary.' London, Kent & Co., 1874–75.

Stanton, Theodore, and Harriet S. Blatch, editors: Elizabeth Cady Stanton, as Revealed in Her Letters, Diary, and Reminiscences. New York, Harper & Bros., 1922.

Swift, Samuel: History of the Town of Middlebury. Middlebury, Vermont, A. H. Copeland, 1859.

—— Vermont Register and Almanac. Middlebury, Vermont, Swift & Chipman, 1811; Samuel Swift, 1812.

Taylor, James Monroe: Before Vassar Opened: a Contribution to the History of the Higher Education of Women in America. Boston, Houghton Mifflin Company, 1914.

—— and Elizabeth H. Haight: Vassar. New York, Oxford University Press, 1915.

Troy Female Seminary Catalogues, 1822–71.

Trumbull, James H., editor: Memorial History of Hartford County, Connecticut, 1633–1884. Boston, E. L. Osgood, 1846.

Vanderpoel, E. N., compiler: Chronicles of a Pioneer School from 1792–1833, Being the History of Miss Sarah Pierce and of Her Litchfield School. Edited by Elizabeth C. B. Buel. Cambridge University Press, 1903.

Waterford Academy Announcement.

Weise, A. J.: History of the City of Troy from the Expulsion of the Indians to 1876. Troy, New York, Young, 1876.

—— Troy's One Hundred Years. Troy, New York, Young, 1891.

Willard, Mrs. John H.: Memorial of the Late Mrs. Emma Willard, in Proceedings of the Seventh Anniversary of the University Convocation of the State of New York. Albany, New York, The Argus Company, 1871.

—— Sketch of the History of the Troy Female Seminary, in Proceedings of the Thirteenth Anniversary of the University Convocation of the State of New York. Albany, The Argus Company, 1876.

Willson, Marcius: Reply to Mrs. Willard's Appeal. New York, Mark H. Newman & Co., 1847.

INDEX

Adams, John, 14, 66–67.
Adams, John Quincy, 100.
Advancement of Female Education, 177, 235.
American Association for the Advancement of Science, 237.
American Colonization Society, 243, 248.
American Journal of Education, 218, 265.
American Ladies' Magazine, 122, 178, 179, 192, 193, 200.
American Literary Magazine, 233.
American Quarterly Review, 179.
American Revolution, 4–6, 15, 48, 102, 124, 126, 185.
Andrews, Reverend, 216.
Anthony, Susan B., 238.
Antioch College, 270.
Anti-Slavery Convention, World's, 244.
Anti-Slavery Society, National Female, 121, 243.
Appeal against Wrong and Injury, An, 229.
Appeal to South Carolina, 250.
Appeal to the Public, An, 229.
Astronography, 240.
Avery, Professor, 240.

Baltimore, 259.
Bancroft, George, 229.
Barnard, Henry, 210–216, 226, 241.
Barnes, Mr., 218.
Barton, Clara, 271.
Beecher, Catherine, 118, 119, 121, 172, 174, 196.
Beeman, Dr., 91.
Bell, John, 249.
Belloc, Madame Louise, 155, 156, 174, 189, 242.
Benton, Thomas H., 245–247.
Berlin, 10–25, 207–216, 267.
Bingham, Caleb, 265.
Blackwell, Elizabeth, 236.
Bleeker, Hermanus, 203.
Bolivar, 116.
Boston, 205–206.
Boston High School for Girls, 119.
Boston Traveler, 125, 126, 229.
Botany for Beginners, 172.

Brandegee, Mrs. Lucy, 11.
Bridge of Louis XVI, 137–138.
Brongniart, Alexandre, 149.
Brongniart, Madame Alexandre, 149.
Brooks, Preston S., 249.
Brown, John, 249.
Buchanan, James, 241.
Burleigh, William H., 267.
Burleigh, Mrs. William H., 267.
Burr, Aaron, nieces of, 96.
Burr, Mrs. Celia. *See* Burleigh, Mrs. William H.
Burritt, Elihu, 211, 260, 261.
Burritt, Elijah, 114.

Calhoun, John C., 48.
Cambridge. *See* Newe Towne.
Campbell, Duncan, 67.
Caroline Westerley, 172.
Cass, Governor, daughter of, 96, 105.
Catherine II, 235.
Chambers, Mrs. Emma Hart Dickinson, 261.
Charlemagne, Packet, 131–132.
Charles X, 140, 141, 145.
Chase, Salmon P., 249.
Cheever, Ezekiel, 265.
Cheever, George Barrell, 174.
Chemistry, 110, 157, 239.
Choiseul, Count de, 169.
Civil War, 252–260.
Clay, Henry, 48, 247, 248, 249.
Clinton, De Witt, 62–65, 80, 109, 113, 114.
Combe, George, 67, 193.
Connecticut Common School Journal, 214, 215.
Cook, Rebecca Hart (Mrs. William Cook), 11.
Cook, William, 11.
Cooper, James Fenimore, 137, 147–148, 154, 157.
Corday, Charlotte, 140.
Cramer, J., 62.
Cramer, Mary, 77.
Crittenden, Senator, 248, 251.
Cuvier, Baron, 149.

Davidson, Lucretia, 186.
Davies, Professor, 253.
Dickinson, Emma Hart. *See* Cham-